Tending the Fire That Burns at the Center of the World

Tending the Fire That Burns at the Center of the World

Beauty and the Art of Christian Formation

DAVID F. WHITE

WIPF & STOCK · Eugene, Oregon

TENDING THE FIRE THAT BURNS AT THE CENTER OF THE WORLD
Beauty and the Art of Christian Formation

Wipf & Stock
An Imprint of Wipf and Stock Publishers
199 W. 8th Ave., Suite 3
Eugene, OR 97401

www.wipfandstock.com

PAPERBACK ISBN: 978-1-6667-4256-5
HARDCOVER ISBN: 978-1-6667-4257-2
EBOOK ISBN: 978-1-6667-4258-9

07/25/22

For Susan

Contents

Acknowledgments

THIS BOOK'S SUBSTANCE HAS long lain in some hidden place within my soul, yet in another sense this "stone soup" of a book has been fed by the work of dozens of friends, colleagues, mentors, and family members. A special and long-overdue thanks goes to my doctoral supervisor, Frank Rogers, whose contributions of friendship and intellectual stimulation can best be measured in quantities of pizza and beer. Thank you to Brian J. Mahan, who endured my ramblings on aesthetics over hot Atlanta "death walks" and amid the oak panels of the New York Harvard Club. More recently, my soul has been fed by the dulcet tones of Paul Hooker's jazz bass, by his poetry, and by his confessions and reflections over mountains of kimchi. I am grateful to my president, Ted Wardlaw, and the brilliant faculty at Austin Presbyterian Theological Seminary, many of whom can, no doubt, by now, recite whole passages of this book by heart. I owe a special debt of gratitude to Fred Edie at Duke, who reminds me of the fundamental significance of the Christian ordo, to which this book can only gesture. Thank you, Fred, for helping me to frame the question to which this book responds, that is, "What kind of knowing nurtures Christian faith?" I am grateful to my friend, the Austin artist and theologian C. D. Weaver, whose art bears prophetic witness to God's own justice. I am eternally grateful to Revs. Billy Still, James Loftin, and Tommy Artmann for a lifelong friendship rekindled by Zoom amid the COVID pandemic.

Perhaps it is axiomatic that persons like me with an artistic bent must rely heavily on editors, those to whom the seeming dark arts of precision are somewhat more transparent. I am immensely fortunate to have benefited from the gifts of editors Ollie Jarvis, Claire Cummiskey, and Kim Boykin. And I am grateful to Peter and Susan Pope for the use of their glorious lodge in rural Pickens, Mississippi—the perfect inspiration for a book on beauty.

Finally, there is no way to describe the enormity of work demanded by a project like this, but even less fathomable is the sacrifice required by family and friends. For writers, ancient thought must be given its rein; complex epistemological problems demand to be solved; antecedent disciplines require mastery; creative responses draw from one's deep reserves, such that one can sometimes descend into dark caverns of thought and mood. A project like this can become a third, and more disruptive, partner in a marriage. To my endlessly patient wife, Melissa Wiginton, I promise to spend what time remains translating this theory into practices of love and beauty with you.

Introduction

Beauty's Urgency

The windows of his room looked onto the garden, and our garden was very shady, with old trees, the spring buds were already swelling on the branches, the early birds arrived, chattering, singing through his windows. And suddenly, looking at them and admiring them, he began to ask their forgiveness, too: "Birds of God, joyful birds, you, too, must forgive me. Because I have also sinned before you." None of us could understand it then, but he was weeping with joy: "Yes," he said, "there was so much of God's glory around me: birds, trees, meadows, sky, and I alone lived in shame, I alone dishonoured everything, and did not notice the beauty and glory of it at all."

—FYODOR DOSTOYEVSKY, *THE BROTHERS KARAMAZOV*

Introduction

IN ONE OF MY earliest memories from around the age of three, I recall peeking through a rusty screen door onto a tree-lined gravel driveway as the late afternoon breeze stirred the autumn leaves in the golden light of the setting sun. The path of translucent stone chippings set aflame by the substrate of red Mississippi clay snaked from the steps below my naked feet to the widening horizon. This is not only my first clear memory, but also of astounding beauty, in which the glory of the world awakened my budding consciousness and commanded my attention. With my whole being I wanted to know this driveway, these stone chips, these trees, this sun, and this world, to drink them in or to be drunk by them. I was enveloped by wonder, a sense that an excess of goodness lay within the ordinary.

Of course, I could not then have articulated this, and even now words are wholly inadequate to capture that moment or the many others like it. My Mississippi childhood was filled with beauty that announced itself in dust motes, dancing sunbeams, languid lakes and rippling streams, noble black dogs, cooing doves, and chirping crickets, my mother's ruby red lipstick and the tickle of my father's beard stubble. As I grew into adolescence, beauty announced itself in my uncle's rockabilly singing, my church's *a cappella* harmonies, the lustrous paintings of my art teacher Mr. Quinn, the adorable girl in my junior high class, and in a well-thrown curve ball. I would come to know beauty in the faces of children and nurturing mothers, the selfless work of teachers and coaches, in heroic acts of justice, and in the story of Jesus Christ and the loveliness of his church. So compelling were my childhood epiphanies that I committed no little energy trying to create and respond to the world's beauty by drawing, painting, and playing musical instruments, however imperfectly.

Yet, somewhere along the way, probably by late adolescence, I was warned—or maybe I breathed it in the air of hard-bitten southern pragmatism—that to yearn for beauty is self-indulgent, while seeking truth and goodness is practical, respectable, even virtuous. I was smart enough, they said, to use my mind to comprehend the world's truth. I had a responsibility, they said, to make the world a better place. Indeed, they said, the gospel of Jesus Christ commands these pursuits. Although I have spent the better part of my adult life pursuing these blessed paths of truth and goodness, I have long suspected that this bipartite canon was incomplete. With this book, I return to memories of my childhood braided in wonder to reconsider the question of beauty for my faith and my calling to Christian education.

Introduction

Throughout this book I will use the terms "education" and "formation" somewhat interchangeably. The term "formation" has historically been understood as more inclusive, connoting such activities as worship, prayer, and spiritual practices, while the term "education" has largely denoted the work of the mind—cognition, intellection, instruction. This book insists, as does any fully Christian notion of truth, that the task of forming Christians must include more than cognitive mastery. Any education that is truly Christian must also engage the heart, body, soul, the whole person. My central concern is how we participate with the Spirit in strengthening Christian faith—how we tend the power that animates us for love of God and neighbor in the way of Christ. This book considers beauty as a way of attending to God's speech that awakens, empowers, and forms us in Christ's lovely way.

As we will see, the impulse to reclaim beauty for Christian formation emerges in response to several contemporary circumstances—including a growing recognition of modernity's tragic reductions, our abiding yearning for transcendence, the consequent gravitation to art and beauty as a haven, and Christianity's insistence upon hallowing the material world as sacramental. Instructional models of Christian knowing and faith do not address the urgencies of this historical moment, much less those of the grand tradition. Beauty, however neglected or trivialized, is a phenomenon that holds an important place in the church's historic thought and practice—but which also resists the reductions of modernity and meets the yearnings of this historical moment for transcendence. Beauty as a category has been explored by philosophers and psychologists, but for purposes of this book constitutes a theological approach to questions of epistemology, teaching, learning, and formation that can be seen as adequate to its object, God's living Word.

The failure of modern rational foundations should not trouble Christianity, since it is grounded in expressive materiality in which the cosmos is imbued with depth, mystery, and glory—and in God's incarnation, which establishes the priority of rhetoric over dialectic, persuasion over argumentation. Christian theology offers an alternate imaginary that revalues beauty and art, an ontology that awakens us to a world enchanted by God's beauty and populates the wonderous depths evacuated by modernity and pedagogies of instruction. Before we can establish beauty as an approach to Christian formation, it will be helpful to rehearse some of the conditions that point to beauty's significance.

3

Introduction

DISENCHANTED MODERNITY LIVED AS A LOSS

Not only does beauty play an important role in Christian truth and formation; it finds a certain urgency in this historical moment. We find ourselves at the far end of a tragic modern period that has failed to found, as promised by Enlightenment thinkers, a peaceful and flourishing society based on reason. Despite Enlightenment hopes, reason was frustrated by the reductionistic mythology it assumed, which narrated the cosmos as a mechanism of efficient causality—a machine with identifiable causes and effects and the mind as its passive mirror. Yet reason, it seems, was never neutral, objective, or innocent, as modernity had assumed. These mythical constructions of a neutral and objective self and world smuggle other hubristic myths—including, for example, nationalistic determinism, racial and gender hierarchies, consumeristic visions of happiness, and eternal economic growth under the guidance of the invisible hand of the market. Ironically, modern reason does not demythologize the world; it offers a rival mythology,[1] a "social imaginary" that now envisions God as a superfluous additive that can be subtracted without loss.

Recently, the concept of "social imaginary" has been popularized by Charles Taylor as a way of designating, not a society's concepts and ideas, but the largely tacit images, narratives, and myths that allow people to imagine or sense the real and true. According to Taylor, the ideas a society accepts as true only have their meaning against the backdrop of its imagination. For Taylor, the social imaginary involves a way of knowing that exists between the mind and the body. As such, social imaginaries are inscribed in us by aesthetic means—stories, images, art, music, liturgies, parables, symbols. If premodernity functioned by the light of narratives, myths, and images in which the cosmos is imagined as open to a transcendent God,

1. As John Milbank states, "Once upon a time there was no secular." Beginning with Max Weber, sociology portrays secularity as a process of "desacralization," the stripping of a sacred covering to reveal pure humanity and nature. This assumes that there is a pure humanity which rests always beneath the surface of the sacred. It assumes that humanism is the natural destiny of history, the inevitable telos toward which all human societies move. Both assumptions Milbank contests (Milbank, *Theology and Social Theory*, 9). Charles Taylor, in *A Secular Age*, provides a genealogy of the evacuation of premodern enchantment and the construction of the modern myth, including historic events such as the Protestant reformers' deemphasis of sacramentality and emphasis on written texts; nominalism that reduced all things as mental signs or conventions without existential significance; deism's evacuation of God from the world's workings; and industrial capitalism that reduced the world to raw resources or commodities.

4

the modern world constructed its own mythology, no less arbitrary than the religious imaginary, in which the immanent cosmos is unhooked from a transcendent God.

Here, at the far end of modernity, we live with a certain sense of loss and alienation at our evacuation of transcendence. According to Charles Taylor, at the heart of modern secularity is a "disenchantment," a source for what many see as a prevailing nihilism. Modern reason concerned itself with extracting the "structures of being," thus obscuring the very concreteness of being itself. For example, if we want to "know objectively" a tree, for the arch-modernist Immanuel Kant, we must disconnect it from its context, from its constant development, from its relatedness with other things, and even from all the stories in which the tree is embedded.[2] But trying to know something with a rational necessity apart from the flux of its relations renders it objectified and necrotic. Anglican theologian Catherine Pickstock suggests that modernity has fostered a necrophilic culture by fetishizing such technical rationality, which obscures things by abstracting them from their concrete material and spiritual relations.[3] Under the guidance of thinkers like Descartes and Kant, modernity impoverishes us by reducing us to thinking things connected to the world only by thought and for the purpose of mastery. They employ an operative metaphor or paradigm that is *assumed but unquestioned*—viz., of a solitary mind "inside itself," as it were, trying to "record" or "represent" an "external" reality. Thus, the Cartesian subject reduces the enchanted premodern world to a closed, mechanical system and opens a fissure between the subject and its body and between self and world. If the premodern soul involved a capacity for feeling ourselves amidst our relations, John Milbank observes, with "Descartes' *cogito* the soul died and the thinking subject was born."[4]

According to Taylor, premodern people existed as "porous" selves, subject to the felt concrete and mystical realities of the world, while as modern people we exist as "buffered" selves, reliant on mental meanings composed internally and applied to the world. The world was laden with supernatural and spiritual realities, with angels and spirits conveying messages back and forth between realms, as people existed as "porous," open and receptive to the mystical, the divine, the "other" beyond the self. This

2. Milbank, Pickstock, and Ward, *Radical Orthodoxy*, 27. Cf. Milbank, *Theology and Social Theory*, 433–34.

3. See Pickstock, *After Writing*, 101.

4. Milbank, "The Soul of Reciprocity," 335.

was accepted unquestioned by nearly all premodern people. The universe was "enchanted," charged with meaning. Power actually resided in the mystery of relations, not entirely divisible as causes and effects.

Taylor characterizes modernity as an "excarnation" in which we now exist at a remove from the corporeal relations of life.[5] Once the mental life of the individual becomes the sole locus of meaning, organic communion is replaced by separate object and selves. The modern buffered self does afford some measure of protection from the terrors and uncertainties experienced by our ancestors due to their vulnerability and openness, but on the other hand we now abide in a closed-off, interiorized state of uneasy disenchantment. Sealed off from the enchantments of the cosmos, the immanent frame of mind is left to ruminate in its own weariness. The separation of the earthly immanent from the transcendent has left us in a somewhat more fragile state. The mythology of modernity opened vast new horizons for science but also closed off the immanent frame from any organic openness to transcendence. No longer is the soul an event; we are now Cartesian thinking things able to exercise power indifferent to "ends underwritten by transcendence."[6]

Lest we imagine that such reductions only appear in certain secular spheres, Roman Catholic theologian Hans Urs von Balthasar once observed modernity's influence in theology. He noted that modern "theologians had reduced it (theology) to the turning of pages in a desiccated catalogue of ideas[,] a kind of butterfly collection for the mind."[7] He insisted that "theology . . . is supposed to be the study of the fire and light that burn at the centre of the world."[8] We might also observe that the modern church has seen an analogous reduction of its ministry of Christian formation to an emphasis on cognitive mastery, to conceptual or moral instruction.[9] In this reduction, God's quickening mystery is subverted by frozen dogma or

---

5. The priority of reason, empiricism, and private faith has led to what Charles Taylor describes as the "excarnation" of Christianity. According to Taylor, modernity effaced older bodily practices to produce "an *excarnation*, a transfer out of embodied, *enfleshed* forms of religious life, to those which are more *in the head*." This problematic is highlighted by Taylor's reflections on the Good Samaritan (Taylor, *A Secular Age*, 554).

6. Taylor, *A Secular Age*, 337.

7. Caldecott, "An Introduction to Hans Urs von Balthasar."

8. Caldecott, "An Introduction to Hans Urs von Balthasar."

9. I am aware that Christian education resources across Christian denominations and nondenominational expressions feature a variety of effective techniques. Yet these seem often undertheorized, lacking a coherent purpose or aim. This book represents a hunch that even these approaches might be improved if the fundamental intellectualist myth is replaced by a better ontological account in which beauty and poiesis play a key role.

equally settled socio-political ideology, and faith formation is envisioned only as rational instruction for cognitive and volitional mastery.

SKYLIGHTS IN THE BRASS HEAVEN

If buffered selfhood protects us from superstitions concerning malevolent spiritual forces, it also inhibits the joy and wisdom that comes with porous communion with the cosmos. This is a loss that we feel deeply. According to Taylor,

> Perhaps the clearest sign of the transformation in our world is that today many people look back to the world of the porous self with nostalgia, as though the creation of a thick emotional boundary between us and the cosmos were now lived as a loss. The aim is to try to recover some measure of this lost feeling. So people go to movies about the uncanny in order to experience a frisson.[10]

According to Taylor, modern post-Christian Westerners find themselves "cross-pressured" by the nagging reality of God, unable to square our yearning for the spiritual with the closed-off, immanent, materialistic world we have created. The nagging reality of God and transcendence has not disappeared but continues to "haunt" our outwardly confident secular world. Despite the disenchantment of modernity, there are cracks, or, as James K. A. Smith says, "skylights in the brass heaven."[11] The Cartesian mythologies that rendered the world inert were sufficiently compelling or ubiquitous enough to erode the influence of organized religion, but could not evacuate our yearning for fullness and transcendence. Just when we think we have exiled the pesky mysteries of angels, holy meals, and the trinitarian God, we see late-modern or postmodern enchantments and misenchantments[12] multiplying and migrating across the culture in legion

---

10. Taylor, *A Secular Age*, 38.

11. This is a descriptive phrase used frequently by James K. A. Smith to denote two things: the accepted modern social imaginary of a closed immanent frame, and the intuition that our life participates in a kind of transcendence or fullness for which we yearn. Smith. *How (Not) to Be Secular*, 93.

12. Or, alternatively, the "mis-enchantments" of the nation-state as preferred by William Cavanaugh, or mammon as preferred by Eugene McCarraher. See McCarraher, *The Enchantments of Mammon*, and Cavanaugh, *Migrations of the Holy*. These authors, strictly speaking, resist Taylor's designation of modernity as un-enchanted; instead, they see the enchantments of the modern world migrating especially to these two sites. In their view, the nation-state and the commodity market are charged with mystical powers.

forms. Our nostalgia for transcendence and porosity can be seen not only in the frisson of movie theaters but is a defining feature of today's culture— it can be seen as an impulse of political activism, yoga, sports, music and the arts, Eastern mysticism, resurgent nationalism, the religious pursuit of commodities—in which we desperately seek the fullness or transcendence for which we are made. William James once characterized this intuition as "something more"—an intuition that things exist in excess of our words and explanations that point to capacities of soul and transcendence.[13]

For our purposes, beauty and art now appear to serve as a key refuge for those who cannot imagine the world open to transcendence but who intuitively resist the reductionisms of secularism. Now may be an opportune time for the church to introduce a new generation, especially those who find a haven in beauty and art, to the apostle Paul's "unknown God" who animates a freshness of heart, the fire and light that burns at the center of the world.

CHRISTIANITY'S CHALLENGE TO EXCARNATION

Here at the end of a long modernity, many Christian theologians see modernity's excarnation—the evacuation of the body, senses, and material relations—as a heretical contradiction of Christianity's hallowing of all incarnate matter. This book will trace theology's resistance to modernity's reductions, especially Christianity's aesthetic tradition. At the heart of this book is the notion that things in the cosmos disclose their materiality not as structures of thought but as forms of art. As Milbank observes, we are only truly able to know things in their material relations with other things, including the infinite mystery in which they are set. The truth of a thing is discerned not by thought alone, but by the soul's engagement with sensed materiality. This sense of relatedness provides the form and depth capable of sparking not only intellection but desire, love, imagination, and empathy.

Amid an age that can't imagine transcendence but hungers for it, we should remember that Christianity constitutes a fundamental challenge to

---

13. James, *The Principles of Psychology*, 305.

excarnate and disenchanted immanence. Christian faith shares with art a resistance to diminished views of human nature, a conviction that human beings cannot be reduced to the material while being nothing less than materially embodied. Christian faith shares with art the sense that the eternal is conveyed in hallowed matter. For Christians, the incarnation and resurrection constitute a testament to the fullness of being human, the hope that embodied joy will be complete. Christ's incarnation and resurrection hallow the tie between heaven and earth, so we should not be surprised to find witnesses to the eternal in painting, poetry, sculpture, fiction, music, and movies, and in the beauty of created being. Musicians and artists seek assiduously to express the light that shines from within the ordinary. Perhaps this late-modern historical moment constitutes an opportunity for our society to recognize beauty and art as "the fires burning in us that have been lit by an eternal God."[14]

Since at least the time of Origen in the third century, Christians have understood "spiritual senses" as our capacities to see, hear, smell, taste, touch that portend an expansion of sensate awareness in the world to come—not as an escape, but an intensification of our senses. Spiritual realities are known not by negating our senses but by attending to them more fully. It is in and through the senses and not upward and away from them that we deepen our spiritual perception. As we will see, the link between our senses and the eternal is not a spurious addition to Christianity but is central to how Scriptures communicate—in parables, narratives, poetry, apocalyptic imagery, and God's own incarnate form. The Christian tradition cannot finally be reduced to a catalogue of ideas or moral duties; it seeks to resurrect an imagination that resists the distortions of the present age and empire. A resurrected imagination sees things as they are, ought to be, and as they will be, a world through which God is mediated and in whom creatures flourish.

Modernity is not impoverished because it retrieves the material world but because it flattens the world to the merely material evacuated of transcendence, without which the world cannot be truly perceived. Late-modern market-driven unrest dissolves everything that is material into thin air. Even as a constant flow of desires and pixels washes over us, the habit of acquiring and consuming things only succeeds in valuing the material as little more than a source of acquisition and distraction. Just as Christian faith testifies that bread and wine reveal the true nature of ordinary things to nurture

14. Smith, "Resurrecting the Imagination."

spiritual life, so does great art and beauty remind us that the material is breached by the immaterial, that matter can be a window to the world's soul.

For example, in the Netherlands and Belgium, the Protestant Reformation took hold in a particular way in Dutch landscape and seascape painting, where creation itself becomes worthy of contemplation.[15] Vermeer and Rembrandt illuminate the workaday world where, just as Jesus' resurrection was announced in the testimony of often-ignored women, we see the laboring women, milkmaids, and mothers invisible to those with power, with their tables laden with the fruit of the harvest and the spoils of the hunt, reminding us that the everyday, even what is usually rendered invisible, is charged with eternal significance. The Christian inheritance of hallowing the ordinary speaks of our hunger to find joy in the quotidian, "to receive the quiet delights on offer right in front of us."[16] This is also the true vocation of art and beauty.

At the heart of the Christian story is a confession about time and history: the Creator of the cosmos incarnates time and history and transforms how we relate to matter and inhabit time. Art and beauty break the flow of mere consumption and receive the material with gratitude, as gift. Like art, Christian existence is punctuated by the fullness of Kairos, not just the tick-tock "one thing after another" of Chronos. God's timeless presence to the world is ever ancient and ever new, as the "long bright shadow cast by the resurrection intersects with the light that reaches us from the kingdom that is to come."[17] The Spirit is present to every age, never reduced to the spirit of the age but groaning for the renewal of all things in the world to come. Art and beauty hallow time and space by illumining the eternal in the expressive groans of material form, of brush strokes, musical intervals, narrative excursions, that gesture toward the world's hope.

What if Christianity is a source of imagination that late-modern culture has forgotten? This book wagers that Christianity's aesthetic sensibilities have something to offer the world. As we witness the exhaustion of late-modern paradigms, the aesthetics at the heart of Christian faith could render this neglected tradition now as a gift. Perhaps post-Christian societies in the West find ourselves at a point where the peculiarities of the Christian belief in incarnation and resurrection can be received anew

---

15. This is a connection observed by James K. A. Smith in "Resurrecting the Imagination."

16. Smith, "Resurrecting the Imagination."

17. Smith, "Resurrecting the Imagination."

as a summons to another way to be human. British novelist Julian Barnes famously declared, "I don't believe in God but I miss him."[18] According to his testimony, Barnes's unbelief is haunted by the great art and music of the medieval church and curiosity about a Reality that lies behind such art. The Christian affirmation that the eternal is embodied in the material is one of the reasons Christianity has generated the great art that haunts Barnes and a great many others. The pulsing heart of Christian hope is the truth of a God-man, a penetrating of the frontier between imminence and transcendence. With the incarnation of Jesus comes a revolution of the imagination, the possibility of paradoxically holding together the otherwise incommensurate.

The circumstances outlined above point to the possibility of a truly "post"-modern way of considering truth and knowing, and a more adequate way of teaching and learning Christian faith. Perhaps this brief account of our historical moment will intrigue readers who will find herein an account of beauty as a phenomenon, its theological articulation, and beginning forays into pedagogies and practices that take seriously the aesthetic nature of Christianity.

A CONFESSION, CAVEAT, AND HOPE

As the reader begins this pilgrimage of ideas, I must make a confession, offer a caveat, and project a hope.

A confession: In over a decade of research I have traversed the thorny brambles of critical literary theory, economic and cultural theory, modern religious history, Greek metaphysics, continental postmodern philosophy, the Patristics, Thomism and Anglo-Catholic theology in general, mid-century *ressourcement* Catholicism, art theory, liturgical theology, a thorough review of religious education approaches, and numerous other rabbit trails that seemed like good ideas at the time. As is evident by this litany, my research followed questions wherever they led, guided by a hunch that beauty matters, if for no other reason (I think there are many good reasons) than for the sake of my own soul. It requires no humility for me to admit that I am not formally trained as a systematic or historical theologian, nor as a philosophical theologian, much less does my expertise lie in Anglicanism, Roman Catholicism, or Eastern Orthodoxy, where some of the most robust theological aesthetics can be found at present. I am a United Methodist

18. Barnes, "Nothing to Be Frightened Of."

practical theologian, a Christian educator by vocation and training. Only with fear and trembling does a scholar publish a work that draws from such a vast body of research that stretches across disciplines and historical eras, many beyond their field of formal training. Because aesthetics remains somewhat arcane as a scholarly topic among educational disciplines, I have judged it necessary to tell the story of beauty and its distinctive place in the history of ideas in a more comprehensive way than might be expected in a book on Christian education and formation. Yet, because this is a book on Christian formation, I promise to move relatively quickly to consider approaches for Christian formation. If beauty and poiesis are to be more than mere techniques to spice up an otherwise didactic pedagogy, we must reconsider the assumptions we have taken on board in our modern social imaginary, with its reductions of the world, the self, and God's mediation. We need a better story, one which cannot be told without a metaphysical and theological account. While there are many excellent books on aesthetics that scholars would no doubt find more satisfying, sadly, few philosophical theologians deign to reflect on its significance for Christian formation. And so into this void I write as a Christian educator who reads philosophy and theology, for better or worse.

A caveat: While I am convinced of the importance of beauty and poiesis for Christian formation, I do not prescribe anything like a complete or seamless approach. In the pages that follow, I point to a larger role for aesthetics, which I hope others will join in developing. Several existing approaches to Christian education, such as narrative or contemplative approaches, engage beauty, even if not theorized with beauty or poiesis as an explicit aim. This book provides new-old ways to theorize existing approaches to Christian formation, especially those involving narrative and contemplation but which should also spark our imaginations concerning unexplored pedagogical practices or aspects of existing practices that may deepen our engagement with beauty and poiesis.

Some might object that frivolous topics like beauty and art are inadequate to address the crying needs of our world for justice; hard times call for hard measures. Is beauty not too ephemeral to ground substantive acts for justice? Others might object that beauty cannot reasonably be expected to ground true, orthodox, devotional piety. Is not beauty subjective, judged only in the eye of the beholder? How does beauty inspire an impulse for communion with God and neighbor, sanctification or theosis? This book constitutes a wager that both justice and/or piety and are best addressed by reclaiming the centrality of beauty and poiesis. Of course, that conclusion lies at the end of a long argument. For now, I hope readers will join me in circumnavigating the world of meaning in which beauty lives.

A hope: As I place the final touches on this book, I feel a bit like a landscape painter who labors over a vista or a musician who intones an inspired musical idea, who then steps back from their work with a degree of satisfaction and concludes, "Yes, that's it! I've captured the mystery I have glimpsed" but who almost immediately recognizes, "No, sadly, the true mystery has eluded me." This book is finally not adequate to the topic because the topic is ubiquitous and eternal in scope and significance, and because at the heart of beauty resides an inaccessible mystery that we only see face-to-face in the eschaton. Nevertheless, sometimes, even artists with meager talent and vision sometimes succeed in taking our breath away, not because of their ability, but because of the exceeding glory of their object, because they succeed in pointing beyond their art to the mystery beyond it. My hope is that this book and the beauty that inspires it will stir some to receive my gift and offer their own in return.

As I write these words, I have the privilege of writing, for a time, in a cabin deep in the rural South. Today is a rare wet wintry day, and I am gazing into a roaring fireplace. The firelight dances and flickers across the pine walls, and I am struck once again by its romance, an unfailing source of longing, wonder, and delight. The glow of firelight provides warmth and softens my mood, placing me at a distance from my cares, more present to my longings. It conjures memories of my youth, of singing songs and telling stories in an aura of warm fellow-feeling, huddling close against the elements and adolescent angst, gaining fleeting access to the world's essential truths. If the fire's delight does not satisfy completely, it nevertheless points beyond itself to the Source of all being, truth, and bliss.

I have known such moments of delight and illumination in the church, even if they sometimes seem all too rare. The modern social imaginary that disenchants the cosmos remains the tacit curriculum of many approaches to Christian teaching and learning. However, as we have acknowledged, there are cracks in the modern brass ceiling. We sense that the world is populated not with objects or thoughts to be mastered. When we linger before a poem, baseball game, pet, beautiful vista, museum masterpiece, concert, child's face, or the incarnation of Christ, we are not first coerced by the rational propositions it spawns; we are first struck by a form that shines forth a radiant mystery and depth. Beautiful forms hold the potential to not only to delight us but to spark our wonder, enlarge our knowing, and prompt acts of poiesis that extend their original beauty and meaning. From the beautiful gesture of Christ's self-giving love, the church built a new form of sociality founded on forgiveness of sins, care for the poor, beatitude, salvation, and eternal life for all. The church is called to be Christ's living body, manifesting God's beauty "in the style of love" and with extravagant gestures of poiesis.

Finally, this book represents a call and a charge. Let us rejoice and participate in the beauty of God's creation and incarnation with a freshness of heart. Let us shed the shackles of abstract argument, pragmatic calculation, and mere didactic. Let us re-enchant finitude with infinity even as we open ourselves to being ravished by beauty. Let us behold the outrageous beauty, the "shook foil" of the created world.[19] Let us find succor in stories, poems, songs, and liturgies that make our hearts explode with delight and compassion. Let us create justice that seeks not merely freedom from constraint but envisions a beautiful life together, including confession, forgiveness, reconciliation, hospitality, charity, and the mutual exchange of good gifts. Let us make room for young poets to speak their rage even as we give voice to hope that can make harmony from dissonance.

We may have been wounded, some severely, within this world of injustice, pain, and discord, yet within each of us there is a child breathlessly awaiting the visceral joy of a setting sun, flaming stone chips, and enormous pecan trees, the joyous release of being carried away by liturgical song or by gestures of care beyond the sanctuary, an awakening by and to the artistry that Christ inaugurated. My fondest hope is that readers will enter fully into the substance of the book, which portrays a world aglow with God's light. Much as the fire in my fireplace ignites my heart with memory, imagination, and wonder, I hope you find something of this light burning in these pages.

The first chapter begins by providing a phenomenology of beauty—its role in awakening, decentering, inviting us to join community, and prompting us to respond—and continues with a survey of beauty through Greek and early Christian thought as antecedent to contemporary theological aesthetics.

The second chapter articulates the pedagogical significance of theological aesthetics focused on created beauty, beginning with Hans Urs von Balthasar's metaphysics and the aims and approaches it suggests.

---

19. Hopkins, "God's Grandeur."

The third chapter articulates the pedagogical significance of the Christ form as understood by von Balthasar along with an articulation of its aims and strategies for Christian formation.

The fourth chapter begins by elaborating the significance of poiesis in the theological writings of John Milbank and concludes by characterizing the aims and strategies implied in his writings.

The fifth illumines the significance of liturgy for Christian formation, drawing on the work of various figures, including the recent aesthetics of James K. A. Smith but enhanced also by phenomenological reflections of art theorists and philosophers, including the telos of beauty.

The sixth chapter considers themes of suffering, lament, and hope, including the significance of theological aesthetics for teaching and learning.

In the conclusion I invite readers to their own kind of poiesis in helping to create approaches and techniques for Christian formation that enhance the aims discovered in the aesthetic reflections of this book. I hope my reflections will spark the reader's own sense of wonder about the possibilities for Christian formation enlightened by beauty and art.

PART I

Beauty as Social Imaginary

ALL REFLECTIONS AND INTENTIONS about teaching and pedagogy contain at least a tacit ontology and anthropology, a set of assumptions about that nature of the human person as we exist in the world, open or closed to transcendence. As this book assumes, in this late-modern or postmodern moment, we have begun to see the limits and risks of modernity which posits the self as a thinking thing, a mirror onto the world gleaning objective and abstracted facts and reasons to be applied to master the world. This book invites readers to imagine a different but no more arbitrary story of the world and self which adapts ancient notions of beauty and creativity. Crafting a social imaginary different from modern rationalism is no simple feat, especially since it has assigned to beauty a trivial and marginal role from which it needs to be redeemed. In order to make a start in imagining a world and a self in which beauty features centrally, this first part invites readers to survey their own experiences of beauty, along with ancient Greek and early Patristic ontologies, and the role of beauty and glory in the Bible. Subsequent theological and pedagogical chapters will make the most sense if we can begin to rearrange the furniture of our imaginations. Teaching and learning will look very different once beauty and creativity are restored to their proper place of theological and pedagogical significance.

1

Remembering Beauty

What Christian thought offers the world is not a set of rational arguments that (suppressing certain of their premises) force assent from others by leaving them, like the interlocutors of Socrates, at a loss for words; rather, it stands before the world principally with the story it tells concerning God and creation, the form of Christ, the loveliness of the practice of Christian charity—and the rhetorical richness of its idiom. Making its appeal first to the eye and heart, as the only way to "command" assent, the church cannot separate truth from rhetoric, or from beauty.

—David Bentley Hart, *Beauty of the Infinite*

WHEN I WAS A small child in the 1960s, most summer Saturday mornings were filled with doing household chores. As my family mopped, swept, cleaned, mowed, and cooked, the air was filled with the lush tones of our white Lucite tube radio blaring out some distant professional baseball game, usually the New York Yankees (I was a young Roger Maris fan; number 9 forever!). I remember being mesmerized by the colorful commentary of Dizzy Dean and Mel Allen.

Around the age of seven, my family traveled from Mississippi to visit relatives in Maryland. To our delight, my uncle had acquired tickets for my father and me to see the Baltimore Orioles play at Memorial Stadium. We sat behind home plate about ten rows up. Nestled between my father and uncle, crunching my Cracker Jacks, I breathlessly awaited the opening pitch. I can still recall the giant halide stadium flood lights, the smell of new-mown grass in the outfield, the red dirt in the batter's box, the cloud rising from the resin bag on the pitcher's mound, the growling Hammond organ, and the chatter of the players. As the players took the field, I was stunned by the beauty of their uniforms, their resplendent knee-breeches, the embroidered orange oriole on their caps and sleeves, the sensual click of their metal cleats. Although Church of Christ kids were expected to suppress such expressions of awe, to me they were gods. As the game commenced, I was immediately drawn into the game's ballet—the pitcher's windup, his dramatic showdown with a defiant batter, the fielders cheating right or left to adjust to the swing of the batter, the baserunners' hook slide, the catchers' surgical throw to second base, the outfielders' over-the-shoulder-catch of a long fly ball. To my seven-year-old eyes, it was the most beautiful thing I had ever witnessed. Ordinary acts of throwing, catching, and running were transformed by artistry that seemed to capture the human longing for excellence, fairness, respect, even love. The roles of each individual player were performed with brilliance, made more so by the harmony of the whole team. I left the ballpark that night with a mysterious but undeniable ache to be a part of such poetry.

The very next week upon returning home from our northern vacation, I convinced my father to buy me a mitt. A few weeks after that he signed me up for my first Little League baseball team. Baseball's goodness was confirmed to me over the next eleven years as I played on various teams and in various positions, with varying degrees of success. While my teammates and I never achieved the beauty or excellence of Roger Maris,

Frank Robinson, or Boog Powell, still we had our moments in the sun; we contributed a bit of our own poietic verse.

Now, many decades beyond my youth, I still have dreams of swinging a bat and solidly connecting with a baseball. The feel of a well-hit baseball is unforgettable. Sometimes from my office I can hear the crack of a bat in a nearby park and am instantly transported. I feel the sun on my face and the wool of my old number 9 jersey; I can smell my leather mitt and my sweat-stained cap from Little League all those years ago.

Not until adulthood did I read those systematic theologies of baseball, such as George Will's *Men at Work: The Craft of Baseball*, *The Numbers Game* by Alan Schwartz, or Bill James's *The New Bill James Historical Baseball Abstract*. Even though these are very good writers, their distilled facts and arguments, in themselves, could never have succeeded in recruiting me to or forming me for the game. The beauty I had earlier beheld in baseball preceded and infused my sense of its goodness and its truth. Glimpsing baseball's beauty sparked in me a desire to participate in its seasonal, liturgical, ethical, physical, and spiritual rhythms. Baseball first appealed to my heart, and later to my body, and only finally as a rationality abstracted from these grounds of experience. If, instead of taking me to a ball game at age seven, my father had given me a book to read on the rules or strategies of baseball, it would never have been nearly as compelling.

Perceiving the concrete beauty of the game set me on a path of lifelong enjoyment, study, and longing for excellence. Awakening to baseball's beauty prompted me to explore its inner nuances—the subtleties of the infield fly rule, where to stand in the batter's box to hit a curve ball, how to play the outfield when a lefthander is at bat, and how to calculate batting averages or a pitcher's ERA. Baseball's beauty called forth in me abilities and virtues—of hand-eye coordination, speed to run bases and catch long outfield flies, cooperation with my teammates, the joy of playing well, and sportsmanship in losing (rather a lot). Baseball's beauty prompted new forms of sociality by compelling me to share nearly every summer afternoon with neighborhood friends in local sandlots and pastures.

Without beauty, baseball would involve mere information or technique. I encountered baseball first as a material form, acts performed with excellence. Some of its internal goods and virtues I would not perceive for many years and only from inside the game, but even from the beginning, in my seat in a Baltimore stadium, the game announced its hidden goodness and truth in its manifest beauty. Ultimately, I was formed as a player, lover, fan, aficionado, and amateur strategist by long hours of play and reflection, but make no mistake, the many layers of my formation were forecast in the first glow of the game's beauty. Whereas rational thought seeks to map reality, beauty invites us to participate in its dance. Reason is a tool for mastery, while beauty claims or masters us, and not just our minds but also our "gut" or heart.

Since the dawn of the modern Enlightenment, the Western world has imagined a more or less direct relationship between reason and a rightly ordered life. We have imagined that right ideas are sufficient to compel right action. Such confidence in reason has defined our view of truth generally and the educational enterprise specifically. Since before the Modern Era, Christian education has manifested a high degree of confidence in reason, in its tasks of instructing in Scripture, doctrine, and moral principles. Ideas are taught by conservative traditions seeking to preserve doctrinal orthodoxy and by liberal traditions to instill just moral/ethical principles. But make no mistake, modern educators all along the theological spectrum have great confidence in the power of ideas to form faithful Christians.

To be fair, instructional approaches to Christian formation have long been critiqued, especially by religious education scholars.[1] Recently, James K. A. Smith asks a question that potentially reframes the important insights of previous scholars by foregrounding the role of imagination. He asks, "What if . . . the primary work of education [is] the transforming of our imagination rather than the saturation of our intellect?" He insists that we are not merely "brains-on-a-stick." Such construals

> belie an understanding of Christian faith that is dualistic and thus reductionistic: It reduces Christian faith primarily to a set of ideas, principles, claims, and propositions that are known and believed. The goal of all this is "correct" thinking. But this makes it sound as if we are essentially the sorts of things that Descartes described us to be: thinking things that are containers for ideas. What if that is actually only a small slice of who we are? And what if that's not even the most important part?[2]

Drawing upon an Augustinian anthropology, Smith asks, "What if (Christian formation) has as much to do with our bodies as with our

1. See Nelson, *Where Faith Begins*; Palmer, *To Know as We Are Known*; Rogers, *Finding God in the Graffiti*; Murphy, *Teaching that Transforms*; Edie, *Book, Bath, Table, Time*; Neville and Westerhoff, *Learning through Liturgy*.

2. Smith, *Desiring the Kingdom*, 32.

minds? What if education wasn't first and foremost about what we know, but about what we love?"[3] We will return to Smith's vision in later chapters, but for now it is important to note his hunch that important aspects of formation occur in our bodies and imaginations rather than our intellects.

To Smith's questions I add my own. What if instructional approaches to Christian formation abstract ideas from their material relations and contribute to a disenchantment of and nihilism in the world? What if an overreliance on the intellect fails to acknowledge the mediating beauty and infinite depth of God's expressive and hallowed creation, and of Christ's beautiful form by which God speaks? What if Christian formation is most adequate to its object, the perfectly beautiful God, not from the distance of rational abstraction, but when we participate in beauty's ecstasy that fosters a knowing that is loving—a freshness of heart, joy of communion, and perpetual creativity? What if the truest aim of Christian formation is to persuade us of a way of living by virtue of its beauty, by the artistry of liturgies, narratives, art, song, and lovely forms of practice?

My questions mirror a growing consensus among theologians who consider that modernity—for example, its tacit ontology, anthropology, and epistemology—now holds a largely problematic significance for theology. In casting a vision for theology, theologian David Bentley Hart states, "The truth of being is poetic before it is rational, doxological before it is systematic. And it is rational only in proportion to its beauty, its poetic coherence and richness of detail, and thus Christian truth cannot be known truly if this order is reversed."[4] In this picture or imaginary, the world in its beauty is a theophanic utterance bearing witness to God, a gift we joyfully receive in liturgy and in ongoing poiesis—in prayer, praise, and praxis. Christianity, marked by God's declaration of creation's goodness and God's incarnate Word, offers a sacramental cosmos in which beauty mediates the depths of being, and which participates in the Holy, thereby marking the path of our ascent in communion with God. Early Patristic and Medieval theologians saw the task of Christian formation as opening our spiritual senses to mysteries disclosed in beauty—in what Hart calls "the Covenant of Light."[5]

In one sense this book asks, "What if reality is God's beautiful poem, the fall the occlusion of that reality, the incarnation restores reality as a poem;

3. Smith, *Desiring the Kingdom*, 18.
4. Hart, *The Beauty of the Infinite*, 132.
5. Hart, *The Beauty of the Infinite*, 125.

and when we let ourselves be written into this poem we are redeemed?"[6] This book constitutes a wager that Christian formation is most appropriate to its object when it attends to God's beauty disclosed in creation, Christ, and church. I hope to convince readers that beauty and poiesis (beauty's necessary correlate) hold a central place in Christian formation.

But again, that comes at the end of an argument, and I do not imagine a single baseball story will suffice to establish a social imaginary that features beauty as an opening to depth, mystery, and transcendence. In the modern social imaginary, beauty has been trivialized as decorative, as having no place in modern priorities of control and mastery. To resist the modern rational imaginary, Christian formation needs an alternate story of beauty—as a phenomenon, a metaphysical notion, and a theological sign—that reveals beauty as an alternative to modern reductions.

BEAUTY AS PHENOMENON

If beauty is to found a new imaginary, it must first be rehabilitated. A quick Google search reveals that contemporary notions of beauty focus largely, if not exclusively, on such objects as home décor, automobiles, fashion, cosmetics, and, of course, human bodies. Consumer culture conditions us to perceive beauty as something to be pursued and acquired, as a momentary distraction without meaning or gratitude. As commodities, things of beauty are consumed, but do not change or affect us. Internet images wash over us and stimulate our senses, but our desire cools quickly and so we must scroll to the next page, post, or picture, chasing the same momentary pleasure. As commodities, things of beauty do not allow for the inbreaking of Kairos time, but as we have seen, only the Chronos of endless desire and consumption as surfaces without depth wash over us. Beauty is rendered superficial and subject to mere personal preference—to "the eye of the beholder." It is no wonder that many consider beauty superfluous in the face of pressing social issues such as racism, injustice, poverty, climate change, or global conflict. And yet, beauty has not always been treated as a triviality plucked from bourgeois cupidity. If beauty is to have a place in Christian formation, we must reclaim it from its modern captivity to consumption, superficiality, subjectivity, and irrelevance.

6. A liberal translation of John Milbank's summary of Augustine's thought in a tweet (Milbank, "Reality is a poem").

Throughout history and across all cultures people have recognized the epiphany of beauty as significant among ways of encountering the world. Navajo tribes once used beautiful sand paintings to restore the sick to harmony with the universe. Physicists and mathematicians claim to be led by elegance into scientific discovery. Albert Einstein once remarked: "I have deep faith that the principle of the universe will be beautiful and simple."[7] The poet John Keats exclaimed "'Beauty is truth, truth beauty'—that is all Ye know on earth, and all / ye need to know."[8] Russian novelist Fyodor Dostoevsky's character in *The Idiot* posits, "Beauty may save the world."[9] Scientists, poets, and mystics testify that beauty is a singular human experience that speaks of the world's mysterious depths and awakens the soul to knowledge and action. Beauty is more than a surface or style subject to personal taste. As we will see, it is a phenomenon with iconic depths key to ancient understandings of being and to the Bible's understanding of God's glory and Christ's incarnation, an event that sparks eros, communion, and insight and which animates the church's joyful worship and mission. If we are to reclaim its priority, we must first characterize its features, our experience of it. In the following section, I will briefly survey the phenomenon of beauty to reveal that it is more significant than is allowed by contemporary reductions.

First, as a phenomenon, beauty is ubiquitous. It appears on the vastest scales (as in the amazing photographs taken by the Hubble telescope of distant galaxies) and on the most minute (as in a floating dust mote in a sunbeam, or the Fibonacci pattern in a head of sunflower seeds). While beauty almost certainly plays some role in natural selection, it is not reducible to this purpose. According to Dutch biologist F. J. J. Buytendijk, "to put it simply, the birds are singing much more than Darwin permits."[10]

Unlike reason, which is subject to endless charges of subjective bias, beauty is objective—it possesses a phenomenal priority. We may quibble over how to interpret it, but we cannot doubt its existence or quality.[11] As John Locke saw, there is more agreement over what is beautiful than what is true.[12] In the Modern Era, beauty comes to be understood as a quality of the

7. Einstein, "Religion and Science."

8. Keats, *The Poems of John Keats*, 194–95.

9. This is, in fact, a statement attributed to the prince by Ippolit. See Dostoevsky, *The Idiot*, 370.

10. Buytendijk, *Het Spel van Mensch*; Portmann, *Biologie und Geist*, 22–29.

11. Hart, *The Beauty of the Infinite*, 17.

12. Locke, *The Works of John Locke*, 519.

subject arbitrarily imposed upon the bare facts of this world, a subjective mood only understandable in the "eye of the beholder." In this view, beauty can say nothing of objective importance, since its meaning is forged in the cellars of our subjectivity. And yet, mysteriously, we never have to explain to small children the attraction of blooming flowers over moldering wood in the garden; their sense of beauty is quite objective. It is so spontaneous and evident that it needs no explanation.

Beauty's authority is manifestly a public announcement, not a gnostic secret. Creation in its beauty overwhelmingly declares God's glory that fills and upholds heavens and earth, the divine goodness that expresses itself in light, flesh, and form, as opposed to any private illumination of spiritual power, such as a gnostic secret spiritualty or the sad remoteness of a call that issues from the distant God of deism. According to David Bentley Hart, "Beauty proclaims God's glory and creation's goodness with equal eloquence and truthfulness in each moment, in each interval within being."[13] Consequently, the Christian story of salvation cannot be partitioned off into the hidden depths of introspection or contemplation; it begins in a world declared "good" by its Creator. Since beauty participates in the infinite, its modalities cannot be exhausted by the endless cultural forms in which it is expressed and felt; still, with a little openness, patience, and tutelage, we can learn to appreciate beauty not native to our experience—whether Japanese modal music, pentatonic Delta blues, the counterpoint of Beethoven, or Hemingway's prose—if we are willing to enter their aesthetic worlds.

Harvard aestheticist Elaine Scarry observes that when we encounter beauty we experience a surplus of aliveness, a "wake-up call" to the plenitude of life. "Beauty quickens. It adrenalizes. It makes the heart beat faster. It makes life more vivid, animated, living, worth living." There is an "overwhelming given-ness in the beautiful, and it is discovered in astonishment, in an awareness of something fortuitous, adventitious, essentially indescribable."[14] It is known only in the moment of response, from the position of one already addressed and only now able to reply. Beauty transcends human language and thought. It cannot be reduced to symbolic representation. Rather than commanding our attention with the force of necessity, inevitability, or utility, the beautiful presents itself to us as an entirely unwarranted, unnecessary, and yet marvelously fitting gift. Beauty is a palpable reminder that the world cannot be reduced to its material causes

13. Hart, *The Beauty of the Infinite*, 21.
14. Hart, *The Beauty of the Infinite*, 17.

and effects, but instead it participates in a mystery, an "invisible nimbus of gratuity"[15] that simply cannot be rationally deduced without remainder.

Beauty provides important clues about the structure of consciousness and the gratuity of being. According to both Plato and Aristotle, the beginning of all philosophy lies in the experience of wonder—in Greek, *thaumazine*.[16] In their view, the beginning of all serious reflection on the world begins in a moment of delighted surprise as things in the world announce themselves to us in their beauty. In every moment of wakefulness, we are confronted by the world given as gift. An amazement lies just below the surface of conscious thought and breaks through only in rare instances. Small children seem to experience the world with an openness to the immediacy and delight of things in the world. Yet, we can't dwell indefinitely in that moment any more than we can forever remain a child. There's a paralyzing fullness to experiences of beauty, a kind of surplus of immediacy that sooner or later we must allow to subside to proceed with the business of life. We may interpret the experience as a kind of passing neurological mistake or a psychological mood, but, in actuality, we have encountered a real, if invitingly brief, glimpse into the deep truth of the world's absolute contingency—the recognition that the world need not be thus, it need not be at all. It is given precisely as gift.

If modernity envisions a thinking mind passively receiving the impress of an inert world, there is now a consensus that human knowing is active and creative. Acts of knowing do not simply receive the world from the senses, as if the mind is a mirror, but they involve an outward intention toward aims beyond the particular object of knowing. In truth, we cannot even walk across a room without some intention toward truth, goodness, or beauty. There is a mystery at the very heart of rational life. In ordinary

15. A phrase coined by David Bentley Hart, who writes, "I may be speaking of something that escapes exact definition here, but it seems to me that the special delight experienced in the encounter with beauty is an immediate sense of the utterly unnecessary thereness, so to speak, of a thing, the simple gratuity with which it shows itself, or (better) gives itself. Apart from this, even the most perfectly executed work of art would be only a display of artisanal proficiency or of pure technique, exciting our admiration but not that strange rapture that marks the most intense of aesthetic experiences. What transforms the merely accomplished into the revelatory is the invisible nimbus of utter gratuity." Hart, *The Experience of God,* 238.

16. Plato has Socrates say, "He was a good genealogist who made Iris the daughter of Thaumas" at 155d of the *Theaetetus* (Bywater, "Aristotles' Dialogue on Philosophy," 7). And at 982b of the *Metaphysics,* Aristotle says, "it is owing to their wonder that men both now begin and at first began to philosophise" (Arieti, *Springs of Western Civilization,* 55).

experience, there is a movement of the self beyond the self, an ecstasy, a sending forth of the mind directed towards an end that resides nowhere within physical nature as an identifiable thing or a closed system of causes and effects. All knowledge is a kind of rapture prompted by a desire that cannot be exhausted by the finite objects that surround us. There is a kind of a deferral of finite desire towards ultimate ends—a greater and more remote purpose for the sake of which one wants whatever one wants. In other words, beauty constitutes an absolute orientation for thought, the horizon of being towards which the mind is always turned. To be seized with a desire for beauty is to yearn to be transformed within oneself into an ever-clearer mirror of its splendor.

As suggested above, beauty holds a certain ethical significance. It conditions our response to others. Beauty is not a product of disinterested contemplation, as Kant supposes; it evokes desire for the other. According to Elaine Scarry, "Beauty establishes a contract or covenant between the perceiver and the beautiful object, compelling the perceiver to attend carefully to and protect the 'aliveness' of the beautiful object."[17] In the words of Simone Weil, beauty requires us to "give up our imaginary position at the center. A transformation takes place at the very roots of our sensibility, in our immediate reception of sense impressions and psychological impressions."[18] In the moment we perceive beauty, we are absorbed into worldly communion with beauty. We are thus recruited by it, beyond ourselves. British novelist Iris Murdoch tells of a day when she was anxious, resentful, and brooding, preoccupied with her problems, but how upon seeing a beautiful kestrel flying above her, all of this fell away. "All of the space formerly in the service of protecting, guarding, and advancing the self is now free to be in the service of something else."[19] Thus there is an aesthetic moment of wakefulness wherein one is moved to cherish and respond to others.

Thus beauty arouses in us a desire for sociality. Beauty invites us into covenant and makes us want to share the experience with others, friends, and strangers, to participate in beauty's own centrifugal movement of eros. Art galleries and museums are filled with people who come to share experiences of beauty. One of the most common responses to beauty, according to

17. Scarry, *On Beauty and Being Just*, 90.
18. Weil, *Waiting for God*, 98.
19. Scarry, *On Beauty and Being Just*, 113.

museum gift shops, is a postcard or phone call to say, "The impressionists are breathtakingly beautiful; I wish you were here! Come as soon as you can."[20]

Beauty prompts an imitative impulse. "The philosopher Wittgenstein says that when the eye sees something beautiful, the hand wants to draw it."[21] Beauty brings copies of itself into being. It makes us want to reproduce it, take photographs of it, or describe it to other people. In museums, we frequently find students with sketch pads; before natural vistas; we find tourists with cameras. Sometimes, the imitative impulse of beauty crosses sensory modes, as when, for example, seeing the smooth cheek of a child prompts a caress, or inspires us to play with or care for the child. This crisscrossing of senses prompted Augustine, when he touches something smooth and pleasant, to think of God, and prompted Dante, inspired by the beautiful Beatrice, to write sonnets of the landscape of salvation in which the beauty of God is met by eternal choruses of praise.

Childhood developmental theorists believe that before the age of three, before the onset of language, young children perceive all stimuli cross-modally—or synesthetically. Daniel Stern observes that the "child directed speech" of a parent to their infant involves rounded—alternating high to low pitch—affect-laden speech, such as "Helllll-ooooo—bayyyyy-beeee."[22] Such aestheticized sing-song words offer an affective embrace that at once invites the infant's attention, attunes to the infant, and draws it near. At a recent university study, researchers ran an endless loop in a special screening room of a recording of Chinese mothers cooing to their infants. They were surprised to find that stressed out graduate students frequently came to sit in the room and listen, to comfort themselves.[23] In addition to its developmental purposes, such sing-song speech seems to be a universal language that crosses cultural-linguistic boundaries. The infants' beauty prompts the mothers' cooing, which, even in an unknown (to them)

20. Scarry, *On Beauty and Being Just*, 6.

21. Scarry, *On Beauty and Being Just*, 3.

22. Stern, *The Interpersonal World of the Infant*, 140.

23. Gopnik et al., *The Scientist in the Crib*. It has been demonstrated that babies' preferences are not linked to the actual words used by mothers because they will turn their heads even if the speaker is using a foreign language. Babies, quite simply, enjoy hearing the higher-pitched sounds and exaggerated speech patterns of parentese. Babies not only enjoy the sounds we make, but they also enjoy watching our faces as we talk to them. Gopnik et al. report that motherese is a comfort language, even if it is listened to in a foreign tongue; for example, graduate students listening to lab tapes found it was therapeutic for end-of-semester stress.

Chinese dialect, traverses fields and crosses modes, affecting moods and behaviors of not only their infants but of stressed-out graduate students in an entirely different culture. Beauty is not, as Kierkegaard supposed, a bourgeois affectation that circles in upon itself, but instead it crosses modes and drives toward the world's complete beautification.[24]

Beauty affects a shift in historical perspective beyond present troubles and contradictions. In *Only a Promise of Happiness*, Alexander Nehamas concludes that beauty manifests a hope that life would be better if the object of beauty were part of it.[25] Theologian David Bentley Hart states that "Beauty seems to promise a reconciliation beyond the contradictions of the moment, one that perhaps places time's tragedies within a broader perspective of harmony and meaning, a balance between light and darkness; beauty seems to absolve being of its violences."[26] In J. R. R. Tolkien's *Return of the King*, when Frodo and Sam are in the shadow land of Mordor, Tolkien writes:

> There, peeping among the cloud-wrack above a dark tor high up in the mountains, Sam saw a white star twinkle for a while. The beauty of it smote his heart, as he looked up out of the forsaken land, and hope returned to him. For like a shaft, clear and cold, the thought pierced him that in the end the Shadow was only a small and passing thing: there was light and high beauty forever beyond its reach.[27]

A final quality of beauty involves the judgment it makes upon us. What distinguishes beauty from modern rationality is that we do not simply make judgments about it; we experience ourselves being judged by it. In every beautiful work we perceive something of the greater mystery we have yet to grasp, something that places us under injunction or verdict. As Eastern Orthodox Christians affirm, "We do not read icons; they read us." So does beauty constitute a challenge to our status quo, urging us toward its greater integration into our lives and toward its referent.

From this summary we can see that beauty as a phenomenon is more than a tool of commodification or a description of mere surfaces. Beauty, in

24. Kierkegaard presents his existential aesthetics in his *The Concept of Irony* as an alternative to Romantic aesthetics. This view is developed further by B in the second part of *Either/Or* as an ethical aesthetics and by Kierkegaard himself as a theological aesthetics, primarily in his *Practice in Christianity*.

25. Nehamas, *Only a Promise of Happiness*, 54.

26. Hart, *The Beauty of the Infinite*, 16.

27. Tolkien, *The Return of the King*, 211.

its concreteness, delights, decenters, crosses modes, points to its transcendent perfection, structures our consciousness, invites community and hope, and publicly witnesses to God's own goodness, to original peace. If the modern social imaginary (which is not to say all modern individuals) forgets, neglects, commodifies, and trivializes beauty, in Christian thought there exists an affirmation of its profundity as key to the purpose of the cosmos.

BEAUTY AS THE LIGHT OF BEING

For ancient Greeks, beauty is that which needs no other justification. For example, cherry blossoms are not beautiful because they bear fruit, their contributions quantified, or because they play some useful role in human evolution. While truth and goodness are desirable for extrinsic reasons—assessed by metrics such as logical coherence, empirical validation, or utility—beauty's value is not dependent on anything else; it is perceived in its immediacy as an unwarranted necessity.[28] Beauty's evidence is simply self-evident, needing no extrinsic validation. For this reason, beauty played a key role in ancient metaphysics. Aristotle concludes that the world's contingency demands that there must be something that moves without being moved, an object of desire and thought.[29] Thus the final cause must have the nature of beauty, since the final cause, like beauty, produces motion by being an object of desire. It requires no other cause or reason. When asked why beauty delights us and why we spend time with the beautiful, Aristotle replies: "that is a blind man's question," since beauty is self-evident.[30] Because there is motion at all, "the first mover exists of necessity; and in this, in necessity, beautifully (*kalos*), and it is in this sense a first principle."[31] For

28. For example, to be considered good, certain conditions must be fulfilled, involving, for example, fairness, justice, respect, and flourishing. To be considered true, a proposition must, for example, logically cohere and resonate with the experience of reality. Beauty, on the other hand, needs no supporting evidence. Its validation is immediate and self-evident.

29. Aristotle, *Hippias Major*, book XII, ch. 7 (1072a 23, 26), as cited in Sammon, "The Beauty of God," 46.

30. Laertius Diogenes, *Lives and Opinions of Eminent Philosophers* V, 1, 20, on Aristotle, as cited in Sammon, "The Beauty of God," 59.

31. Aristotle, *Metaphysics* (1072b 12). According to Sammon, "the fact that the Greek word *kalos* has been translated most often as 'good' reveals how scholars of Aristotle tend to ignore the role that beauty performs in his understanding of the good" (Sammon, "The Beauty of God," 49).

the Greeks, the moving contingencies of the world find their source and end in beauty that needs no contingent reasons or principles.

For the ancient Greeks, beauty was ethically significant. Beauty and love are bound together. Plato (in a speech of Agathon) affirms that love requires some form of loveliness to be loveable. Beauty constitutes "love's loveliness," as it were.[32] In Plato's *Symposium*, Phaedrus praises love as the "ancient source of all our highest goods," as that which alone "will make a man offer his life for another," and as "the oldest and most glorious of the gods, the great giver of all goodness and happiness to men, alike to the living and the dead."[33] Agathon brings love and beauty together when he declares that "although all the gods are blessed, love is the most blessed since it is the loveliest, the youngest, capable of kindling in the souls of others a poetic fire."[34] In a similar way, much later, Dionysius characterizes beauty as the divine perfection that accounts for the allure of the good.[35] Beauty is the divine perfection that serves as the basis for love and establishes the good's attraction. The good is surely what all things desire, but without the concreteness provided by beauty, the good requires extrinsic justification. Beauty is thus a unifying power that exists preeminently in love, drawing us to its delighted consummation. If love is prompted by beauty in an object, it is also true that love's extravagance is itself beautiful.

According to Dionysius, divine beauty communicates itself in the form of the multitude of beautiful things in the world. Its intention is to elevate the soul toward the higher, intelligible realm where the originals of beautiful things reside. He concluded that contemplation of created beauty directs the soul to God. Dionysius writes:

> And, as in the case of sensible images, if the artist looks without distraction upon the archetypal form, not distracted by sight of anything else, or in any way divided in attention, he will duplicate, if I may so speak, the very person that is being sketched, whoever he may be, and will show the reality in the likeness, and the archetype in the image, and each in each, save the difference of substance; thus, to copyists who love the beautiful in mind, the persistent and unflinching contemplation of the sweet-savored

32. Plato, *Symposium*, (196b). as cited in Sammon, "The Beauty of God," 31.

33. See, e.g., Sheffield, Plato's *Symposium*, 35.

34. Plato, *Symposium*, 195b, 195c 196a, 196e, as cited in Sammon, "The Beauty of God," 32.

35. Dionysius the Areopagite, *On Divine Names*, 4, 7 (701C), as cited in Sammon, "The Beauty of God," 112.

and hidden beauty will confer the unerring and most Godlike appearance. Naturally, then, the divine copyists, who unflinchingly mould their own intellectual contemplation to the superessentially sweet and contemplated comeliness, do none of their divinely imitated virtues "to be seen of men" as the Divine text expresses it; but reverently gaze upon the most holy things of the Church, veiled in the Divine Muron as in a figure.[36]

For the Greeks, beauty (along with unity, goodness, and truth) is a transcendental property which every particular being has by virtue of existence, but which is perfected in God. Just as beautiful art points beyond itself to a referent—an object, feeling, circumstance, or person—so Dionysius observed in the beautiful things of the created world a Referent which they express. As such, beauty joins finity with infinity, this world to the mysteries of God, as a path of ascent.

In book VII of the *Republic,* Plato famously offers his allegory of prisoners in an underground cavern, shackled since birth such that they can only see shadows cast on the distant wall of the cavern.[37] A released prisoner would gradually recognize different planes of reality. First they would see the objects and the light inside the cave, later they would emerge from the cave and see the reflections of objects on the water, and eventually real objects. Finally, they would see the sun and determine that it rules the realm of visible objects, the cause for all the prisoners see. The last object they achieve is the idea of the good (represented by the sun), which is the reason for all the good and beautiful things of the world. Yet the philosopher's ascent from the sensible to the intelligible level is not primarily intellectual, nor does it end in calculations of the good. Propelling this ascent is desire (*eros*) and its object, beauty. Thus, Plato sees the shadow world as materially linked to the real, which is ruled by the sun, but beauty finally holds an erotic sway over all things. According to Plato, prior to "coming to earth," the soul contemplates visions, which, when recalled in reality, are the objects of remembrance. Only beauty, the brightest of these visions, gives itself to sensuality and cognition and provides to the lover of beauty the capacity to 'reconnect' with the true being, the primordial conditions of existence.[38]

---

36. Dionysius the Areopagite, *The Collected Works,* 131.

37. See Plato, *The Republic,* 365–401.

38. Plato, *Phaedrus* 250d, in Pieper, *"Divine Madness,"* 42.

Plato's metaphysics of analogical participation, which makes beauty central, survived in various forms well into Patristic and late medieval theology. Thomas Aquinas, for example, represents the height of medieval theological thought. His *Summa Theologica* is divided into three major parts: the first deals with the *Exitus* or going forth from God; the second involves humankind's *Reditus* or return to God; and the third explains the return to God as taught by Christ. With Augustine, he saw that God is Love, hence the best way to know God is through the heart, a methodological assumption that excludes a rational grasp of God and points to love of beauty. As he sees it, all creatures were created good by a perfectly good God, beautiful by a perfectly beautiful God, thus God is present to each creature in their own way. In his exposition on Dionysius, Thomas holds that God, the supreme Beauty, is his own existence, *ipsum esse subsistens* (subsisting only in himself), hence all things only have their being by participating in God's beauty.[39] Citing Dionysius, Thomas insists that God is the cause of being's brilliance. God with a "flash sends down to all creatures a share of His luminous ray, the source of all light."[40] These dazzling communications of the divine shaft are "pulchrifying"—producing beauty in things.[41] Every form by which a thing has being is a participation in divine brilliance.[42] In his *Quaestiones Disputatae De Veritate*, Thomas states that the object of knowledge is truth, while the object of desire is the good, yet truth and goodness radiate a splendor from their forms that captivate the one who sees with love, drawing them into ecstatic contemplation and wisdom.[43] Beauty, "which shines with dazzling light," bears witness to the spiritual reality of being, awakening the most intimate depths of the person by captivating the

---

39. A term meaning "being itself subsisting." Aquinas derives this as a description of God from Aristotle (through Avicenna) and also from Exodus 3:14. Basically, it is the distinctive characteristic of God in Aquinas's metaphysics. All created beings are composite in their essence and existence (*esse*). Thomists call this "the real distinction." This means that what creatures are and the fact they actually exist are not identical in them, while in God, what he is and the fact that he is are truly identical. God is his own existence or act of being. Thus, God can be described as *ipsum esse subsistens. Expositio in Dion. De div. Nom. 4.5–6*, as quoted in Aquinas, *The Pocket Aquinas*, 269.

40. Aquinas, *The Pocket Aquinas*, 269–70.

41. Aquinas, *The Pocket Aquinas*, 269–70.

42. Aquinas, *The Pocket Aquinas*, 272.

43. "*Cognitio et voluntas radicantur in substantia spirituali super diversas habitudines eius ad res*" (Aquinas, *De verit.* 23.1, in Aersten, *Medieval Philosophy and the Transcendental*, 247).

mind and will in wonder and ecstatic contemplation.[44] For Thomas, beauty signifies that God is closer to us than we are to ourselves, *"intimior intimo meo."*[45] We are caught up in the things themselves, outside of ourselves in an attitude of receptivity—that is, love—in the splendor of truth and goodness being revealed.

Due to the potential risk of idolatry, early and Patristic Christians were cautious of identifying God with ordinary things. By the late fifth century, Dionysius, in *The Divine Names,* navigated this prohibition by identifying qualities in the created order, including beauty, that may be viewed as praiseworthy names for God. He saw Christ's incarnation as providing a warrant for earthly names and qualities of the divine. Dionysius made a crucial theological contribution by identifying beauty as a concept capable of mediating the intelligible plenitude of God within the restrictions of human perception, a "porosity" between the material and the spiritual. He avoided the risk of idolatry by designating divine names such as beauty as "dissimilar similitudes." Once we announce a similarity to the divine, a negating mechanism immediately reveals a greater dissimilarity.[46] Like many other Patristic scholars, he adapts Neoplatonic notions of the One (unity of God) and Nous (God's self-communication) as language befitting the Christian Trinity in which the Father is hidden in light inaccessible, and the incarnation as God's self-communication.[47] In God's self-communication, beauty's material form lifts the gaze to immaterial divine beauty. The divine name of beauty serves to draw the heart and mind toward God, while its greater dissimilarity prevents our idolatry. Ascent through beauty's material form to divine beauty does not involve leaving behind materiality but engages it more profoundly since it analogically discloses the spiritual.

---

44. Dionysius the Areopagite, *Theologia mystica,* from John Paul II, "The Trinity,."

45. Augustine, *Confessions* III, 6, 18.

46. Dionysius feels it necessary to clarify that these images ought not be taken in the literal sense but in the more spiritual sense found in Pauline theology. "By no means do I affirm, after the statement of antiquity, that as being God and Creator of the universe, the sun, by itself, governs the luminous world, but that the invisible things of God are clearly seen from the foundation of the world, being understood by the things that are made, even his eternal power and deity." These statements indicate Dionysius's intention to extend the divine names to the sensible properties found in material things without univocally identifying any particular divine perfection with those material things. Dionysius, *CH* 2, 2–4 (137 D–140A–C, 141C, 144A, 145A), as cited in Sammon, "The Beauty of God," 92.

47. See Sammon, "The Beauty of God," 95.

If beauty is a philosophical first principle, it is not without significance for our thinking minds. As early as Plato, beauty was seen as inspiring and containing the impulse for intellection. Plato asks, "What sort of phenomenon could be so capable of attracting intellectual curiosity with such vigor only to leave the intellect unrequited in its desire for determination?"[48] He sees beauty as such a phenomenon, since it transports the questioning intellect beyond its normal modes of analysis to a dimension where failure of intellectual comprehension may indicate transcendent success. In *Phaedrus*, Socrates distinguishes beauty from common modes of thought by classifying it as a mania—that "heaven-sent madness" that communicates and bestows "all blessings."[49] As he explains, this divine mania occurs in four modes. The first is a mania associated with prophecy, which he proclaims the greatest of the arts and which "comes from the gods" and "is more beautiful than sanity, which is of human origin."[50] By connecting prophetic mania with beauty Plato suggests that it is precisely in this "loss of rational sovereignty that we gain intuition, light, and insight into reality, all of which would otherwise remain beyond our reach."[51] A second mode of the mania of beauty, the "cathartic mania," "appears among the sick and inspires prayer and worship, establishing the means of purification."[52] Cathartic mania reorders the disorder that erupted on account of sickness. Thirdly, poetic mania takes hold of "a gentle and pure soul, arouses it and inspires it to songs and other poetry, and thus by adorning countless deeds of the ancients nurtures later generations."[53] Plato suggests that poiesis involves a double purpose: it extends itself beyond the bounds of discursive reason, immersing itself in mystery, and returns to the jurisdiction of discursive reason to express what was perceived in its transcending. The fourth mode, the desire of those who love beauty, transforms them into lovers—the "sum and substance of all our discourse."[54] Pope Benedict summarizes Plato thus: "Indeed, an essential function of genuine beauty, as emphasized by Plato,

48. Plato, *Hippias Major*, 304e, cited in Sammon, "The Beauty of God," 28.

49. Plato, *Phaedrus*, 244b, cited in Sammon, "The Beauty of God," 36.

50. Plato, *Phaedrus*, 244c, cited in Sammon, "The Beauty of God," 37.

51. Pieper arrives at the same interpretation through an application of the findings of modern psychoanalysis. Cf. Pieper, *"Divine Madness,"* 17. Cited in Sammon, "The Beauty of God," 37.

52. Plato, *Phaedrus*, 244e, cited in Sammon, "The Beauty of God," 38.

53. Plato, *Phaedrus*, 245a, cited in Sammon, "The Beauty of God," 39.

54. Plato, *Phaedrus*, 249e, cited in Sammon, "The Beauty of God," 40. Also see Pieper, *"Divine Madness,"* 38.

is that it gives man a healthy 'shock,' it draws him out of himself, wrenches him away from resignation and from being content with the humdrum—it even makes him suffer, piercing him like a dart, but in so doing it 'reawakens' him, opening afresh the eyes of his heart and mind, giving him wings, carrying him aloft."[55]

While beauty resists precise definition, Thomas Aquinas in *Summa Theologica* offers three distinguishing characteristics of beauty—integrity, proportion, and radiance. For Thomas, each created thing has its own form or integrity, its own distinctive beauty. In his words, "Everything is beautiful in proportion to its own form."[56] A tree is beautiful to the degree in which it perfectly attains to the form of a tree. To be beautiful the parts of the whole must be well-balanced in harmony with one another. "We have only to think of the symmetry of the petals of an orchid, the balance of a mathematical equation, the mutual adaptation of the parts of a work of art, to realize how important the factor of harmony is in beauty."[57] A chief characteristic of beauty is *claritas* or radiance—the luminosity that issues from a beautiful object, which initially seizes the attention of the beholder and illuminates our intellects with an intuition of understanding. "Radiance belongs to being considered precisely as beautiful: it is, in being, that which catches the eye, or the ear, or the mind, and makes us want to perceive it again."[58]

Thomas Aquinas formalized for Christian theology what remains tacit for the Greeks in an ontology of *analogia entis* (the analogy of being) which sees that the world participates analogically in God. If no language can be adequate for talking about God (equivocity), that makes God entirely unthinkable, but if we say that our language and concepts are identical with God's (univocity) then that makes God all too thinkable, potentially reduced as an idol.[59] Thus, the world we encounter, including its beauty, participates by analogy in God's own perfection. For Thomas, analogy applies not only to our speech but to our very being in God. He envisions the cosmos as participating in God in a similarity that involves an always greater dissimilarity.

55. Benedict XVI, "Meeting with Artists."

56. Aquinas, *Summa Theologica* I.5.5.

57. Maurer, *About Beauty*, 10–11.

58. Gilson, *The Arts of the Beautiful*, 35.

59. See especially Aquinas, "On the Principles of Nature," and *Summa Theologica* Ia Q. 13, a. 5.

For Thomas, the world cannot simply be flattened for mastery as Descartes imagined, since it testifies of God's beauty. In its existence it bears witness to and praises God. Contrary to the modern reduction or objectification of the cosmos, being is theophanic in both the classical and Pauline sense, dependent upon God and subsisting in the luxuriant plenitude of finite forms through which God speaks.[60]

As we can see, for the Greeks, this cosmos is no brass canopy, a closed loop of efficient causes, since all things in their beauty reveal their openness to God. It cannot be simply spatialized or mapped for cognitive mastery; all things vibrate with eternal meaning and significance. In Taylor's terms, the world is "enchanted."[61] It demands a different quality of attention than is required for mirroring, mapping, and mastering; to know the world requires, as we will see, something more like love. In this abbreviated survey of the ancient metaphysics of beauty, we see that beauty is intrinsic to all created being and participates in God's perfect Beauty. Beauty is the unmoved mover, the source and telos of desire and love; as such, beauty directs us to God, sparks our intellect, sets us outside ourselves, and assimilates us in love.

BEAUTY AS BIBLICAL WITNESS

Beauty is not only key to Greek metaphysics; it also finds support in the biblical tradition, especially in its analog, glory. The God of Scripture is

60. "The wrath of God is being revealed from heaven against all the godlessness and wickedness of people, who suppress the truth by their wickedness" (Rom 1:18). "Paul then stood up in the meeting of the Areopagus and said: 'People of Athens! I see that in every way you are very religious. For as I walked around and looked carefully at your objects of worship, I even found an altar with this inscription: to an unknown god. So you are ignorant of the very thing you worship—and this is what I am going to proclaim to you. The God who made the world and everything in it is the Lord of heaven and earth and does not live in temples built by human hands. And he is not served by human hands, as if he needed anything. Rather, he himself gives everyone life and breath and everything else. From one man he made all the nations, that they should inhabit the whole earth; and he marked out their appointed times in history and the boundaries of their lands. God did this so that they would seek him and perhaps reach out for him and find him, though he is not far from any one of us. For in him we live and move and have our being. As some of your own poets have said, "We are his offspring." Therefore since we are God's offspring, we should not think that the divine being is like gold or silver or stone—an image made by human design and skill'" (Acts 17:22–29).

61. The notion of an enchanted premodern and a disenchanted modern world is first developed by Max Weber (See Weber, *The Sociology of Religion*, 270) but is a central concept of Charles Taylor in *A Secular Age*.

envisioned as an artist creating in sheer delight a world woven through with beauty. Genesis (1:31) speaks of God creating and consecrating the world as good (*tov*), which can be translated as "beautiful" or "harmonious." The Bible highlights the concrete sense of God's loveworthy beauty or glory. The Song of Songs refers to the writer's beautiful lover, which is eventually taken up in allegorical fashion as an analogy that points to Christ, the beautiful lover, and his beloved, the church.[62] Psalm 19:1 proclaims, "The heavens are telling of the glory (*kavod*) of God; And their expanse is declaring the work of His hands." In the Old Testament, "glory" (*kavod*) communicates God's power, radiance, character, and presence, often through physical manifestations, like the burning bush and the cloud at Sinai. In the Exodus, God's glory is manifested in pillars of cloud and fire.[63] In Deuteronomy, the construction of the temple combines God's glory in the Ark of the Covenant with the beauty created by the artisans who wove cloth and applied the gilding.

Israel's literature, according to Gerhard von Rad, "brims over in sheer delight in God's creation" (Ps 114, 143; Job 9:3, 26:5),[64] but the highest form of beauty seems to be reserved for the unmerited redemptive work of God in history. According to von Rad, while Israel knew the beauty recognized by all people—in the human form, the moon, forms of speech, artistry, narrative, and poetry—her most intensive encounter with beauty was in the religious sphere, and because of this "Israel occupies a special place in the history of aesthetics." He states, "For Israel, beauty was something that happened rather than something that existed."[65] In the priestly tradition especially, the focus of Israel's rapt delight was the glory of God perceived as a reflection of transcendent (1 Kgs 8:11), or otherworldly brilliance—"the heavenly robe or light in which glory is clothed which, though fatal to mortal eyes, must with the divine triumph fill the whole earth (Ezek 38:18; Isa 6:3; 40:5; 60:1ff.)."[66] In Scripture, God's glory (*kavod*) manifests itself before any word is heard—i.e., in the great epiphany on Sinai, the vision in the burning bush, the visions through which Isaiah and Ezekiel received their

---

62. Hippolytus of Rome, Origen, Athanasius, Gregory of Nyssa, Theodore of Mopsuestia, Theodoret of Cyrus, and Maximus the Confessor all compose commentaries on this text contributing to the development of desire's relationship to God's beauty.

63. Exodus 13:21–22.

64. Von Rad, *Old Testament Theology*, 368.

65. Von Rad, *Old Testament Theology*, 368.

66. Eichrodt, *Theology of the Old Testament*, 1.277.

callings, the visions on Tabor and Damascus, and the apparitions of the Son of Man of the Apocalypse.[67] According to Hans Urs von Balthasar, glory distinguishes God from created beings. God's glory signifies none other than God's own divinity. The more fully a creature is allowed to encounter God's glory, the more this creature will long to extol God's glory over all creation. The triumph of the divine purpose in history eventuates in a full experience of the divine glory in the whole earth.

With the emergence of the prophetic tradition, the term "glory" comes to be charged with moral-ethical significance, and this understanding of holiness would continue to be a part of its meaning for subsequent traditions in the West. It would come to signify a "holy people" obedient to God's "holy will." In the later messianic tradition, there was a unification of the priestly and prophetic threads in the "figure of divine glory" who, in bringing the historical process to fulfillment in peace and justice, would at the same time bring all of creation into participation in the divine glory.

The beginning of the Christian religion is the self-communication of the wholly other God and the thanksgiving offered by the creature overtaken by what it has received. For Balthasar, perceiving the ineffable glory of God is the beginning of all truth and justice. With Karl Barth, Balthasar insisted that there is no neutral stance from which to reflect on ethics. Only when one is overawed by God's divine glory can we love our neighbors—hence we love others in the measure of love with which God loves us (1 John 4).

In the Bible, the whole earth is seen to groan to be lifted out of the realm of the profane. God does not hold his divinity to himself but "offers it as the space . . . in which Israel is henceforth to dwell after being transported out of itself."[68] By his glory, at the consecration of the Tent of Meeting, God hallows what is not himself. For Balthasar, the hallmark of the true God, which renders the mission of Christ wholly credible as God's decisive engagement with the world, is love that radiates the quality of "excess," the "ever greater," the "yet more."[69] In the face of the recklessly self-forgetful character of God's crucified love, the most fitting response is summed up in the exhortation, "so we ought to lay down our lives for our brothers"(1 John 3:16). The more the Christian grasps the lengths to which the triune God is involved on our behalf, the greater grows their ambition to live no longer for themselves. The aesthetic form and measure of God's action in Christ

67. Balthasar, *The Glory of the Lord: 1*, 12.

68. Balthasar, *The Glory of the Lord: 1*, 63.

69. Balthasar, *My Work in Retrospect*, 41.

provides the model for Christian action. Balthasar anticipates our protests: "It will be objected that such a program of action demands the character of a saint. This may well be; but from the very beginning, Christian living has always been most credible, where at the very least it has shown a few faint signs of true holiness."[70]

Genesis 1:26 reveals that humans are created in the "image and likeness" of God. Karl Barth insists that humans, having been made in God's image, are thus ordained to be God's creaturely co-respondent or covenant partner—for such is an expression of the lordship of God *par excellence*. If this image is to resemble its archetype, then it must bear certain traces of glory, which is the theme of Psalm 8: "You have made them a little lower than the angels and crowned them with glory and honor. You made them rulers over the works of your hands; you put everything under their feet." Humans are thus to be seen as God's art. The goal of the incarnation consists in making image (human) and glory (God) coincide in Jesus Christ so that in the embodied human form the supraformal divine fullness may dwell (see Col 2:9: "For in Christ all the fullness of the Deity lives in bodily form").

In the Bible, perceiving God's glory is no incidental matter. Witnesses of glory respond by falling to the earth, their eyes downcast or shielded, or in Paul's case blinded. As such, encounters with glory are perceived as a grace the Spirit of God brings to people as a kind of death and new life. Balthasar suggests that this is the experience of every hearer of God's word; the hearer "perceive(s) God by being transported outside of himself or herself . . . They are no longer their own but are conscripted for obedience in mission, thus revealing God's holiness to the world."[71] While Balthasar does not finally collapse the notion of glory into the phenomenon of beauty, he sees that glory and beauty are alike in that they contain palpable qualities that speak of what is at once intelligible and sublime, true and mysterious, delightful and untamed.

* * *

This chapter has attempted to characterize beauty not by proposing a precise definition, but by providing numerous observations and insights. If we cannot precisely define beauty, there is still a good deal to say for its significance. It should be clear that beauty does not refer merely to the appearance or

70. Balthasar, *Engagement with God*, 43.
71. Balthasar, *Engagement with God*, 13.

to surfaces, nor to prettiness, symmetry, or calculable order. Neither do we encounter beauty disinterested or unaffected; it transports us beyond ourselves and makes demands on us. It is known through concrete forms—of sight, sound, words, materials, movements—that resist one-to-one rational or abstract summary. It delights but does not sate us; it lifts our gaze to its ground and telos. It invites wonder and prohibits totalizing finalities or easy essentialism. It does not circle in upon itself, but extends the reach of its eros across modes, in creativity, gifts, worship, and practical response.

I have attempted to provide new perspectives and historical resources with which to understand ordinary experiences. Understood in light of these sources and reflections, beauty is not trivial, but participates in the very movement of the world toward God. If baseball awakened and called me beyond myself to love, that would be profound enough, but my testimony is that baseball not only recruited me in love but constituted a kind of parable in which my desire comes to be directed to God. The beauty of baseball lifted my gaze toward a more excellent beauty in Christ and Christ's church. If this is true, then the methods of Christian education and formation have been far too limited, and beauty deserves greater consideration.

PART II

Beauty as a Foundation for Formation

ALL APPROACHES TO CHRISTIAN formation, beyond their assemblage of techniques, assume some vision or myth concerning the nature of the world, God, and human selves. As we have seen, modernity introduces a story in which humans are thinking things inclined to rationally master concepts—and indeed, the world. In this model, cognition is scaffolded, involving certain tasks—for example, remembering, understanding, applying, analyzing, evaluating, and creating—to incrementally clarify and achieve cognitive mastery of ideas.

In the account I am developing from ancient, Patristic, and modern sources, beauty constitutes a way of knowing that does not allow mastery but evokes the mystery and depth of the material world and lifts our gaze to God. To encounter beauty is already to intuit, without incremental tasks of development, its hidden depths and to respond creatively. (As we saw, the Bible depicts the human response to God's glory as immediate humility, surrender, and active commitment.) In this account, beauty frames the world, God, and human personhood very differently from modernity and demands its own approaches and techniques. Beauty's account of knowing and being is confirmed and deepened when seen as key to the Christian understanding of the cosmos created in glory and to John's notion of Christ as God's Art.

Because beauty is a phenomenon that unifies human experience—perception, feeling, evaluation, knowledge, commitment, and action are known in a moment—any attempt to identify discrete and rigid pedagogical tasks will be problematic. Thus, any attempt to systematize the tasks of Christian formation in light of beauty must be considered relative and suspect, taken only as heuristic. Yet this does not mean that Christian formation is random and accidental. Christian educators have learned much from artists and mystics about how to give focused attention to mysteries hidden in the world's materiality that cannot be exhaustively distilled and abstracted by reason or instructed as principles.

Because the modern story of thinking selves and inert matter has been exhausted, Christian formation needs a more adequate account; thus, I have chosen to reflect on Christian formation and pedagogy through the lens of theological aesthetics. We can gain a sense of the aims of Christian formation by considering theological visions that emphasize themes such as beauty, Christology, poiesis, liturgy, and prophetic art. This volume does not pretend to craft a unified pedagogical approach from the ground up, but instead draws from existing techniques and a variety of pedagogical approaches—including narrative, contemplative, and practical theological approaches. Many educators have intuited the importance of beauty, mystery, and creativity in Christian formation. The following chapters survey concepts from a small selection of theologians, especially those that shed light on knowing and formation that is Christian. Each chapter will also deduce from these theological underpinnings aims and practices consistent with them.

Finally, deducing practices consistent with the experience of beauty is akin to rationally systematizing the Sistine Chapel, that is, destined to be incomplete and partial, subject to alternate interpretations. Predictably, others will see alternate ways to parse the possible aims and learning activities. I see my role rather as an art critic—drawing attention, illumining possibilities, inviting more adequate perception and engagement. Also, since the following chapters feature theological accounts that relate to and build from each other, there will thus be some redundancy in the pedagogical techniques that flow from them. When this is the case, I have tried to note the overlaps and resist repeating my practical reflections except as they vary significantly in focus and intent.

2

Creation Announces Itself

[St.] Francis helps us to see that an integral ecology calls for openness to categories which transcend the language of mathematics and biology, and take us to the heart of what it is to be human. Just as happens when we fall in love with someone, whenever he would gaze at the sun, the moon or the smallest of animals, he burst into song, drawing all other creatures into his praise. He communed with all creation, even preaching to the flowers, inviting them "to praise the Lord, just as if they were endowed with reason." His response to the world around him was so much more than intellectual appreciation or economic calculus, for to him each and every creature was a sister united to him by bonds of affection. That is why he felt called to care for all that exists. His disciple Saint Bonaventure tells us that "from a reflection on the primary source of all things, filled with even more abundant piety, he would call creatures, no matter how small, by the name of 'brother' or 'sister.'" Such a conviction cannot be written off as naive romanticism, for it affects the choices which determine our behaviour. If we approach nature and the environment without this openness to awe and wonder, if we no longer speak the language of fraternity and beauty in our relationship with the world, our attitude will be that of masters, consumers, ruthless exploiters, unable to set limits on their immediate needs. By contrast, if we feel intimately united with all that exists, then sobriety and care will well up spontaneously. The poverty and austerity of Saint Francis were no mere veneer of asceticism, but something much more radical: a refusal to turn reality into an object simply to be used and controlled.

—POPE FRANCIS, *LAUDATO SI'*

"Oh, earth, you're too wonderful for anybody to realize you," Emily cries as she leaves to return to her grave. She then looks at the stage manager and tearfully asks, "Do any human beings ever realize life while they live it?—every, every minute?"

"No," he answers. "The saints and poets, maybe—they do some."

—THORNTON WILDER, *OUR TOWN*

LONG BEFORE EMILY RETURNED to Grover's Corners from the other side, even before St. Francis preached as brother to the flowers, Christians beheld a world whose beauty testifies to God's own perfect beauty. Once, in this tradition, the world in its beauty was seen to subsist in praise of the Creator, while the human calling inaugurated in Eden was, as Alexander Schmemann suggests, to receive God's gifts and name them—to respond to God's blessing with our blessing.[1] As Scriptures testify, sacred beauty lies

---

1. Schmemann states, "the unique position of man in the universe is that he alone is to bless God for the food and the life he receives from Him. He alone is to respond to God's blessing with his blessing. The significant fact about the life in the Garden is that man is to name things. As soon as animals have been created to keep Adam company, God brings them to Adam to see what he will call them. And whatsoever Adam called every living creature, that was the name thereof. Now, in the Bible a name is infinitely more than a means to distinguish one thing from another. It reveals the very essence of a thing, or rather its essence as God's gift. To name a thing is to manifest the meaning and

in ordinary things—in bread and wine, sheep and shepherds, vineyards, fig trees, seeds, fathers and prodigal sons, importunate widows, children, the generosity of boys with fish, humble servants, weeping mothers, friends, simple meals, and self-giving love unto death. These ordinary things constitute parables that point toward Christ's paradigmatic beauty, even as Christ points to the beautification of all things in God.

Despite modernity's evacuations of mystery, we find the spirit of St. Francis in odd little outposts of saints, mystics, and artists. For example, J. R. R. Tolkien's fantastic creatures of Middle Earth—sage wizards, ethereal elves, rapacious orcs, soulless dragons, crafty dwarves, solemn Ents, and pragmatic hobbits—were not trivially or accidentally fashioned. Tolkien expressed in his sub-creations the conviction that God's cosmos is outrageously wondrous, a peculiarity best described as magic. Tolkien maintained:

> The definition of a fairy-story—what it is, or what it should be—does not, then, depend on any definition or historical account of elf or fairy, but upon the nature of Faërie: the Perilous Realm itself, and the air that blows in that country . . . Faërie itself may perhaps most nearly be translated by Magic—but it is magic of a peculiar mood and power, at the furthest pole from the vulgar devices of the laborious, scientific, magician. There is one proviso: if there is any satire present in the tale, one thing must not be made fun of, the magic itself. That must in that story be taken seriously, neither laughed at nor explained away.[2]

G. K. Chesterton pronounced, "[Fairy] tales say that apples were golden only to refresh the forgotten moment when we found that they were green. They make rivers run with wine only to make us remember, for one wild moment, that they run with water."[3] In Faërie, Tolkien warns, the one thing that we must not mock is magic,[4] and yet in our disenchanted modern world this is precisely the thing we have forgotten. Jürgen Moltmann reminds us that this excess of "play" woven into the created world reflects God's own delighted play, that "even the birds sing louder than Darwin

---

value God gave it, to know it as coming from God and to know its place and function within the cosmos created by God." Schmemann, *For the Life of the World*, 15.

2. Tolkien, "On Fairy-Stories," 145.

3. Chesterton, *Orthodoxy*, 81.

4. By magic, Tolkien and Chesterton do not mean to include black magic—the notion that by manipulating earthly objects we can bend God to our will. Instead, what they mean by magic is the sacramentality of all things that disclose God and invite communion. Here, they are pointing to the iconic or theophanic function of all created things.

would allow."[5] All creation, in its beauty, exists in praise of God, such that "even the stones cry out" (Luke 19:40). An adult who has learned that the world unfolds of its own accord or by force of will may forget such things as wonder, joy, or gratitude. The fairy stories of Tolkien awaken us to an outrageous creation that reveals more than is allowed by the reductions of modern science, economics, or the Cartesian thinking self. Scripture tells us of a God who creates the world *ex nihilo,* from nothing, and for no reason save playful delight. In his delightful fourth chapter from *Orthodoxy,* "The Ethics of Elfland," G. K. Chesterton writes,

> The sun rises every morning . . . Now, to put the matter in a popular phrase, it might be true that the sun regularly rises because he never gets tired of rising. His routine might be due, not to a lifelessness, but a rush of life. The thing I mean can be seen, for instance, in children, when they find some game or joke that they especially enjoy. A child kicks his legs rhythmically through excess, not absence, of life. Because children have abounding vitality, because they are in spirit fierce and free, therefore they want things repeated and unchanged. They always say, "Do it again"; and the grown-up person does it again until he is nearly dead. For grown-up people are not strong enough to exult in monotony. But, perhaps God is strong enough to exult in monotony. It is possible that God says every morning, "Do it again" to the sun; and every evening, "Do it again" to the moon. It may not be automatic necessity that makes all daisies alike; it may be that God makes every daisy separately, but has never got tired of making them. It may be that He has the eternal appetite of infancy; for we have sinned and grown old, and our Father is younger than we.[6]

Against the modern imaginary that renders the world inert and necrotic, Christ's redemption involves a redemption of human senses. At least as far back as Origen, our spiritual senses were not seen as gnostic endowments but a quickening of our natural senses of sight, sound, touch, taste, smell, which awakens spiritual qualities of wonder, awe, conviction, joy, or glory in which the infinite is disclosed.[7] Theologian Hans Urs von Balthasar

5. Moltmann, *A Theology of Play,* 5.

6. Chesterton, *Orthodoxy,* 61.

7. Hans Urs von Balthasar picked up on the theme in the 1930s, building his understanding of the spiritual senses largely on his interpretation of Origen. See, for example, Balthasar's anthology *Origines Geist und Feuer.* The spiritual senses became an important theme within his masterwork, *The Glory of the Lord: A Theological Aesthetics.* More recently, Mark McInroy has offered a thoughtful reassessment of modern scholarship on

insists that faith is not only, as Karl Barth imagines, a gift from above; it is also a gift from below, discerned in the concrete beauty of incarnate life by our senses. Hence, it is crucial that we restore something like St. Francis's sense of the world alive in beauty if we are to refresh our hearts, restore our worship, and deepen our faith, if we are to perceive creation and the incarnation as gifts.

Hans Urs von Balthasar is arguably the most important modern thinker to articulate beauty's theological significance, and his seminal contributions are enduring. Certainly, Balthasar's thought does not exhaust the possibilities for considering aesthetics, but he does provide a basic grammar of the big ideas constituting current epistemological discussions. In this chapter, we will survey the thought of Balthasar to clarify how ways of knowing, especially for Christian formation, can appropriately participate in created beauty. I will elaborate key points of his aesthetic epistemology and make a start at articulating pedagogical aims and practices for attending to beauty and re-enchanting the spaces between beings and God.

THEORETICAL UNDERPINNINGS

Hans Urs von Balthasar was born on August 12, 1905, in Lucerne, Switzerland, to a patrician Catholic family. His aesthetic interests, including his obsession with music, began in his childhood with his training at the hands of Benedictine monks. He eventually chose a religious life over what might have been a promising career as a concert pianist.

In 1928, Balthasar entered the Jesuit novitiate for two years, after which he spent two years studying with a Jesuit faculty near Munich, followed by four years of theology near Lyon. He was trained in both philosophy and theology but was dissuaded from a theological doctorate because he felt himself "languishing in the desert of neo-scholasticism"—a theological approach that relied heavily on systematic reason.[8] Instead, he completed his doctorate *summa cum laude* in literature. His thesis, *The Apocalypse of the German Soul*, was a massive study of the eschatological implications of the major philosophies, dramatists, and poets of the late eighteenth through early twentieth centuries, focusing especially on the conditions of

---

the matter. See McInroy, *Balthasar on the Spiritual Senses*, 20–35.

8. Biographical details in this section are drawn from two articles by the Jesuit bishop Peter Henrici, a nephew of Balthasar: "Hans Urs von Balthasar A Sketch of His Life," and "Hans Urs von Balthasar: His Cultural and Theological Education."

modern nihilism. He saw that in the collapse of transcendence, the proper relationship between God and humanity is destroyed, as human thought submerges transcendence into immanence to the point of glorifying death.

In the years just prior to World War II, Balthasar formed a lifelong friendship with Protestant theologian Karl Barth. In 1950, as a result of an Ignatian retreat, Balthasar left the Jesuit order and found an ecclesiastical home in the diocese of Chur where he began developing his views on theological aesthetics, a project that he would not complete until 1985. In 1988, Balthasar was invited by Pope John Paul II to become a cardinal, an honor he accepted out of obedience after refusing twice before. However, on June 26, two days before his elevation as a cardinal, Balthasar died of heart failure as he was preparing to celebrate morning Mass.

Balthasar attempted to bridge what he saw as the "fatal cleavage" between theology and spirituality in contemporary Christianity. In a memorable quote, he believed theology properly to be the study of the "fire and light that burn at the center of the world . . . while theologians had reduced it to the turning of pages in a desiccated catalogue of ideas—a kind of butterfly collection for the mind."[9] He insisted that "the living God, if he is anything, must be supremely concrete. By losing the priority of beauty, by closing the spiritual senses that grasp the colors and contours, the taste and fragrance, of truth in its radiant body, the theologians had betrayed even the very master they claimed to serve."[10] In Balthasar's view, the reason beauty seems to recede into the background is not because it's less important but because it forms the very context in which truth and goodness make sense. Only by virtue of beauty is truth evident and goodness palpable.

Balthasar's writings amount to well over eight thousand pages, making any inclusive summary impossible, but for purposes of considering its implications for Christian formation, we can point to a few key aspects of his metaphysical account.

Form and Splendor

If, as we have seen, modern rationality parses the "structures of being" abstracted from their constitutive relationships, artists know that things in the world can only be truly seen as integrated "wholes" or forms. A character in a play, a note in a song, or the colors of a landscape only have their

9. Caldecott, "An Introduction to Hans Urs von Balthasar."
10. Caldecott, "An Introduction to Hans Urs von Balthasar."

true meaning in the context of the whole form. Neither do we encounter the world as fragments of sensation or facts but as forms that have aesthetic unity. According to Balthasar, form is the exterior shape of an interior depth that shines through it. Form is what distinguishes rock from plant, plant from animal, animal from human being, one musical score or poem from another, poetry from philosophy, etc. Apart from form, the human *eros* towards knowledge would be futile. It is the rich detail of the lovely world that draws us to curiosity and pursuit of knowledge and a desire to be good.

Balthasar's concept of "form" is drawn from an array of sources: classical sources, German romanticism, and the English poets, especially Gerard Manley Hopkins. Drawing from Goethe, Balthasar understands form as possessing a "distinct inner finitude" (*deutliche innere Endlichkeit*).[11] His understanding is also rooted in two ancient Greek concepts: *eidos* (image, idea) and *morphe* (shape). For Goethe, form is not static but is in dynamic movement toward its potential, its true telos. Goethe saw form as shaped by an "inner law of self-realization" (*inneres Gesetz der Selbstverwirklichung*), in which the form at once already possesses and is realizing a movement towards fulfilling its potential.[12] With Augustine and Aquinas, Balthasar concludes that a thing cannot be truly known apart from its final cause and fulfillment in God.

Humans encounter form as a capacity of soul which participates with God, perceiving essences and depths. For Gerard Manley Hopkins,

> everything in the universe was characterized by what he called *inscape*, the distinctive design that constitutes individual identity. This identity is not static but dynamic. Each being in the universe "selves," or enacts its identity. And the human being, the most highly selved, the most individually distinctive being in the universe, recognizes the inscape of other beings in an act that Hopkins calls *instress*, the apprehension of an object in an intense thrust of energy toward it that enables one to realize specific distinctiveness.[13]

When we see forms—trees, flowers, skies, faces, etc.—we do not see them as arbitrary constellations of color, light, and movement, not mere facts. When we encounter the forms of God's creation, we perceive them as *inscapes* or expressed unities, that can only be fully known in their relation

---

11. Balthasar, "Personlichkeit und Form," 1–15. For a discussion of this article, see D. C. Schindler, *Hans Urs von Balthasar*.

12. Balthasar, "Personlichkeit und Form," 1–15.

13. Greenblatt et al., "Gerard Manley Hopkins," 2159.

to God, their true end. We perceive inscape by the powers of our souls. By means of our souls we are capable of expressing *inscape* to others, which Hopkins calls *instress*.

The Greeks, according to Balthasar, were right to see the world as radiant or epiphanic. To truly know a thing does not involve simply mapping its facts but perceiving its expressive light. This light shines from form, from shapes and patterns that permit our souls access to meaning. For Balthasar, a thing discloses two poles or aspects—form (or *species*) and splendor (or light, or *lumen*). These two poles are inextricable and constitute our experience of every created thing. Balthasar writes:

> As form, the beautiful can be materially grasped and even subjected to numerical calculation as a relationship of numbers, harmony, and the laws of Being . . . Admittedly, form would not be beautiful unless it were fundamentally a sign and appearing of a depth and a fulness that, in themselves and in an abstract sense, remain beyond both our reach and our vision.[14]

Form, the first pole of beauty, denotes a thing's integrated materiality in which its parts that can be grasped and even calculated. For example, musicians study tones, intervals, keys, chordal patterns, and their complex relations; painters study color, shadow and light, and composition.

The second pole of a beautiful object is the light that shines from beyond it, its lumen or splendor—the more mysterious pole. For Balthasar, beautiful objects are not mere feats of artistic engineering, but manifest a mystery, a unifying principle that draws us to and beyond it—a mystery he calls "depths." Regarding the second pole, he writes:

> We "behold" the form; but, if we really behold it, it is not as a detached form, rather in its unity with the depths that make their appearance in it. We see form as the splendor, as the glory of Being. We are "enraptured" by our contemplation of these depths and are "transported" to them. But so long as we are dealing with the beautiful, this never happens in such a way that we leave the (horizontal) form behind us in order to plunge (vertically) into the naked depths.[15]

14. Balthasar, *The Glory of the Lord: 1*, 115.

15. Balthasar, *The Glory of the Lord: 1*, 116.

Form and splendor are always beheld together.[16] We catch sight of the form (as a whole) precisely in the illumination of its splendor (a striking clarity). For example, we might read a poem over and over again and it makes no impression, but then suddenly we have a moment of clarity and see how the threads are connected together. An illumination occurs as its form coheres. If we were to behold only form and fail to recognize the splendor, we would fall into a dry and objectifying theory of beauty, while an excessive focus on splendor might lead to subjectivism.

In beholding a beautiful form there is also in that moment of perception a conjunction of subject and object. Confronted by beauty's form and splendor, there is an ecstatic rapture, a self-emptying or *kenosis* of the heart to make room for the beautiful. It is not that we first see beauty and then respond as a deliberative second act; rather, when we are catching sight, we are already being lifted in motion by its splendorous depths. We do not master beautiful things; we are assimilated to them. Beautiful things announce their beauty, draw us into them, and compel our response in a covenant of joy, gratitude, and creative response. If the Cartesian *cogito* comprehends an object by abstracting and calculating its rational structure, it fails to recognize the light that shines forth from its form, allowing disparate elements to be seen as a unity, in terms of what it is becoming. The priority Balthasar gives to this understanding of form may sound odd to moderns but should not be foreign to artists who seek to express the soul of a thing, its inner light and feeling that outstrips its mere appearing.

Wonder and the Appearing of Depths

Wonder is an abiding disposition in Balthasar's epistemology. Wonder at being is not only the beginning of thought but the permanent element in which thought appropriately moves. David Schindler says that, for Balthasar, "Wonder is not a merely subjective experience, but it is rather the objectively adequate response to the reality of being. Likewise, since it is the nature of being to cause wonder, being cannot be perceived as it is except from within this experience."[17] However, this wonder "is possible only where the horizon of being itself is not closed but is constituted in such a way as to include a 'more': in other words, to include a difference."[18]

16. Balthasar, *The Glory of the Lord: 1*, 115.
17. Balthasar, *The Glory of the Lord: 5*, 615.
18. Schindler provides a clear description of what Balthasar means by contrasting

Difference is that element within relationality that takes us beyond simple admiration to that which is unexpected and surprising. In the example of St. Francis, we may admire a bird that has decorated our lawn, but when we address her as sister, we are perceiving her as a surprising "something more"—an alterity, a difference, an agency, not reducible merely to our use or the machinations of our egos. Wonder discloses in beauty the hidden agency of an "other" through which God speaks.

Whether we are encountering the face of a child, a majestic oak, a seascape, or an act of kindness, there is more to our encounter with beauty than can be attributed to evolutionary biology, psychological projections, or efficient causality. When we perceive the splendor of a beautiful form there is an "appearing of depths"—a mystery that becomes manifest.

When Balthasar says the depths are appearing in the form of beauty, he means, inseparably, three different things. First, the depths reveal the thing itself. For instance, when the beauty of a tree strikes us, we perceive something like the very life principle of the tree, its own inner being manifesting itself to us. Second, the depths reveal something of the mystery of being. Reality is making itself known to us in its thick web of relationships. Third, the depths reveal a glimmer of God's inaccessible glory.[19] These are not intellectually deduced but are sensed immediately as inseparable and simultaneous. Beauty's splendor discloses a thing's depths, its inner principle, the gratuity of being itself, as a gift of Benevolence. As such, beauty lies at the very intersection of God and the world. Those who have surrendered in love to another person will know the experience of a light being shone on the object of love, on the entire world, revealing its goodness, and sometimes even the divine Beloved who gives good gifts. When beauty is truly perceived, we "experience the cosmos as the revelation of an infinity of grace and love."[20]

---

freedom with "necessity of Being." In analyzing Balthasar's comparison of genuine wonder with admiration, Schindler argues, "Admiration is the astonishment one experiences that 'everything appears so wonderfully and "beautifully" ordered from within the necessity of Being.' What is lacking here—even if we grant that such admiration is indispensable and may itself be a profound experience—is precisely the element of surprise. Let us take the term necessity, which Balthasar uses in this context. It is a word to be contrasted with freedom, understood not in the psychological sense of having choices and not being under constraint, but rather in a metaphysical sense connected with a notion of 'positivity,' that is, the arrival of an unanticipated 'more.'" Schindler, *Hans Urs von Balthasar*, 32.

19. Schindler, *Hans Urs von Balthasar*, 15, 16, 26.

20. Schindler, *Hans Urs von Balthasar*, 109.

For Balthasar, while the incarnate Christ is the highest form of beauty disclosing God and the world, all beautiful things are analogues of the Christ form. Beauty moves us by eros toward the world and toward God. As such, Balthasar sets beauty as the first word of theology.

The Mother-Child Image

While Balthasar was critical of aspects of modernity, he appreciated the modern "turn to the subject" which emphasized the interiority of human personhood as an opening for theology. Balthasar sees in modern anthropology a microcosm of the whole, a self that opens in wonder to God.[21] He illustrates this in a phenomenology of the "mother-child" relationship in which the wonder of "difference" reveals the whole structure of finite being.[22] For Balthasar, the mother-child relationship is pregnant with significance for epistemology, ontology, anthropology, and theology. D. C. Schindler has said that Balthasar's insight into the mother-child unity constitutes a singular contribution to philosophy.[23]

The analogy of a mother's smile, in its broadest strokes, details how a mother smiles at her child before her child can smile back at her. For Balthasar, this analogy is a primordial indicator of the nature of all reality as founded on prior love. Balthasar states:

> After a mother has smiled at her child for many days and weeks, she finally receives her child's smile in response. She has awakened love in the heart of her child, and as the child awakens to love it also awakens to knowledge: the initially empty sense impressions gather meaningfully around the core of the Thou. Knowledge (with its whole complex of intuition and concept) comes into play, because the play of love has already begun beforehand, initiated by the mother, the transcendent.[24]

21. In his view, the modern turn to the person presents an opportunity, as we will see, to clarify the significance of Christ's personhood in the incarnation.

22. Of course, as most of us would acknowledge, the role of the caregiver, as mother, is not absolute nor necessarily gender specific. There are many ways in which caregivers of any gender can show this quality of relationship to infants. Even though Balthasar's image or metaphor has been problematized, still it holds value in what it reveals about aesthetic epistemology. Schindler, *Hans Urs von Balthasar and the Dramatic Structure of Truth*, 51.

23. Schindler, *Hans Urs von Balthasar and the Dramatic Structure of Truth*, 51.

24. Balthasar, *Love Alone Is Credible*, 54. Balthasar contextualizes the smile of the

Balthasar characterizes the mother-child relationship as including the following dynamics:

1. As the mother beholds the child, she does not perceive the child as mere fact, but as a beautiful other worthy of love. Therefore, the mother's beautiful smile is a reciprocating gesture of love that "welcomes" the other, her child. She is not imposed as a smothering or dominating or demanding presence, but as an enabling invitation. As children, we awaken to love only through a love that is prior and greater than ours; "The little child awakens to self-consciousness through being addressed by the love of his mother."[25]

2. Not only does the mother perceive a beauty that is worthy of her love; the mother also beholds in the child a visage, an image of the child's true selfhood—who they are, who they are becoming. In her loving gaze, a mother discerns, crafts, guards, and bears an "image" of her child in the "creative mirror" of her loving knowledge. In loving her child, she gives her child that image in return. According to Aidan Nichols, "This is why Balthasar says that the love of the mother is a creative call; it is a spontaneous receptivity that gives rise to a receptive spontaneity."[26] In response to the image she discerns in the child she crafts an environment that anticipates and suits the child's unique development. This creativity can be seen, for example, in child-directed speech, in affect-attunement, and in their play together. Thus, knowing and loving bear the same presupposing conditions; they require a flexible openness that permits the beloved "space" to be, while also giving the beloved back to themselves in an act of free artistry.

---

mother in this way: "God interprets himself to man as love in the same way: he radiates love, which kindles the light of love in the heart of man, and it is precisely this light that allows man to perceive this, the absolute Love . . . In this face [of Christ], the primary foundation of being smiles at us as a mother and as a father. Insofar as we are his creatures, the seed of love lies dormant within us as the image of God (imago). But just as no child can be awakened to love without being loved, so too no human heart can come to an understanding of God without the free gift of his grace—in the image of his Son" (Balthasar, *Love Alone Is Credible*, 76).

25. Balthasar, "Movement toward God."

26. I refer to Aidan Nichols's work in defining how Balthasar uses these terms. He states, "Since the revelation of an object has its meaning only when it is offered to a knowing subject, we can even say that the object finds its own full sense only in that subject. Created knowledge for Balthasar is therefore at once receptive and spontaneous, or, in his preferred vocabulary, 'measured' and 'measuring'" (Nichols, *Say It Is Pentecost*, 15).

3. The mother's gaze and the creative image she projects calls forth from the child a mutual gaze of the lovely and loving infant in free response. The infant perceives in the mother's gaze an image that reflects the child's love-worthiness, inviting a return response of love. Balthasar writes, "In the creative mirror of the subject, the object sees the image of what it is and of what it can and is meant to be." When successful, the child will respond with her own creative acts, for example, of chatter, play, and exploration.

4. It is not only the infant whose self is perceived, given, and called forth by the care of the mother; the mother's self is also enhanced by the returned gaze of the child as the image that calls forth the mother in new ways. The two are determinative for each other's selfhood; they serve as a creative mirror for each other's unfolding response to their difference, beauty, and creativity.

5. As the child is awakened to consciousness by the love of the mother, the child is simultaneously captured by the wonder of being. Similarly, the mother also is struck by wonder at the fact that her experience is not merely interpersonal but a response to wider Being. Their mutual unfolding prompts wonder at the gift of existence, the fact that there should be anything at all. Balthasar states, "The fact that I find myself within the realm of a world and in the boundless community of other existent beings is astonishing beyond measure and cannot be exhaustively explained by any cause which derives from within the world."[27]

6. Finally, they sense their life as gift and the possibility that its source lies beyond. They will wonder at the source of goodness, truth, and beauty upon which their being subsists. The mysteries they have encountered in each other and in being now open to the depths which speak of God. The mother's task of measuring or intuiting an appropriate sense of the child—who she is, who she is becoming, and the space required to flourish—remind the mother of her finitude and God's infinitude. In the mother's own measuring, she comes to the realization that her experience of the child is not an unlimited experience of Being. She realizes that in the act of measuring, she is being measured by the encompassing truth of Being which comprehends her.

27. Balthasar, *The Glory of the Lord: 5*, 615.

For Balthasar, the dynamics of the mother-infant encounter are analogous to the mutuality of the Trinity, to our co-respondency with God in Christ, and ultimately to how we know all things. The mother-child relationship cannot be comprehended by a Kantian disinterested subject or the Cartesian *cogito*, but only from within the dialectical flow of aesthetic experience—through beauty, wonder, and poiesis.

A mother's smile is a primordial indicator of the nature of all reality because all reality is founded on an unconditional, prior, and signifying love perceived in its beauty. Analogous to the mother-child dyad, the created world is to be known in beauty, wonder, love, and creativity. If beauty is the "self-showing" of being, then everything we encounter offers its inner word to us. Thus, creation is not to be mastered but perceived in wonder and beauty, creatively imagined and allowed to unfold according to its mysterious depths. Objects in the world radiate beauty and wonder into the knower's space for their completion. True knowledge of an object can unfold only in the subject making itself available in an attitude of service for the completion of the object.[28] There is a curious suitedness of the human mind for the created world, and the created world to the human mind.

In summary, for Balthasar, the subject is not simply a mirror capturing objective states of affairs. Every created object in its form shines forth its depths, which must be lovingly discerned by humans as a creative image if it is to develop in its fullness. For Balthasar, "Receptivity means accessibility to another's being, openness to something other than the inner dimension of one's own subjectivity, the possession of windows looking out on all being and truth. Receptivity signifies the power to welcome and, so to say, host another's being in one's own home."[29] As Balthasar observes, "One knows oneself simultaneously with actually being addressed by another's truth."[30] Here Balthasar is acknowledging the role of our creative encounter with other creatures as constitutive of our selfhood. This is a theme we will develop later in the chapter dedicated to poiesis.

As we can see, Balthasar's epistemology—his notions of participation, form, wonder, depth, and the reciprocity of the mother-child image—constitutes a dramatic shift away from Descartes's mastery of an object. His epistemology constitutes a foundation in which Christian formation can attend to the beauty of things in the world.

28. Balthasar, *Theo-Logic*, 1.66.
29. Balthasar, *Theo-Logic*, 1.44–45.
30. Balthasar, *Theo-Logic*, 1.47.

EDUCATIONAL AIMS

Balthasar's theological aesthetics articulates created beauty as open to wonder and participating with God. If we are to perceive the truth of towering mountains or trees, the delicate beauty of a child's face, or the ecstasy of a Mozart concerto, as they disclose the depths of themselves, being, and God, we must learn to see them not as mere objects but as openings for our spiritual senses, as something other than the inner dimension of one's own subjectivity. Artists, saints, and mystics have historically cultivated practices that reliably open them to the world's beauty and its spiritual significance. Below is a set of aims to guide pedagogical practices that engage created beauty and awaken us to a knowing that is loving. Pedagogies for engaging creation's beauty seek to accomplish the following aims.

1. *They seek to train us to perceive the world as a plentitude of beautiful forms that announce their depth and mystery and invite mutual participation.* To break the spell of modern excarnation, we must cultivate practical habits of contemplation that restore our attention to the sacramental world and awaken our spiritual senses. Walter Burkhardt defines contemplation as "a long, loving look at the real."[31] When we look lovingly at the real in its beauty, we can know it as an "invisible nimbus of gratuity."[32] The quality of attention required to enhance our engagement with created beauty is at once outward and inward. Outward attention awakens us to the world's concrete forms; inward attention awakens us to how these forms surprise us with wonder, alterity, desire, and gratitude.

2. *They seek to help us perceive created forms with splendor and depth that disclose things in themselves, the glory of being, and the Creator.* Created things in their beauty hold a kind of wisdom that doesn't reduce wholly to concepts, but which speak eloquently beyond words in each moment. Just as artists learn to perceive the essence or inscape conveyed in their art, so must Christians discern wisdom that discloses things in themselves, being, and God.

3. *They seek to foster a creative encounter in which we craft images that approximate a thing's true ends, even as we discern in its wisdom the possibilities for our own completion.* As a mother perceives the true

31. Burghardt, "Contemplation," 91.
32. Hart, *The Beauty of the Infinite*, 283.

ends of a child and holds this image in her gaze, conditioning her response in creating the child's environment, so does our encounter with the world's beauty invite us to creatively express the ends and wisdom we intuit in its forms.

Even though practices that allow us to perceive the wonder and wisdom in created beauty have not always been an explicit part of the toolkit of many Christian educators, still some have explored techniques that can nurture beauty, wonder, and creativity. Below are four educational practices that can help us to attend to the above aims.

FOUR EDUCATIONAL PRACTICES FOR ENGAGING CREATION'S BEAUTY

The first practice involves giving attention to concrete particulars. If Balthasar is to be believed, all art—natural and created—shines a light on spiritual mysteries. Things in their material concreteness allow the Spirit to speak. If, as Walter Burghardt suggests, contemplation involves "a long, loving look at the real," artists and contemplatives know how to give this kind of attention to objects.[33] Artists and mystics testify that grasping the mysteries of the world begins with seeing the world in its material beauty with fresh eyes. Learning to see the world in its gratuity and depth requires engaging its concrete materiality in patient practice in an attitude of love. While practices of giving attention are specific to forms of art and prayer, we can observe some similarities.

Julia Cameron, author of *The Artist's Way,* suggests arranging regular "artist dates" in which to set aside time to immerse ourselves in an unfamiliar context—other cities, or communities, for the purpose of noticing, sensing, feeling the strangeness that can awaken us from our forgetfulness of ordinary life.[34] Cameron suggests that we "capture" as much as we can. Cameron's practice of attending to the unfamiliar seems consistent with Balthasar's affirmation that sources of beauty in the buzzing, blooming world of creatures can spark wonder and desire and point to God.

Contemplative theologian Richard Rohr adapts a similar practice for prayer. Richard Rohr suggests the following:

33. Burghardt, "Contemplation," 91.
34. Cameron, *The Artist's Way.*

Go to a place in nature where you can walk freely and alone. If you can, find some place where human impact is minimal. But if you're not able to travel to wilderness, visit a neighborhood park or tree-lined street where you can walk safely. If you are unable to walk, sit in a place where you can gaze at nature and move within your imagination, your inner vision.

Begin your wandering by finding a threshold (perhaps an arched branch overhead or a narrow passage between rocks). Here offer a voiced prayer of your intention and desire for this time.

Step across the threshold quite deliberately and, on this side of your sacred boundary, speak no words, but watch and listen for God's presence. Let the land, plants, and creatures lead your feet and eyes. Let yourself be drawn, rather than walking with a destination or purpose in mind. If you are called to a particular place or thing, stop and be still, letting yourself be known and know, through silent communion with the Other.

Before you leave, offer some gesture or token of gratitude for the gift nature has given you. When it is time to return to the human world, find your threshold again and cross over—and now you have learned to watch for God in all things.[35]

Contemplative artist Jean Wise uses the following exercise to behold the hidden depths of created beauty.

Quiet your mind and ask God to meet with you and speak to and teach you through the natural beauty or piece of art you are contemplating. Spend some time with the form of natural beauty. Gaze at it. Spend some time keeping your eyes on the part of the natural form or art that captured your attention first. If your eyes were deterred from a part of the whole form, spend some time with your eyes looking there as well. Study the details, the colors, the relationship of where things are placed. Notice what is in light and what is in shadow, what is fully included in the "frame" and what is only partially included.

Now spend some time reflecting on the following questions:

- *What captured your attention?*
- *What did you want to avoid looking at?*
- *What emotions are you feeling?*
- *Does this stir up any memories or bring any person or situation to mind?*

35. Adapted from Rohr, *A Spring Within Us*, 64–65.

- *Do any Scriptures come to mind or specific words?*
- *What are your other thoughts?*

Bring all of these to God. Let the prayers form within you. Speak to God about what you are experiencing from this natural form. You may also want to record some of your thoughts and insights in your journal. Thank God for speaking to you.[36]

Contemplative writer and spiritual director Anthony De Mello invites us to engage our memories to perceive the beauty in other people and in ourselves. Here is one of his many guided meditations, entitled "Judge Not."[37]

It is a sobering thought that the finest act of love you can perform is not an act of service but an act of contemplation, of seeing. When you serve people, you help, support, comfort, and alleviate pain. When you see them in their inner beauty and goodness, you transform and create.

Think of some of the people you like and who are drawn to you. Now attempt to look at each of them as if you were seeing them for the first time, not allowing yourself to be influenced by your past knowledge or experience of them, whether good or bad. Look for things in them that you may have missed because of familiarity, for familiarity breeds staleness, blindness, and boredom. You cannot love what you cannot see afresh. You cannot love what you are not constantly discovering anew.

Having done this, move on now to people you dislike. First, observe what it is in them that you dislike, study their defects impartially and with detachment. That means you cannot use labels like "proud," "lazy," "selfish," "arrogant." The label is an act of mental laziness, for it is easy to stick a label onto someone. It is difficult and challenging to see this person in their uniqueness. You must study those defects clinically. That means, you must first make sure of your objectivity. Consider the possibility that what you see as a defect in them may not be a defect at all but something that your upbringing and conditioning have led you to dislike.

If, after this, you still see a defect there, understand that the origin of the defect lies in childhood experiences, past conditionings, faulty thinking, perception, and, above all, in unawareness—not

---

36. Wise, "How Does Art Enhance Prayer?"

37. The practice as it appears here can be found on the official website of Anthony De Mello; see De Mello, "The Finest Act of Love." The practice found online is only slightly modified from its original text in De Mello, *The Way to Love*, 128.

in malice. As you do this, your attitude will change into love and forgiveness, for to study, to observe, and to understand is to forgive.

Having made this study of defects, now search for the treasures buried in this person that your dislike prevented you from seeing before. As you do this, observe any change of attitude or feeling that comes over you, for your dislike has clouded the vision and prevented you from seeing. You can now move on to each of the people you live and work with, observing how each of them becomes transformed in your eyes when you look at them in this way. By seeing them in this way, it is an infinitely more loving gift that you offer them than any act of service. For you have transformed them, you have created them in your heart and given a certain amount of contact between you and them. They will be transformed in reality, too.

Now, make this same gift to yourself. If you have been able to do it for others, this should be fairly easy. Follow the same procedure: No defect, no neurosis is judged or condemned. You have not judged others; you will be amazed now that you yourself are not being judged. Those defects are probed, studied, and analyzed, for a better understanding that leads to love and forgiveness. And, to your joy, you will discover that you are being transformed by this strangely loving attitude that arises within you toward this thing you call yourself—an attitude that arises within you and moves out through you to every living creature.

These and many other practices of artists and mystics engage the created world announcing its beautiful otherness, disturbing our settled identities with its wisdom. Contemplative practices cultivate what Martin Buber called "I-Thou" relationships, where other people, events, and things are beheld as subjects and not merely as objects for use or enjoyment.[38] Unless we place ourselves in unfamiliar places or perceive the world afresh in its depth and alterity, we risk obscuring the surprising beauty and wisdom disclosed in its concrete particulars.

The second educational practice involves imaginative free play with created beings. Contrary to modern knowing, meaning is not harvested in a neutral process, nor are human minds simply mirrors upon that world. As Balthasar saw, humans make meaning in a creative field of play analogous to the gaze between the mother and child. The mother and child find meaning in each other not because of an analysis of bare facts, but in a creative field of play in which they grasp the aesthetic unity of the other and hold

---

38 Buber, *I and Thou*.

a created image to which the other responds creatively. He saw that all our knowing involves a similar aesthetic process, a free play of perception, imagination, and creation. Just as the mother creates and holds an image of the child to which the child responds, so our engagement with created beauty evokes our creative response in words or actions that express its truth. As suggested above, artists and contemplatives do not truly know the world's wisdom apart from their artistic creations—their play—that render and express it. Truly perceiving the hidden depths of beauty necessitates this kind of free play which grasps and gives form to what we intuit in our souls. Christian education practitioners employ tactile play to better perceive beauty's depths. Only in such play is their meaning rendered. Practitioners and practical theologians have long employed a range of contemplative and artistic methods for spiritual purposes.[39]

Most notably, in Jerome Berryman's *Godly Play* approach children encounter the tactile and narrated stories of Christian texts and tradition, which teachers envelop in wonder by asking questions and by creating space for children to playfully render by drawings, paintings, and play with the manipulable objects of their stories. In his approach, the Christian tradition provides the general boundaries of the "game" but allows free play in which the meanings of God and self can emerge. While Berryman's approach does not, strictly speaking, play with creation's beauty, his approach sheds light on a pedagogical role for play and poiesis. The role of play with Christian stories in Berryman's approach is analogous to the beauty of ordinary things in God's creation.

For example, Kaisa Stenberg-Lee's practice of praying with children illustrates an approach that plays with created beauty in a straightforward manner. Her practices involve the following:

1. Go Outside
   An overwhelming body of research shows that most children's earliest and most profound experiences of God or "the

39. It is the nature of beauty to involve a creative process of play and poiesis. It would be insufficient to elaborate a pedagogical approach to beauty that does not acknowledge the crucial role of play and poiesis; but for the purposes of this book, it will be helpful in this chapter to foreground beauty in a way that includes its background dynamic of play, but in the next chapter play and poiesis will be foregrounded with beauty as its background. As we will see, poiesis in the thought of John Milbank requires more thorough consideration than will be helpful here, but it already punctuates Balthasar's understanding of beauty. For this reason, this section will provide enough theory and practical hints to suggest its role, while a more adequate understanding of play and poiesis should also consider the entire next chapter.

Transcendent" have been recorded to take place in nature. As we enable the child to experience nature and the natural world (even if it's just through indoor plants, collected sticks and rocks, or family pets, on some days) we let children read the first book of God (creation). Children and adults naturally are drawn to encounter their Maker in and through nature. Being in nature nurtures our wonder for all of life and God in the world.

2. Engage the Senses

Studies have also shown that being outdoors helps children to awaken their senses and improve their awareness of their environment. Children explore the world through their senses. This is how they naturally learn and make sense of their environment. It is no different when it comes to their friendship with God. When I pray with children, I try to encourage a full range of sensorial experiences and sensory engagement. When we ask curious questions such as, "What smells or sounds make you think of God?" or "I wonder if you wanted to show God how you feel inside by drawing a picture or using watercolors?" We honor and nurture children's natural ways of encountering God in and through their physical bodies.

3. Connect through Play

Play is children's native language and the way through which they give and receive love. Child-parent attachment specialists encourage parents to build safety, trust, and connection with their children through play. God made children, and surely God too knows how to "speak the language of play". As you observe children's play, you learn what their natural, preferred ways of connecting are. Consider those to be and become their gateways to prayer. For example, children who enjoy making and creating things most likely will naturally enjoy praying through arts and crafts. We honor children's unique developmental gifts and needs when we are willing to "relearn" the language of play alongside them and join them in play as spiritual companions. This communicates the important message that they matter just the way they are right now to us and to God.

4. Embrace Mystery

Finally, there is a lot of mystery around the ways God and children come to connect and share their hearts with each other. While we can be eager to get peeks into children's lives with God, we won't ever fully come to know or understand them. My encouragement to adults who accompany children in prayer is to be faithful in our own secret lives with God. Let us remember our childhood faith and cultivate curiosity, faith, and wonder in order to make space for the praying children among us in all of the sacredness that they deserve.[40]

Narrative arts have long been a means by which Christians have played with sacred mysteries in the created world. As we have seen, J. R. R. Tolkien expresses through his fiction wisdom of the created world by playing with language, fantastic creatures, dramas of good and evil, and unexpected heroic figures. Contrary to the misunderstanding that fiction represents mere flight of imagination, he insists that "[fairy] tales say that apples were golden only to refresh the forgotten moment when we found that they were green."[41] Literary play can awaken us to other worlds in which creatures are partners, where courage is found, good triumphs over evil, the world which Christian liturgy establishes at its font and table. In the play of writing and reading fantasy literature our desire is strengthened and our hope is bolstered. For this reason, writing and reading fantasy and poetry should be seen as formative spiritual practices.

The everyday stories and testimonies of people can also be playful means by which meaning is discovered in the created world. When we tell the stories of our lives, we are not simply offering systematic accounts of empirical facts; instead, we are playing with characters, events, plots, tensions, and resolutions that highlight mysteries that do not always yield to rational calculations. Our stories and testimonies constitute our play with the meaning of our lives amidst the materiality of our concrete experiences and various cultural and religious meanings. Our testimonies are not rational articulations of historical realities but also our hidden desires, intuitions, and visions that animate and heal us. In Dori Baker's story theology approach, for example, each session begins with a story told as an artful expression of a slice of life.[42] Participants are then asked to give focused attention to their felt responses to everyday stories, enveloping them with wonder and playing with their meanings. In this approach, not only is a storyteller playing with meanings, but a gathered community of participants are playing with the meanings hidden in the stories. This notion of narrative play undergirds a number of educational and spiritual approaches, including Frank Rogers's typology of religious, social, personal identity,

---

40. Stenberg-Lee, "Wonder Walks and Listening to God with Children."

41. Chesterton, *Orthodoxy*, 81.

42. Baker, *Doing Girlfriend Theology*.

critical, existential/contemplative, and creative contexts.[43] Approaches to spiritual direction have long existed that involve journaling and storytelling as a means of narrative play to access hidden spiritual meanings.[44] Contemplative approaches invite participants to play with the mystery they glimpse in the materiality of their daily lives. The Ignatian Examen, for example, involves a prayerful review of the events of the day, giving expression to experiences of consolation and desolation, which is a way of imagining, naming, or expressing how God is at work in our lives.

Theatre arts have their own tools for playing with meanings. In Augusto Boal's games theater is a language for expressing the wisdom hidden in our bodies as they are shaped by situations in our environment.[45] Boal's warm-up games help participants access their felt experiences as inspiration for their theater images, tableaus, or skits. In techniques of silence, guided imagery, and warm-up games, participants access the felt "sense" of a past lived situation, enveloping it with wonder. Participants are then led in creative play—creating images and scenes—to express and reinvent the situation. Creating skits and living sculptures helps participants to play with created forms in all their beauty and ugliness and the wisdom they disclose. Boal's *Rainbow of Desire* approach seeks to express and play with the inner drama of a person's life and its complicity in lived situations of oppression.[46] Just as the mother sees in the beauty of her infant an image that guides her care, so for Boal do we theatrically play with our created and social worlds. Just as a mother perceives in the infant the image of a self that wants to become, in Boal's theatre approach we glimpse "ideal" images—what things (persons and events) in their beauty want to be.

The third practice involves attending to the wisdom of created beings. Beautiful things are not simply inert, to be consumed or mastered; they speak a gracious word of wisdom. A beautiful garden, a beautiful child, a majestic forest, a beloved pet may give us delight, yet they also have wisdom to share and a partnership to enjoin. In depths of the world's being new awareness can be attained and expressed in halting words and gestures in excess of our concepts.

43. Rogers, *Finding God in the Graffiti*.

44. See, for example, Progoff, *At a Journal Workshop*.

45. Boal, *Theatre of the Oppressed*.

46. Boal, *The Rainbow of Desire*, 86–88.

Elizabeth Liebert assumes that God speaks wisdom in and through created things. Liebert, in her book *The Way of Discernment*,[47] suggests the following practice of discernment before a creature that discloses its wisdom:

1. Go outside. Walk or sit in a place where you feel comfortable.

2. Seek, once again, the inner freedom to desire what God desires and follow it once it becomes clear.

3. As you walk or sit, notice your surroundings. Let your attention be drawn to something natural in the environment, living or nonliving. Be present to it as completely as you can. Allow it to be just what it is without trying to change it or use it for your purposes.

4. In the presence of that natural object, restate the decision you are discerning, without describing it in detail or rehearsing its aspects. Simply let your discernment question be present alongside you as you ponder this natural object.

5. Wait, in the presence of this bit of nature, listening for what it might share with you. Note it in detail in your journal.

6. What does your experience of being present to the natural object suggest about your decision?

7. Bring any new awareness about your decision back to your desire to follow God's call. Notice what happens to your thoughts and feelings. Perhaps an image comes to you. Does your decision feel different from this perspective? Record in your journal any shifts.

8. Offer your tentative decision to God.

Perhaps more than any other religious educator, Mary Elizabeth Mullino Moore has emphasized that our teaching ministry needs to inspire a sense of holy connectedness between human beings and the rest of the created order. Moore's writings, especially *Ministering with the Earth* and *Teaching as Sacramental Act*, demonstrate her commitment to *tikkun olam*, "repair of the world." Moore does not call only for ministry in which human beings strive to take better care of the earth but also ministry with the earth as partner in helping to fashion God's reign on earth. In *Teaching as a Sacramental Act*, Moore expresses the conviction is that it is in the "concrete stuff of creation"—through our connections with people and the earth, through our practices, through our stories—that God's grace is mediated to human

47. Liebert, *The Way of Discernment*, 134.

beings.[48] For Moore sacramental teaching equips people for sacramental living, in which our very lives "mediate divine grace in the church and world".[49] Moore emphasizes the sacredness of hopes, creation, meetings, confrontation, journeys, partners, and vocation as sources of inspiration toward the metaphorical project of assembling a quilt of sacrality. Moore names seven acts of sacramental teaching: expect the unexpected, remember the dismembered, seek reversals, give thanks, nourish new life, reconstruct community, and repair the world. While Moore does not explicitly develop the aesthetic dimensions of these reversals, the mystery of created beauty might be seen as fundamental as a source and telos of wisdom and healing. Moore's practices of sacramental teaching can be seen as ways to mine the wisdom found in creation's beauty.

To eyes awakened by beauty the world remains endlessly open to fresh meaning, to wisdom. In the same way that artists learn to perceive what its object is expressing—that outstrips its rendering—so may we attune our senses to perceive and render the spiritual wisdom of creatures in our world.

The fourth practice involves engaging in creative praxis. Axiomatic to Christian faith and formation is that it is embodied and active, not held as a gnostic secret or a mere ideological dogmatism. As we saw above, for Balthasar our action is intimately bound up with responding creatively to beauty and the ends toward which it points. When a mother perceives the beauty of her child, she is glimpsing a vision of the child as it is becoming. The mother sees the child's emerging personhood in their speech, behavior, the activities and objects to which they gravitate, and the gifts they manifest, if only nascently. Drawing from these materials the mother renders an image of the child which she holds in her eyes, and in her response to the child—in child-directed speech, in the caring environment she creates. A mother's creative rendering of her child's image—who they are and are becoming—determines her active response. Further, the actions of the mother are perceived by the child as an aesthetic unity, which in turn conditions the child's active and creative response to the mother and the world.

Balthasar's vision of the action of the mother constitutes a rejection of other possibilities—for example, that the mother asserts her personality onto the child, that the mother's actions are but rational calculations, or else a laissez faire relationship which renders the mother passive and the child the primary active agent. For Balthasar, both our knowledge of

48. Moore, *Teaching as a Sacramental Act,* 10.

49. Moore, *Teaching as a Sacramental Act,* 22.

the world and our developing personhood and action are reciprocal and interdependent. Human knowledge and personhood are constituted in loving aesthetic perception, creativity, and creative action. As indicated in Balthasar's paradigmatic example of the mother and child, our encounter with the world's created beauty involves a quality of action rendered in response to beauty and its ends.

In recent decades a number of praxis or "revised correlational approaches" have been introduced as Christian education pedagogies.[50] While they differ on many finer points, many resemble Richard Osmer's praxeological approach with its four moments: descriptive-empirical (What is going on?), interpretive (Why is this going on?), normative (What ought to be going on?), and pragmatic (How might we respond?).[51] These practical theological approaches feature descriptive, contextual, and theological analysis and culminate in a strategic moment for active response. Considered positively, they constitute an important pedagogical development that extends normative theological concepts to faithful action. Negatively, they can reduce these various mediations to rational conclusions that evacuate them of their beauty and ends. If we fail to lovingly contemplate the beauty of people, situations, and their ends, then our practical responses risk being determined by mere rational calculations of dogma or utility, or else projections of our egos.[52] If Balthasar is right, better practice involves contemplation of the other's beauty and their ends. Attending to beauty's depths resists our flattening of people, things, and Christ's gospel for mere instrumental purposes. Of course, this critique does not apply universally;

50. A representative sample of those articulating practical theological methods might include, for example, Browning, *A Fundamental Practical Theology*; Groome, *Sharing Faith*; Anderson, *The Shape of Practical Theology*.

51. Osmer, *Practical Theology*, 4. Similarly, in *Sharing Faith*, Thomas Groome identifies the following as key moments of praxis pedagogy: naming/expressing present action (movement 1); critical reflection on present action (movement 2); making accessible Christian story and vision (movement 3); dialectical hermeneutics to appropriate story/vision to participants' stories and visions (movement 4); and decision/response for lived Christian faith (movement 5).

52. It is important to note that this critique of praxis approaches—the possibility of a rush to action, reductionistic conclusions, evacuation of aesthetic depths—is more a problem with how these approaches are implemented than how they are envisioned. Osmer, *Practical Theology*, for example, refers to these mediations as "spiritualities" of presence, wisdom, prophetic discernment, and servant leadership. With this language, Osmer is pointing away from rational reduction and toward the guidance of Spirit.

many practical theological approaches include techniques that attend to beauty's hidden wisdom.

As suggested earlier, Dori Baker's approach involves a kind of *lectio* or holy reading that contemplates beauty within a slice of life. Anne Wimberly's story-linking approach invites participants to draw from ordinary life stories, biblical stories, heritage stories to find in them "liberating wisdom," a concept open enough so as to not foreclose meaning or action too quickly.[53] Wimberly's approach avoids reductive conclusions by diversifying the field of narratives.

Augusto Boal's theatre approach invites participants to imagine and rehearse alternate creative responses to limit-situations with their hidden beauty and their "ideal image." The richness of multiple interpretations can serve to prevent scripted or simplistic responses, giving participants the opportunity to contemplate beauty and wonder in each story. Each of these approaches hold a place for active praxis without reducing the engagement with beauty's mystery and depth. At their best, the action they allow is a kind of rendering or naming that is not merely addressing a problem with a solution but is instead an extension of creation's hidden beauty and its ends.

In this chapter, I have argued that natural beauty should be a substantial dimension of our Christian formation and education. In the Christian theological tradition, the beauty of the created world must not be objectified, reduced as commodity, or instrumentalized toward some predetermined end. The beauty that lies around us is not inert; it is alive, dynamic, and wise. The above pedagogical aims and practices serve as a starting point for considering pedagogies that takes the beauty of creation seriously. When such pedagogies are employed well, often, and lovingly, over time, participants may cultivate spiritual senses alive in wonder, perceiving God in all these places in and through their beauty and responding faithfully, guided by love. As Balthasar saw, to neglect such formation risks missing even the formal, material reality of God's revelation in Jesus and the church, God's decisive revelation of beauty, to which we now turn.

---

53. Wimberly, *Soul Stories*.

3

The Surpassing Beauty of Christ's Form

In its fundamental articulations—his Incarnation, his preaching of the kingdom and preparing of the Church, his suffering, his solidarity with the dead and re-union with the Father, his return at the end of history—Christ's dramatic form is the simple self-presentation of a single attitude, which is the effective expression of God's love for the world.

—HANS URS VON BALTHASAR, *THEO-DRAMA*, VOL. 2

THE CREATOR OF ALL things emptied himself and entered the world he created, a child born to a humble carpenter and his young wife. Christ healed the sick, fed the hungry, lifted up the downtrodden, cast out demons, rebuked moneychangers and hypocrites, and taught in parables that confounded expectations. In his life and words, he articulated a message of grace, forgiveness, and peace. So hungry were people for the good news of God's shalom that his followers grew, for a time, into a great multitude, threatening the gatekeepers of power and religion, who colluded to kill him in a cruel spectacle. Even as he was dying, he forgave his executioners, cared for his mother, and surrendered his will to the Father. Three days later, he was raised from death, gathered his followers, and founded his church in a style approximating and extending his love. Even in its frailty and corruption, many amazing acts of healing and reconciliation have been done in Christ's name by the church. So powerfully does Christ's love bear witness to God's glory that, according to Scripture, one day all things will be drawn into God's complete redemption.

This is a narrative simple enough for even a child to understand, yet so profound that scholars and saints spend their lives mining its significance.

The meaning of Christ's incarnation has been interpreted variously throughout history. In addition to endless scholarly interpretations, he is celebrated in the arts. Da Vinci, Rembrandt, Caravaggio, Raphael, Bloch, Velazquez, Michelangelo, Durer, Gauguin, Dali, and so many more have been inspired to express the inner feeling of their encounter with his form. The 1970s play *Godspell* portrayed Christ as a hippy innocent. In *Jesus Christ Superstar,* he took a stand against political power, while *Jesus of Montreal* confronted the evils of commercialism. For mystics and evangelicals, he is the lover of my soul or the payment for my debt of sin. For progressives, he is the champion of social justice, liberation, and peace. For liturgical traditions, he is the always-arriving gift that we eternally receive, a name we are continually trying to express more adequately in our praise and practice. Early Jewish converts saw Christ as the fulfillment of the Hebrew Law and Prophets. Greek philosophers saw him as the fulfillment of Platonic ideas or the Neoplatonic pattern of the material world. Latin American base communities see in him the ground of their liberation. Despite many attempts to decisively articulate Christ's significance, the plurality of ways and reasons he is loved bear witness to his surpassing power to move and inspire.

Hans Urs von Balthasar sees in Christ's incarnation something more fundamental—a form that in beauty poetically harmonizes and fulfills

Hebrew, Greek, and all religious and cultural antecedents, myths, and narratives.[1] For Balthasar, Christ's incarnate form discloses an aesthetic idea, a unity of the sort beheld in works of art—and, as we have seen, in all creatures. Balthasar insists that the methods of theology and biblical study must be adequate to their beautiful and glorious object, Christ's incarnation.[2] For this reason, Christian formation does not only entail mastering a body of facts or systematic ideology but must be taught and learned in ways most adequate to its beauty. Balthasar interprets the encounter with Christ as an aesthetic epistemology in which truth resonates and persuades rather than forces or argues.

Over against the reductions of modern reason—its propensity to flatten, disenchant, and evacuate—I will in this chapter offer a survey of Balthasar's understanding of the Christ form, especially for the church's ministry of formation, as one that enchants with desire and freshness of heart. Since Christ is constituted as a form, much of what we said about the structure of the aesthetic experience in the previous chapter will apply to how we attend to the incarnation.

THEORETICAL UNDERPINNINGS

For Balthasar, Scriptures bear witness to God, who is palpably revealed in glory, beauty's analogy. In a sense, all of Balthasar's writing can be seen as clarifying the prologue to John's Gospel, which proclaims: "And the Word became flesh and took up residence among us, and we saw his glory, glory as of the one and only from the Father, full of grace and truth" (1:14). He seizes on the notion that here the primary way Christ is known is by a palpable sense of his glory. This chapter will focus on Balthasar's notion of the

1. Balthasar in *Glory of the Lord* suggests that all world myths and religions find their fulfillment in the Christ form. Obviously, this is a confessional statement of a Christian. In the contemporary context where we encounter great religious diversity, it seems as reasonable to wonder analogously if Christianity is preliminary to the hopes of other religions. Either way, the confession is speculative, and formation best happens in the context of coherent traditions, with particular stories and practices.

2. Balthasar acknowledges that his Christological account of truth may be accused of being methodologically sloppy. But he embraces this accusation, claiming that there is no other way that a genuine account of truth could be. Cf. Balthasar *Theo-Logic*, 2.363. For a study that develops a saintly epistemology in light of Balthasar, see Schindler, "Sanctity and the Intellectual Life," 652–72.

Christ form and our entry into Christ's theo-drama, especially as it suggests adequate approaches to Christian formation.

The Christ Form

Although Balthasar insists that the created world participates sacramentally in God, his theological aesthetics is not a naïve form of natural theology. His thought can only be properly understood in terms of his Christology. In his life, death, and resurrection, Jesus Christ is the image or form that discloses God as God's artwork as well as the true form of creation. Previously, we unpacked Balthasar's notion of form that draws significantly from aesthetic theories, including those of Goethe and Hopkins, yet his notion of form is deeply imbued with theological meaning, since God is incarnate in Christ's form.

According to Balthasar, the love revealed in the Christ form as beauty is part of a threefold kenosis. There is a prior Trinitarian love that constitutes the "first kenosis," in which the Father gives himself to the Son and Spirit. God creates the cosmos as a "second kenosis," which means that the Trinity is archetypal for creation. The "third kenosis," of which Philippians hymns, involves God emptying himself into history in love unto death. Junius Johnson, in his analysis of Balthasar's metaphysics, observes that the Trinity's "openness for the world portrays in it the fundamental behaviors [of creaturely existence]: reception and giving, service and creation, justice and love, which are all just different forms of self-giving."[3] As we have seen, for Balthasar, romantic love, mother-child mutual love, and all forms of charity, point to creation's participation in God's intra-Trinitarian "being-for-another." All creaturely forms are "sacred veils" of the divine wisdom which is their foundation,[4] but which, because fallen, must be restored to be more perfectly transparent to the original Trinitarian love and beauty. Thus, Christ is the Word, the "super-form," in whom the beauty of the triune God is definitively revealed, but which also reveals the true telos of all other created forms.[5]

---

3. Johnson, "Christ and Analogy," 152.

4. Balthasar's account of this theme works out at the end of the medieval period with Nicolas of Cusa in *The Glory of the Lord: 5*, 205. For a Protestant attempt at reclaiming this tradition, see Boersma, *Heavenly Participation*.

5. This understanding, grounded in the thought of Patristic thinkers such as Irenaeus, Athanasius, the Cappadocian fathers, and Maximus the Confessor, has come to influence

Aidan Nichols summarizes Balthasar's understanding of the decisive role of Christ's incarnate form:

> This self-revelation of God in Christ is not a mere prolongation or intensification of the revelation given with creation. The personal substance of the Father in his Word is now lavished on the world. And yet, because the creation was from the beginning orientated towards its own supernatural elevation, and because too the incarnation, taken in the fullness of its unfolding, from the annunciation, through the resurrection to the Parousia, entails the bringing together of everything in heaven and on earth under one divine-human Head, it follows that the self-manifestation of God in Jesus Christ brings the form of the world to its perfection, and in that way uncovers the fullness of its significance for the first time.[6]

Balthasar alludes to a Patristic tradition that culminates in the writings of Maximus the Confessor in which the human person is seen as a microcosm of the cosmos potentially synthesizing cosmic disparities—for example, material, sensate, spiritual, intellectual. For Maximus, being a microcosm is the human's vocation, since God has appointed us as representatives over a divided creation[7] and has entrusted us with the task of leading the cosmos into union with its Creator—so that the human person might "[gather] up all things to God . . . [bringing about] the union of all things in God, in whom there is no division."[8] While our vocation of unifying the divided creation in God was corrupted in Adam's fall, it is fulfilled in Christ, the new Adam. Therefore, Balthasar sees in Christ's "form" the unification of all creation, revealing to creatures their true unity.

Recalling the previous chapter, the Christ form must be received as a whole, not as a collection of discrete or divided facts abstracted from the unity of Christ's form. The New Testament is a unity because the authors had all been impressed by a shared sense of the glory of God in the form of Christ.

---

many contemporary reflections. See Balthasar, *The Glory of the Lord: 1*, 432.

6. Nichols, *The Word Has Been Abroad*, 34–35.

7. In Maximus's "Ambigua 41," all existing things are "marked by five divisions." The first is between uncreated nature (i.e., the Godhead) and created natures—the numerous essences of the cosmos are unified by their common source of existence in God. The second division is between the intelligible and the sensible or, in other words, the immaterial and the material. Material reality is further divided into the heavens and the earth. Maximus locates the final division within human nature, namely, between man and woman, a distinction that he does not think existed prior to the fall. See Maximus, "Ambigua 41," 103.

8. Maximus, "Ambigua 41," 105.

For this reason, Balthasar thought that modern historical-critical study of the Bible is hampered by its atomistic approach which parses the whole into fragments and risks ignoring the beauty of the whole that unites them. This approach he deems inadequate to its object, the revelation of Jesus Christ as unified form. Only a contemplative or artistic reading of the New Testament is adequate to its object, the glory of God shining in Jesus Christ.[9]

Balthasar permits a good deal of discontinuity between the Old and New Testaments, since their themes are taken up, transformed, and unified by an entirely unexpected fulfillment in the person of Jesus Christ. In Christ, we do not see the Old Testament promises and themes merely replicated. Christ's incarnation takes up these antecedent themes in a surprising new way, much as a poem takes up existing images to express something entirely new. According to Balthasar, "Whatever God used as an instrument for his Son's coming was taken up by him in the great recapitulation brought to pass in Jesus Christ."[10] Christ takes up into himself everything on earth—all created being, Old Testament prophecies and promises, Greek philosophy, cultural mythologies, human history, even other religions—because "the revelation in Christ was to bring together under one divine and human Head everything heavenly and earthly."[11] All partial forms of earthly love and all prior testaments are transfigured by Christ's form. Balthasar's Christological reading of the Old Testament emphasizes the theme of the "descending God," who comes to his people in covenantal relationship. As the mother's smile discloses an abundant love to her child that prompts its loving response, so in the covenantal relationship between Yahweh and Israel, the "I AM WHO I AM" makes God's self to be known, and in turn, the people of Israel recognize themselves as a "Thou."[12] In creation and covenant, God binds himself to the world out of love. These Old Testament themes are emphasized and clarified by Christ's form.

By "Christ," Balthasar always means the "total Christ" (*totus Christus*): Christ himself, his life, death, and resurrection; and Christ's body,

9. Balthasar, *Mysterium Paschale*, 6.

10. Balthasar, *Word and Revelation*, 55. The notion of *anakephalaiosis*, bringing all together under one head, was key in the theology of Irenaeus, the church's first great theologian. The term is derived from St. Paul (Eph. 1:9) and goes back to the oldest strata of Christian doctrine; it is in essence a development of the scriptural doctrine of the two Adams, an idea that is also a favorite with Balthasar. See Balthasar, *Word and Revelation*.

11. Balthasar, *The Glory of the Lord*: 2, 431. This idea is elaborated by Aidan Nichols in *The Word Has Been Abroad*, 34, 35.

12. Balthasar, *The Glory of the Lord*: 6, 134–97.

the church, which in unity with him in the Spirit continues the totality of his life, death, and resurrection both on earth and in heaven. If Christ is a poietic figure capable of reconciling Hebrew Scriptures and completing all partial forms of love, then the church lives under the sign of Christ and unfolds eternally as a poem, not rigidly seeking to reclaim a pristine past but giving expression to new and surprising forms of truth, goodness, and beauty. We will return to this theme of poiesis in the next chapter.

Theo-Dramatics

The ethical significance of the Christ form is elaborated in his theo-dramatics. In the opening of his *Theo-Drama*, Balthasar remarks that this beautiful form of Christ is not a static image, icon, or artwork "crystallised in immobile perfection," but a dynamic event, a dramatic act, an embodied performance that reveals to us, along with God's glory and beauty, God's unbounded goodness.[13] In perceiving the beauty of the *Gestalt Christi or the Christ form,* it becomes clear that who Christ is cannot be separated from what Christ does. God's beauty and glory come to expression through Christ's actions that are aimed at bringing about the good "for us" and "in us."[14] Balthasar writes that there is "nothing ambiguous" about what the beautiful form of Christ does on earth: "it is simply good."[15]

According to Balthasar, in the moment of perception, when we are enraptured by the beauty of Christ, we respond through action to follow and imitate Christ in performing the good in our own lives, to play our part in God's redemptive activity in the world. Balthasar's linking of ecstatic perception and action recalls our first chapter, when we observed that there is not normally a deliberative interval; beauty as an event prompts action, crosses modes in response, whether to reproduce, recreate, protect, support, or enjoin in covenant communion. Balthasar holds that the "good which God does to us" can only be experienced as the truth "if we share in performing it," if we also "embody it increasingly in the world."[16] He asserts that God's "saving drama" is not "a self-sufficient armchair drama" and that neither "faith, contemplation nor kerygma can dispense us from action."[17]

13. Balthasar, *Theo-Drama 1,* 15. Nichols, *A Key to Balthasar,* 49.

14. Balthasar, *Theo-Drama 1,* 19.

15. Balthasar, *Theo-Drama 1,* 18.

16. Balthasar, *Theo-Drama 1,* 20.

17. Balthasar, *Theo-Drama 1,* 22.

Our response to the Christ form involves an ethics internal to it. According to Balthasar:

> In Christian faith, the captivating force (the "subjective evidence") of the artwork which is Christ takes hold of our imaginative powers; we enter into the "painterly world" which this discloses and, entranced by what we see, come to contemplate the glory of sovereign love of God in Christ (the "objective evidence") as manifested in the concrete events of his life, death and resurrection. So entering his glory, we become absorbed by it, but this very absorption sends us out into the world in sacrificial love like that of Jesus.[18]

Subjectively, "before the beautiful . . . the whole person quivers. He not only 'finds' the beautiful moving; rather, he experiences himself as being moved and possessed by it."[19] This ecstatic absorption into Christ's form orders our imagination and sends us out into the world in sacrificial love, in creative response to the new creation we encounter in Christ. This subjective decentering occurs as the result of a genuine clash with the dramatic, historical revelation of the Triune God in Jesus Christ. This is the power of an occurrence that "demands the name of not just beauty, but of glory—that irreducibly other, uncontainable splendor which breaks forth at the advent of divine presence."[20] It involves a receptivity to the object of faith wherein one is so "impressed" that obedience necessarily ensues.[21]

In *Theo-Drama*, Balthasar rejects the modern notion that beauty is subject to the attitude of a spectator, an entertainment that avoids action. *Theo-Drama* elaborates a triadic structure in which creating, directing, and performing the drama on the world stage can be seen in Trinitarian terms, with the Father as Author, the Son as Actor, and the Spirit as Director. The entire dramatic production is for the benefit of the audience who are drawn into the action on the stage. As Balthasar points out:

> Human beings go to the theater . . . [to meet] a twofold need and a twofold pleasure: we project ourselves onto an ultimate plane that gives meaning, and thus we are given our selves. It can also be described as the twofold need to see and to surrender ourselves

---

18. Balthasar, *Mysterium Paschale*, 6.

19. Balthasar, *The Glory of the Lord: 1*, 247.

20. Mongrain, "Balthasar's Way from Doxology to Theology," 61.

21. Here, Mary, the mother of Christ, is the model for such obedience in her *"fiat"* to God's word—an active receptivity analogous to the receptivity of the womb.

to something that transcends and gives meaning to the limited horizon of everyday life.[22]

The Son is not merely a passive recipient of the expressive will of his Father, since passive reception is not yet love or truth. Passive receptivity lacks both mission and creative obedience, two defining characteristics of the Son. Balthasar claims that the determining characteristic of divinity is surrender, the giving over of oneself.[23] The Father gives himself to the Son and the Spirit, whose reception "is enacted only in the mode of a return gift to the 'Person' who gives himself over, the Father."[24] The eternal Son is both the recipient of the Father's word and the content of that word, the expressive truth of the Godhead and love itself. Jesus' farewell prayer in John 17 illustrates the eternal I-Thou relationship between the eternal Son and the eternal Father, "in which the Son turns to the Father in knowledge, love, adoration, and readiness for the Father's very wish"[25] and in which the Son submits to and discovers his mission in response to the "Thou" of the Father, a creative gift given out of love and praise. "The Son's form of existence," Balthasar says, "which makes him the Son from all eternity, is the uninterrupted reception of his very self from the Father. It is indeed this receiving of himself which gives him his 'I,' his own inner dimension, his spontaneity, that sonship with which he can answer the Father in a reciprocal giving."[26] The Son's vocation as the expressive Word of God is obedience to his mission to testify to the truth of the Father. The willful poverty that Christ adopts is an expression of his kenotic being, which leads to

---

22. Balthasar, *Theo-Drama* 1, 308.

23. *Selbstübergabe* is an especially Ignatian idea, though it also has a legacy even in Eckhartian thought. See Balthasar, *Theo-Logic*, 2.137.

24. Balthasar, *Theo-Logic*, 2.137.

25. Balthasar, *Theo-Logic*, 2.126. Balthasar sees this passage as an indication of the eternal I-Thou relationship between the eternal Son and the eternal Father "in which the Son turns to the Father in knowledge, love, adoration, and readiness for the Father's very wish": "Father, the hour has come. Glorify your Son, that your Son may glorify you. For you granted him authority over all people that he might give eternal life to all those you have given him. Now this is eternal life: that they know you, the only true God, and Jesus Christ, whom you have sent. I have brought you glory on earth by finishing the work you gave me to do. And now, Father, glorify me in your presence with the glory I had with you before the world began" (John 17:1–5).

26. Balthasar, *A Theology of History*, 30.

his perfect solidarity with the poor of every form.[27] Christ enters into the chasm of forsaken solitude bearing all of creation in the community of his flesh.

Quoting Maximus the Confessor, Balthasar says that Christ "reestablishes the continuity between heaven and earth and 'proves that heavenly and earthly beings join in a single festive dance, as they receive the gifts that come from God.'"[28] In the performance of Christ's reception of the Father's love, Christ provides the pattern for humanity in which we also become God's art.

In an encounter with God's Divine Love, exegeted by Christ's beauty, a person goes through a conversion in which self-love is transformed into love for God and neighbor. Thus, as Timothy J. Loder puts it, "an individual achieves personhood through accepting and enacting his or her mission."[29] Such participation is possible through faith, which involves a surrender of the whole person before the glory of Christ's form in a radical availability to do the will of God.[30]

Humans are called to bear in themselves the fullness of creaturely and divine truth through their dialogical relation with God, first glimpsed when Adam walked and talked with God in the cool of the garden. This dialogical relationship, the relationship of discipleship, is one in which we are compelled to return again and again to the endless source of Christ's form, to be taken into its aesthetic world, allowing it to spark our imaginations in which our mission and selfhood take new shape. The saints, through the Holy Spirit, perceive that Christ is the truth that pulses in the heart of Being, and they are enraptured into it. They share in Christ's kenosis, his impoverishment, and his petition and are led along the path to truth that

27. Balthasar notes the way Christ acts in solidarity with all of the forms of the poor of ancient Palestine: Christ takes the side of the tax collectors and sinners (Luke 15:1–32); children (Luke 18:15, 16); the persecuted (Luke 6:22). The scandal of Christ's solidarity expresses the Father's perfect love for "those who have lost their way." The "weakness" of the Father's heart for the poor is made visible in the life of Christ. See *The Glory of the Lord: 1*, 7, 137–38.

28. This language of the "Christological synthesis" is derived from Balthasar, *Maximus*, 273.

29. Cf. Yoder, "Hans Urs von Balthasar," 112. Yoder adds: "Balthasar does acknowledge the importance of self-love. However, it is only 'a byproduct of that moment when we truly understand what we mean to God. Within this kind of kenotic framework, our identity is no longer threatened by the other, but realized in a "we" that transcends self-love completely'" (Yoder, "Hans Urs von Balthasar," 115).

30. O'Donnel, "Hans Urs von Balthasar," 213–14.

is Christ himself.[31] For Balthasar, saints are the true theologians because their living "words about God" are founded in their spiritual participation in the truth of the expressive Word himself.

Harkening again to his favorite image of the dialogical relationship between mother and child, Schindler summarizes Balthasar's notion of mission this way:

> The mother's smile is the outward expression of her love for the child and thus her "self-gift" to the child . . . it is a mediated immediacy, a presence that bears within itself an "open space." This open space within the positivity can be put more concretely: the spontaneous gift of self on the part of the mother is not mere spontaneity, which would in fact smother the child, and force his consciousness into the ill-fitting mold of a pure passive receptacle for the mother's own self. But this is not consciousness at all. Rather, the content of the mother's self-gift is her receiving her child. Her spontaneity has the form of receptivity.[32]

The mother's smile embodies the ability to give herself away to another and create a space in which the child is called into realization of its own being. Schindler adds, "This is why Balthasar says that the love of the mother is a creative call; it is a spontaneous receptivity that gives rise to a receptive spontaneity."[33] Just as the mother's face invites the gaze of the child, so does Christ offer his incarnate and beautiful form as God's loving face to the cosmos. Just as the mother's smile signifies reception of the child, so does Christ's form signify God's reception of humanity and all creation. Just as the mother's smile presents to the child an "image" of itself, so does Christ's form, as God's face, offer to humanity an image of its own perfection. Just as the gaze of the mother projects an image of the child, which is received by the child as a clue to its fullness, so do we receive in the Christ form

31. See Balthasar, *Theo-Drama,* 5.111–12: "At the same time he is visibly on his way back to heaven, taking his earthly body and his entire earthly fate with him. Yet, nullifying the distance between heaven and earth, he remains on earth, invisibly, to the end of time, thus in a more concrete manner than ever before (cf. Is 55:10–11), in order to promote the exchange between heaven and earth; indeed, he is this exchange."

32. Schindler, *Hans Urs von Balthasar and the Dramatic Structure of Truth,* 114–15.

33. Schindler, *Hans Urs von Balthasar and the Dramatic Structure of Truth,* 115. Aidan Nichols uses these terms to characterize Balthasar's notion of receptivity. He states, "Since the revelation of an object has its meaning only when it is offered to a knowing subject, we can even say that the object finds its own full sense only in that subject. Created knowledge for Balthasar is, therefore, at once receptive and spontaneous, or, in his preferred vocabulary, 'measured' and 'measuring.'" (Nichols, *Say It Is Pentecost,* 15).

images of our true personhood, clues by which we may respond creatively in mission and personhood in dialogue with God.

While these few pages have not by any means exhausted the substance of Balthasar's thought, I have summarized some of his central concepts concerning the Christ form and the theo-drama that potentially hold significance for formation and pedagogy. In Christ's form we are always awakening to new depths of God's beauty and our own creative responses. As with all art, encountering the Christ form involves a harmonized whole that resonates in our bodies and hearts, moving us in ecstatic response beyond ourselves, in identity and mission. The Christ form establishes a dialogical relationship, which, like the mother-child dyad, blurs boundaries between subject and object, prompts a sense of wonder, invites creative expression, and compels us to respond in creative identity and mission.

EDUCATIONAL AIMS

Given the surpassing power of Christ's form to delight, attract, and order our lives in identity and mission, pedagogies that teach the Christ form seek to do three things:

1. *They seek to render and engage Christ in a material aesthetic form—in word, story, song, theatre, sculpture, painting, architecture, liturgy, as ecclesia—that holds an inner unity and mediates God's beauty and the true ends of humanity and creation.* Just as an artistic masterpiece is revealed in the unity of the material it harmonizes—its colors, brush strokes, musical tones, melodies, counter-melodies, words, architectural angles, textures—so the Christ form has a material density that includes complex characters, dramatic plots, images, parables, narratives, and counter-narratives—all of which are taken up and harmonized, rendered expressive in form. Christ's form is also rendered in the concrete life of saints and in the church (the *totus Christus*) animated by Christ's original donation.

2. *They seek to facilitate an ecstatic encounter, an entry into the aesthetic field of Christ's form, a creative call that gives rise to a creative response of identity and mission.* Just as the mother's smile presents an "image" of the child, so does Christ's form represent and offer an image of our true personhood in which we see ourselves and to which we may respond creatively in personhood and mission.

3. *They seek to foster, in response to ecstatic encounter with Christ's form, active responses that participate in his form.* As we have seen, the truth of Christ's form cannot be known at a distance, but only from within its dramatic field. Approaches that seek to awaken participants to Christ's form facilitate them in bearing witness, in creating art, music, liturgy, practices, acts of justice, peace, and communion that not only express but extend Christ's beauty into the world.

Churches and Christian educators have engaged people in formative encounters in a number of ways, such as, for example, in St. Ignatius's imaginative exercises in which Christ is engaged as form in imaginative dialogue to which pilgrims respond. The fine arts in general—music, film, paintings, sculpture—have also proved effective ways of engaging people in the materiality of Christ's form. Narrative is an especially effective way to create worlds in which the Christ form can be imagined and responded to. Generally, there are four movements listed below that facilitate the aims of entering the field of Christ's form and responding in action.

FOUR EDUCATIONAL PRACTICES FOR ATTENTING TO THE CHRIST FORM

The first practice involves engaging the materiality of Christ's beautiful form. As Christ's incarnate materiality reveals God's glory and humanity's true form, so must our teaching attend to artful materiality. The Christ form is not simply a ladder of material form to be kicked away upon arriving at abstracted doctrines. The Christ form is, in David Tracy's terms, "a classic," containing an "excess of meaning" that provokes understanding in the present with a kind of "permanent timeliness" to which we return throughout our lives.[34]

Just as we enter the world of any artistic masterpiece and move among its materials in order to experience and comprehend its beauty, so must we engage the materials of the Christ form if we are to be truly formed by it. Balthasar's aesthetics point to the use of art, poetry, song, liturgy, architecture, new forms of communal sociality, historic practices including those that seek justice and peace, in rendering the beauty of the Christ form. We must enter its drama and meet its characters and the depths they disclose.

---

34. This is how David Tracy characterizes the significance of the Bible as a classic. Tracy, *The Analogical Imagination*, 104.

Learners should feel Mary's fear, Peter's impulsivity, the adulterous woman's desperation, and Pilate's hubris, but also the agony of Christ's vulnerability unto death, the joy of communion he offers, and the plenitude of God's grace. Churches must render the Christ form concrete to honor the depth of feeling and meaning conveyed in the unity of its material form, even if only partially and haltingly.

Throughout history, Christians have contemplated the Christ form by many means—silence, guided imagery, *lectio* or *visio,* collaborative reflection, and art. As mentioned above, in the Spiritual Exercises of St. Ignatius, participants accompany Jesus through his life by imagining scenes from Gospel stories.[35] They are instructed to visualize the details of the events of Jesus' life—the sights, sounds, tastes, smells, and feelings. They are asked to give full rein to the imagination. So when Jesus is speaking to a blind man at the side of the road, we feel the hot Mediterranean sun beating down; we smell the dust kicked up by passersby; we feel the rough clothing we're wearing, the sweat rolling down our brow, a rumble of hunger; we see the desperation in the blind man's face and hear the wail of hope in his words; we note the irritation of the disciples. Above all, we watch Jesus—the way he walks, his gestures, the look in his eyes, the expression on his face. We imagine the words Christ spoke and might have spoken, other deeds he might have done, and our response to him. Ignatian practices seek to represent Christ as concrete form for the purpose of encountering him dialogically, to ask him questions, to respond to his questions, to allow his concrete form to affect our lives.

Balthasar frequently emphasized the significance of saints whose lives express and replicate the Christ form in a wide variety of material conditions across cultures and historical eras. Saints are those whose lives are animated by Christ's form and in which his form is rendered visible for a new generation and context. There are many saints, not all of them canonized, whose lives participate in the Christ form and inspire us in their beauty. The lives of saints have been memorialized in anthologies and in films, including *St. Anthony: Miracle Worker of Padua; Blackrobe; Thérèse; The Flowers of St. Francis; Francesco; Mother Teresa: In the Name of God's Poor; Molokai; Brother Sun, Sister Moon;* and *Romero.* Many others throughout the church's history have participated in gestures of care, hospitality, justice, forgiveness, repentance, and joy in ways that make Christ's form concrete,

---

35. Ganss, *The Spiritual Exercises of St. Ignatius.*

material, and articulate. In the materiality of these stories, learners perceive Christ's form, the form of the Trinity, and the true human form.

As stated earlier, Balthasar does not focus exclusively on the historical Jesus but on the *totus Christus,* which includes the church as Christ's body, continually expressing Christ's form. Christian education that teaches the Christ form should make liberal use of these stories and their materiality. As Frank Rogers observes in *Finding God in the Graffiti,* communities of faith are founded on canonical stories that give them meaning and purpose. The form of Christ is not only manifest in gospel accounts; many living exemplars in their historical circumstances introduce Christ's form and provide the community a sense of narrative identity and unity, along with practical and ethical guidance, and make the community appealing.[36] Rogers suggests the importance of perceiving Christ's form in many guises, collecting and proclaiming these stories, and constructing new stories that give form to Christ for new contexts. In an opening chapter, Rogers tells of a congregation celebrating the retirement of its longtime pastor. To educate and encourage the congregation, the young people presented a play featuring heroic figures such as Harriet Tubman, Thurgood Marshall, Rosa Parks, Ruby Bridges, Martin Luther King, Jr., and Malcom X but also included local members of the congregation who had loved and sacrificed themselves for the good of the community.[37] These characters were given words and actions that not only serve and advocate for the good of the community, but harken to Christ's love. The act of creating, rehearsing, performing, and witnessing their play served to engage them as actors and participants in Christ's form.

Jewish educator Peter Pitzele's Bibliodrama approach invites participants to dramatize biblical scenes to resist their flattening from overfamiliarity.[38] With Christian participants, the Bibliodrama approach asks participants to recreate biblical scenes, including those featuring Christ. Bibliodrama participants "workshop" each character, assigning them desires, fears, inhibitions, virtues, and other qualities drawing from Scripture and from their imagination. When characters are given this dimension, the words of Scripture, and those improvised by participants, such a process

36. These themes are elaborated in his chapter titled "How do stories transmit a faith tradition? Narrative pedagogy and religious literacy." Rogers, *Finding God in the Graffiti,* 21.

37. Rogers, *Finding God in the Graffiti,* 21–50.

38. Pitzele, *Scripture Windows.*

renders Christ as a concrete form to which other characters relate and respond.

The second practice involves fostering openness and humility before Christ's form. Harkening back to Balthasar's paradigmatic example of the mother-child dyad, he observes that "the object surrenders itself to the subject and the subject in an attitude of receptivity surrenders to the object." And as Aidan Nichols puts it, "without this attitude of selfless surrender, truth cannot happen."[39] As we have suggested throughout, beauty ordinarily prompts a decentering of the ego. Christian education approaches can support this intrinsic effect by cultivating a receptive humility that sets aside the totalizing narratives of our culture in order to allow the beauty of the Christ form to evoke wonder. Educators and practitioners have utilized a variety of practices for fostering humility before the Christ form.

For Eastern Orthodox, praying with icons is a receptive experience where practitioners gaze into and beyond the image, humbly subjecting themselves to God's own gaze. The aesthetic images of the icon draw the gaze but point beyond its surface to God. Practitioners are instructed to look at the icon, remain silent and still, and recognize where your eye is drawn. What effect does the color have on you? What feelings does the icon stir up? Notice the eyes of the individual in the icon that are looking back at us. Let the eyes of Jesus, Mary, or one of the saints penetrate your soul. What are they trying to tell you?[40] Praying with icons creates a space in which the egoistic will can be decentered. Praying with icons of Christ can help cultivate habits of humility in which we perceive others not as mere mirrors reflecting back to us our own egos but as icons open to God and through which God speaks.

All Christian practices embody Christ's form in microcosm; they teach us to meet God beyond our egos in spaces where ordinary things are rendered extraordinary. Christian practices create open but not unbounded spaces for humility. For example, practices such as hospitality, confession, forgiveness, charity, justice seeking, holy conferencing, worship, singing, prayer, and contemplation all engage us in goods beyond our egoism and use. Singing decenters us by joining our voices with the voices of others, lifting our hearts in praise. The practice of showing hospitality to

39. See Nichols's description of Balthasar's examination of truth as a combination of the Hellenic notion of *aletheia* (unveiledness or revelation) and the Hebraic notion of *emeth* (fidelity). This combination of ideas becomes a critical link to Balthasar's understanding of the encounter of subject and object. Nichols, "The Theo-logic," 161.

40. Material summarized from Kosloski, "How to Pray with Icons."

strangers demands that we inventory our resources for what we can provide for the stranger, humbly opening our lives to her influence. Practices of confession and repentance compel us to regularly notice our distortions and to make amends.

Leaders in theater education often invite participants to create a community covenant in which they identify fears that inhibit full participation and establish an expectation to withhold judgment and give support to each other in free play and attentive learning. Covenants of this sort can provide a form of communal accountability that can encourage our openness and prevent fear and hubris.[41]

Brian J. Mahan, in his book *Forgetting Ourselves on Purpose*, suggests that our inhibitions are often embedded so deeply in our preconscious that rigorous effort is required—including, for example, journaling, attending to our rationalizations, conversations with trusted others, dream work, etc., to make conscious internalized scripts that prevent our self-forgetful humility. One helpful exercise is Mahan's "distraction diary," in which participants are asked, while reading a text, to notice their wandering thoughts and write them down.[42] As participants record these thoughts over time, they recognize the various preoccupations and inhibitions that reside in their preconscious minds. Once they are noticed, they can be studied and resisted. This kind of work is necessary to understand our alienation from God's beautiful world and can help restore us to a self-forgetful flow response to beauty's depths. The struggle to attain openness and humility is never-ending, therefore we must not imagine that we can awaken our spiritual depths apart from such resistance as a habitual part of our practice with beauty, wonder, and creativity.

The third practice involves imaginative free play with Christ's form. For Balthasar the Christ form is significant for its own playful and poetic strangeness. In harmonizing Old Testament themes, Greek philosophy, other religions, and the created order, the Christ form transforms these antecedents in surprising new ways. The gospels portray Christ "playing" with cultural and religious expectations—as a boy teaching adult leaders in the temple, feasting with sinners, dignifying women, harrowing hell, and preaching love of our enemies which upends the prevailing ethic of an-eye-for-an-eye. In the same way, our response to Christ's play is to engage in our own play with the Christ form.

---

41. See, for example, Boal, *Games for Actors and Non-Actors*.

42. Mahan, *Forgetting Ourselves on Purpose*.

According to Balthasar, the Christ form uniquely sparks a kind of play. While Balthasar sought to reclaim the fire and light of Christian faith, the significance of Christ has at times been frozen, rendered identical to the "sameness" of causes such as nationalism, middle-class niceness, or partisan politics. Against such familiarity, the task of Christian formation is to play with, thus "make strange," the Christ form.

Playful artistry alerts us to forgotten or surprising aspects of Christ by creating images, stories, songs, and liturgies that juxtapose other experiences into which the Christ form speaks, shedding new light upon its original donation of the Christ form. In our own day we see Christ in surprising guises—standing in a breadline in a woodcutting by Fritz Eichenberg,[43] as a jester in *Godspell*, as the lion Aslan in C. S. Lewis's *Chronicles of Narnia*, in the sacrificial type of Jean Valjean in *Les Misérables*, or James Cone's Christ of the lynching tree. In these examples, the Christ form is made fresh and strange by insertion into the experience of hunger and homelessness, fantasy literature, nineteenth-century France, and in the worst aspects of racist brutality. Such playful juxtaposition continually accesses the endless depth of Christ's form.

Liturgy ordinarily juxtaposes the familiar with the unfamiliar—Scripture readings are juxtaposed with songs, prayers, gestures, sermons, testimonies, and sacraments. Rev. John Leedy at University Presbyterian Church in Austin, Texas, recently designed an Easter vigil in which the young people of the church present murals, tableaus, or skits depicting various Old Testament stories given new meaning by Christ's death and resurrection.[44] In this vigil, these stories are given their own voice, yet because they are juxtaposed with Christ's resurrection, they are given surprising new meanings that shed light on contemporary issues. The congregation thus comes to perceive how Christ is their King, prophet, priest, liberation, sacrifice, lamb, light, wilderness, desert, holy mountain, law, bridegroom, and shalom, as Old Testament stories point to their completion in Christ. These stories performed by youth serve to gather the Old Testament themes in the person of Jesus Christ, shed new light on his strangeness, and set him apart from cultural familiarity.

One religious educator, Courtney Goto, sees play as central to Christian formation. In her book *The Grace of Playing: Pedagogies for Leaning*

---

43. Fritz Eichenberg's woodcutting from 1951 called *The Christ of the Breadlines*.
44. White and Farmer, eds., *Joy*, in ch. 2, "Beauty: The Light of Joy," 47.

into God's New Creation,[45] Goto's theological frame is provided by a revision of Jürgen Moltmann's *Theology of Play,*[46] in which play is seen as God's nature and the impetus for creation ex nihilo, woven into the fabric of the world and manifested in the incarnation, pointing toward God's new creation, inviting Christians to playful transformation and recreation of themselves and the world. She describes a psychological-spiritual state she calls "revelatory experiencing" that occurs in playing games or creating art, a state analogous to Mihaly Csikszentmihalyi's "flow" experiences that decenter and recenter participants in a new reality. As Goto notes, "the faithful do not know the good news simply because they have read or been told about it. They experience it in relating to others, knowing it in their bodies, with the senses, in heartfelt imaginings, and authentic exchanges that hit home."[47]

In Goto's view, there is a middle zone between subject and object in which imaginative play happens and we experience revelation. She employs Donald Winnicott's account of transitional objects, which are imbued with life, desire, and character by the child's "as if" imaginings.[48] For Winnicott, play first occurs in the liminal space between the child and the mother's gracious care, which allows the freedom necessary for the child to experiment in the zone between self-occupation and reality—toward the end of achieving identity in the real world. Thus, playing involves "losing and finding oneself in engaging reality and one another 'as if,' exploring freely a world of possibilities bounded by structure that facilitates relationship."[49] This definition grounds Goto's theological, historical, and aesthetic analysis of playing as a pedagogy for "leaning into God's new creation."

For Goto, play can happen in the space between teachers and learners, learners and transitional objects, learners and artistic media, learners and created seasons and rhythms, learners and the future, learners and God, but her examples of the Rhineland nuns and the medieval holy fool tradition bring into focus play with the Christ form. Goto reports that the Rhineland Catholic nuns in fourteenth-century Germany played with infant Christ dolls in order to imagine anew the humanity of Christ and their own. In

---

45. Goto, *The Grace of Playing.*

46. Moltmann, *A Theology of Play.*

47. Goto, *The Grace of Playing,* 128.

48. Obviously, Milbank would reject the notion that there is any such thing as a realism that is not imbued by the imagination.

49. Goto, *The Grace of Playing,* 15.

their play with Christ dolls they imagined his holy qualities of love, which became a means of interrogating their own lives. Medieval people played with the image of holy fools as an expression of Christ's upside-down rationality as possibilities for their own lives. In each of these cases, engagement with Christ's form illumines tensions and potentials, awakens our desires, and prompts spiritual wisdom. The theme of play will be given special consideration in the following chapter under the category of poiesis.

The fourth practice involves fostering creative receptivity. The Christ form sparks our imagination, enlivens our desire, and opens a space for our responsive creativity. According to Balthasar, the mother's gaze represents a form of attunement that invites the child's responsive creativity. Just as the child's response to the mother's attunement is receptive and creative, so the "gaze" of the Christ form invites our creative response to the image held in his form. Our personhood is animated in a playful, poietic process in which we respond to the Christ form with the historical materials and gifts at our disposal. If the Christ form constitutes an attunement with our humanity, so is the form of life we give in return an attunement to the Christ form.

Christian educators have long sought to cultivate space for such encounter and play—a space for wonder in which to imagine our lives as an attuned response to Christ's form. Christian educators can ask questions to spark wonder and creative response. Questions serve to resist merely reducing Scripture or the Christ form to ideas or reasons by creating zones for wonder. For example, when Bible stories are told, Godly Play storytellers signal the end of the lesson and the opening of a time of reflection by pausing for a moment and then raising their eyes to make contact with their listeners. They say, slowly, thoughtfully, "I wonder, what was your favorite part of the story?" "I wonder where you are in this story, or what part of the story is about you?" For the parables, storytellers ask, "I wonder what this seed (tree, pearl, etc.) could really be?" Children are provided art materials to make their own wondering response to the stories told by the teacher, and the storyteller asks each child individually, "I wonder what work you would like to do today?" Each child then has the chance to choose among the different story materials and art materials for their work. Jerome Berryman describes the response time as "deep and personal play," a way for children to make existential connections between the stories and their own lives.[50] The creative process provides a space for children to recapitulate the

---

50. Berryman, *Teaching Godly Play*, 66.

story and its themes, to perceive their inner spiritual meanings and depths, and to artistically express their response.

In a very similar vein, Elisabeth Caldwell, in her book *I Wonder: Engaging a Child's Curiosity about the Bible,* recommends the following wondering questions:

1. "Who is in the story and what happens to them?"

2. "What do you think this story is about?"

3. "What kind of story is this?"

4. "How is this story different from the time and place in which we live?"

5. "Why do you think this story is important?"

6. "How do you connect with the story or what does this story have to do with your life? Or, when would be a good time to remember this story?"[51]

Creating pedagogical spaces in which students are invited to wonder serves to cultivate a kind of responsive creativity in which children receive the gift of the narrative and engage imaginatively in a response that deepens their comprehension of the story and its call upon their lives.

Another example of such playful attunement can be seen in Walter Wink's *Transforming Bible Study* approach, which moves back and forth between aesthetic play and critical exegetical discussions.[52] Wink's Bible study approach is theorized in his book *The Bible in Human Transformation,*[53] which seeks to engage both right-brain and left-brain ways of knowing. Wink connects historical-critical scholarship and discussion with artistic ways of knowing. His Bible study approach begins with silence and bidding prayer, proceeds with performing a roleplay of the Scripture text and discussing its significance and ends with prayer or art exercises in which participants are encouraged to "not think their way through" but to respond playfully with clay, art, journaling, or prayer in response to the Scripture story. In this way, Wink's approach allows for participants to respond creatively to the texts, including the Christ form. While Wink's approach features serious intellectual study his application,

---

51. Caldwell, *I Wonder,* 40–41.

52. Wink, *Transforming Bible Study.*

53. Wink, *The Bible in Human Transformation.*

exercises feature art and contemplative exercises that engage in the kind of creative response that can animate personhood and mission.

As suggested above, Pitzele's Bibliodrama approach invites participants to recreate a biblical scene, which, when adapted as it often is for a Christian context, can include dramatic depictions of Jesus Christ or parables in which his form is rendered.[54] As a biblical scene is workshopped, the leader facilitates playful conversation among the characters, moving back and forth between the realism of the biblical scene and the realism of participants' present world and lives. Bibliodrama honors the written text while deeply exploring and challenging usual biblical meanings. This establishes a space in which participants may play with the Christ form and attune their responses as persons in mission.

* * *

In this chapter, I have articulated Hans Urs von Balthasar's central ideas related to the Christ form and its significance for Christian formation. Balthasar's key insight is that Christ is a surpassing mystery that cannot be reduced to concepts or doctrines. He is a historical, material, aesthetic form—a work of art crafted by God to reveal God's self and humanity's true vision and purpose—that demands a different quality of appreciation that is felt in our senses and in our imagination. Like art, we are taken up by Christ's form into its radiant body before we give our rational consent. I have tried to suggest what it might look like to encounter the Christ form in a variety of pedagogies. I have drawn from a variety of pedagogical approaches which acknowledge the aesthetic or contemplative aspects of teaching and learning. These and many other approaches might be adapted to more fully accommodate the aims and movements outlined here.

54. Pitzele, *Scripture Windows.*

4

Poiesis under the Sign of the Cross

The truth of being is "poetic" before it is "rational" (indeed, it is rational precisely because of its supreme poetic coherence and richness of detail), and thus cannot be known truly if this order is reversed. Beauty is the beginning and end of all true knowledge: really to know, one must first love, and having known, one must finally delight; only this "corresponds" to the Trinitarian love and delight that creates.

—David Bentley Hart, *The Offering of Names*

I ask them to take a poem
and hold it up to the light
like a color slide

or press an ear against its hive.

I say drop a mouse into a poem
and watch him probe his way out,

or walk inside the poem's room
and feel the walls for a light switch.

I want them to waterski
across the surface of a poem
waving at the author's name on the shore.

But all they want to do
is tie the poem to a chair with rope
and torture a confession out of it.

They begin beating it with a hose
to find out what it really means.

—BILLY COLLINS, "INTRODUCTION TO POETRY"

LIKE MANY PEOPLE, I share a home with a dog. Lulu (Christian name, Luisa) is a two-year-old, ninety-pound Golden Retriever that my wife and I raised from a small pup. All my adult life, I have been privileged to live alongside dogs, usually Border Collies, but as my wife and I get older, we have wondered if perhaps a Border Collie might be too athletic for us, what with our bad backs and work schedules. As expected, Lulu is a beautiful, big, yellow, furry throw pillow who lounges on any bed or sofa she chooses (how indulgent we are!). We pass her dozens of times each day wherever she is enthroned; we speak to her, rub her ears, take her on walks, throw the ball for her, and ply her with treats. Although Lulu is terribly proud when she succeeds in finding and returning the ball, she is not a serious athlete like our Border Collies, Wink and Jackson of blessed memory, who took great delight in catching frisbees and herding us around the neighborhood.

95

Lulu is content to sit near at hand and gaze adoringly between naps and treats. Each night she jumps (all ninety pounds) onto whatever sofa or chair I am sitting on and lays her head in my lap, within easy reach of my caress.

Here's the thing—please don't judge—sometimes I do not perceive her as a mere dog. When I look at her soulful eyes, her loving gaze, her flowing golden curls, her noble muzzle, I see—well, royalty. I sometimes imagine that she is a royal emissary, perhaps from a wise and benevolent planet, sent to heal my twisted soul and those whom I love.

Moreover, she "speaks" to my wife, Melissa, and me. And I don't mean in dog whines or yelps but in perfect English, with a slight Mid-Atlantic accent (think Kate Hepburn). Okay, strictly speaking, the actual words issue from my mouth, but I am convinced that I am accurately channeling the intent of her soul. Sometimes she asks, ever so politely, "What is for dinner?" or "When might I expect a walk?" She inquires about my day and offers sympathy for my hardships. When I come home beleaguered, she crouches in her play stance and says, "Hey come on, sad sack. Life is good! Catch me if you can!" Novelist Dean Koontz describes her thus:

> Golden retrievers are not bred to be guard dogs, and considering the size of their hearts and their irrepressible joy in life, they are less likely to bite than to bark, less likely to bark than to lick a hand in greeting. In spite of their size, they think they are lap dogs, and in spite of being dogs, they think they are also human, and nearly every human they meet is judged to have the potential to be a boon companion who might, at any moment, cry, "Let's go!" and lead them on a great adventure.[1]

She comes to my bed each night to tuck me in, wish me blessed dreams, and pray for my safety. Never does she miss a night offering me this blessing.

In the morning, she entreats me to go with her on a walk to survey her parish and to minister to her parishioners. On our mission, every new scent betokens late-breaking news; she carefully hoists her muzzle in the morning breeze, as if to pluck every bit of available gossip. As we approach each neighbor, they greet her dotingly by running their hands through her golden mane, and she returns their affection in sloppy kisses. She inspects each of her dog friends with a few courtesy sniffs, after which she gives a single bark and runs with them in a game of circle tag, until they run out of breath and fall back into heel beside their humans.

1. Koontz, *The Darkest Evening of the Year*, 79.

On these walks, she is my spiritual guide. She shows me things I would not normally notice—babbling streams, frogs, egrets, our neighbor's red poppies, the neighborhood squirrel bandits, the best lawns for legs-in-the-air back scratching, the flora and fauna of our little piece of the planet. She introduces me to the neighbor children, to widows who furnish her with treats, and especially to college students—whom she seems to recognize as members of her own secret monastic order or lost tribe of pups—who cut through our neighborhood on their way to campus.

My confession is that whatever virtue I have would not be nearly so without her. Somehow, amidst our walks, blessings, treats, and ministrations, my heart grows a tiny bit larger. I simply cannot walk beside such a beautiful creature and be mean or petty. She does not allow me to retreat inside my introversion or fearful egoism.

I have read a good bit of psychoanalytic theory, so I know how all of this sounds to a Freudian or Jungian. Perhaps what I perceive in Lulu is actually some hidden part of my psyche projected onto the flat screen of her material "dog-ness." Okay, sure. But try as I might, I simply cannot believe our partnership is meaningless. I am fully aware that the way I describe our relationship is aesthetic and not technical, poetic and not scientific. The thing is, while I may find other metaphors or images to better describe our truth, I am not convinced that our life together can be adequately expressed in other than poetic terms. To insist that Lulu's significance—"what she really means"—can be reduced merely to facts of evolutionary biology or psychodynamics is to deny the true significance of her beauty, the poetic shape of our relationship, and her influence upon my soul.[2] I am convinced that we humans keep pets not simply to remind us of our materiality, as some suggest, but quite possibly the opposite, to remind us of our spirituality. In the language of poet Billy Collins, such a reduction would be like extracting a "confession" from a poem that demands instead to "open a room" and "turn on a light." Because Lulu's beauty has recruited me, made covenant with me, and called me into communion with the world,[3] beginning with

2. My relationship with Lulu might be understood in the context of the long history of literature, such as *Wind in the Willows* and *Winnie the Pooh*, in which animals are portrayed as a source of wisdom, as spiritual guides. Even the most jaded atheist can be found distributing internet memes celebrating the grace of dogs. So common are such experiences that elude the mechanistic model of the self-enclosed mind that we pass them by without reflecting on their significance.

3. Some may object that dogs are a unique subject, specially evolved for such domestication. That may be partially true, but many people find such poietic significance in

my neighborhood, I am awakened to the reality that beauty invites me beyond myself into love with God and neighbor.

My story about Lulu also points to an aesthetic epistemology that emphasizes poiesis—creative making—as how we ordinarily know the world and its mysteries—revealing a stronger role for creative poiesis in Christian formation. To truly know Lulu involves a "naming" that is poetic and mutually constitutive. My creative characterization—my naming—of her as "benevolent emissary" bears on her well-being and my own. We are both created amidst my poetic rendering of her.

The concept of poiesis as articulated by Plato and Aristotle is reimagined by theologian John Milbank as creative "making" which encompasses all our knowing and acting.[4] Milbank is an emeritus professor in the department of theology and religious studies at the University of Nottingham and a founder of the radical orthodoxy movement which extends the aesthetics of Balthasar to include a larger role for creativity. For Milbank, along with others such as Alexander Schmemann and Rowan Williams, our human vocation involves creatively naming the world, as Adam did in the garden, in a doxological gift of blessing.[5] Theological aesthetics constitute a challenge to commodification and objectification of our world and the Christ form.

If Balthasar articulated a theology of beauty for the modern world, John Milbank stands on Balthasar's shoulders and emphasizes that beauty

---

other creatures. For example, my colleague Carolyn Helsel has a similar relationship to her chickens and monarch butterflies.

4. The term "poiesis" or "poietic" has generally referred to the creative process of making, while "poesis" or "poetic" has connoted a relationship with poetry. In other words, poetry is a specific example of poiesis; not everything that involves poiesis is poetry. However, readers will notice that some authors cited herein also use the term "poetic" to denote creative making, which can be confusing. Throughout this volume, insofar as it is possible, I will endeavor to use the term "poiesis" for creative making, except when specific authors use the term poesis, and I will use the term "poetic" to refer to poetry.

5. Schmemann states, "the unique position of man in the universe is that he alone is to bless God for the food and the life he receives from Him. He alone is to respond to God's blessing with his blessing. The significant fact about the life in the Garden is that man is to name things. As soon as animals have been created to keep Adam company, God brings them to Adam to see what he will call them. And whatsoever Adam called every living creature, that was the name thereof. Now, in the Bible a name is infinitely more than a means to distinguish one thing from another. It reveals the very essence of a thing, or rather its essence as God's gift. To name a thing is to manifest the meaning and value God gave it, to know it as coming from God and to know its place and function within the cosmos created by God." Schmemann, *For the Life of the World*, 15.

prompts an ecstatic response in which we are moved to creative response in doxological poiesis.[6] As we saw in the previous chapter, Balthasar's notion of receptive creativity already acknowledges that the beauty of the created world and Christ's incarnation prompts an active response of "making" or poiesis which extends God's beauty in the world. Both Milbank and Balthasar view knowing as inherently a creative act and a way we participate in God's own making. But Milbank foregrounds creative poiesis as a key aspect of God and true human vocation.

To understand poiesis as a way of knowing demands a revision of how we understand Christian formation and pedagogy. Christian formation that acknowledges the role of poiesis emphasizes a more active role for beauty, a more constructivist anthropology, a more participatory ontology, and an expanded role for cultural mediation. This chapter explores Christian formation in terms of responsive and creative "making." First, we begin by articulating the theological significance of poiesis and its significance for knowing.

THEORETICAL UNDERPINNINGS

As Balthasar already recognized, beauty is not passive but prompts active creativity—that beauty is only truly known in a creative response. It is therefore not surprising that theologians who stand on Balthasar's shoulders emphasize beauty's more active and poietic dimensions. If Balthasar emphasized beauty for a modern world evacuated of mystery, Milbank emphasizes poiesis for a postmodern world that has learned that rationality is always reliant upon a background of story or myth. Like Charles Taylor, he insists that secularity is in fact a product of poiesis and should thus have no privileged status over religious myth. Religion and modern secularity both rely on background myths—of a cosmos open to transcendence on one hand or one enclosed within the immanent frame. Modern secularity is thus revealed to be essentially religious in nature, and as such is no less arbitrary than religion.[7] For Milbank, modern secularity is constituted by a founding myth that must now be "out-narrated."[8] What is required, Milbank suggests, is attention to rhetoric, narrative, and aesthetics—which should not be a problem for Christianity, since poiesis already lies at the

6. Milbank's theory of poiesis is most fully elaborated in *The Word Made Strange*.

7. As William Cavanaugh has written, secular institutions such as the nation-state appropriate their mythic authority from the church. Cavanaugh, "A Fire Strong Enough."

8. Milbank, *Theology and Social Theory*, 279.

heart of the tradition. As we will see, theology that features poiesis offers an alternate vision of Christian formation from the Enlightenment account that features foundational ideas to be transmitted.

Poiesis as Native to Christianity

First, it is important to recognize that poiesis or creative making is not a novel or late addition but lies at the heart of the Christian tradition. An emphasis on poiesis, or "creative making," grows from ordinary understandings and experiences of Christian life and liturgy. (a) The divine-human poiesis essential to Christianity is seen in Christ, whose life, death, and resurrection is God's poietic response to Hebrew narratives and hopes; (b) the liturgy, which is the prayer of the religious community that embraces everything from the rhythms of cultic movement to hymns, architecture, prose, and poetry; (c) mythmaking or storytelling, including Holy Scripture, the narratives of the church, the stories of the saints, and works of Christian theology, such as Dante's *Divine Comedy,* the *Confessions* of Augustine, and Pascal's *Pensées;* and (d) making and being the church, which is everything from entrance into, life in, and extension of the sacred community in its practices, the edifying care it extends to its members, to humanity, and to the world, as the steward of God's reign. As religious educator Maria Harris observes in her book *Fashion Me a People,* the church's ministries—*koinonia, kerygma, didache, diakonia,* and *leiturgia*—are themselves artistic forms that create us even as we create them.[9] As such, that poiesis is the ordinary character of religious life should be uncontroversial. Milbank observes:

> The very first "creative artist" was seen by western Europe to be Christ himself and in his wake the figure of the Pope ... who had the power of drastic creative innovation, because he mediated first of all liturgically, but then legislatively, the trans-creation of Christ himself, Christ's deployment of fictions, Christ's institution of new birth at baptism, and finally Christ's act of transubstantiation on Maundy Thursday ... The power [to share in creation and to originate creation] is restored to us in the Incarnation and even newly augmented by it.[10]

9. Harris, *Fashion Me a People,* 170.
10. Milbank, *Theology and Social Theory,* 198.

Here Milbank signals that poiesis is not a mere supplement but is essential to our understanding and practice of Christ and his church which speaks to the contemporary world in specific ways. Christianity shares with art the project of subverting modernity's disenchantment and nihilism. The banal materiality of late-modern society evacuates the material of significance, reducing it to a gnostic veil that is constantly rewoven by the next image, show, post, tweet, or performance—an object for consumption or a source of distraction but little more. Late modernity, despite its desire to avoid religion by collapsing all things into the material, nevertheless reduces the material to nothing. It flies through our fingers or across our gaze as we scroll, purchase, and consume. Its satisfactions are fleeting, enduring only as long as the next form is consumed, and so we must continually scroll, shop, or reload.

An emphasis on poiesis can be seen as part of Christianity's revolutionary transvaluation of the material in which God is mediated in the goodness and ongoing recreation of the material order in God's kingdom. In the eighth century, St. John of Damascus saw that the incarnation was a watershed moment in history when there could no longer be any reluctance about God's sanctifying of the material because God became material; the sculptor became the clay. Amidst the iconoclast controversy, St. John says:

> When I revere images, I do not worship matter. I worship the creator of matter who became matter for my sake, who will to take his abode in matter, who worked out my salvation through matter. God's body is God because it is joined to his person by a union which shall never pass away. Because of this I salute all remaining matter with reverence because God has filled it with His grace and power.[11]

It is no mystery that Christianity has produced such enduring art. The creative arts have long played a role in spiritual practice and formation because they transcend and make strange the everyday, allowing us to return to the world with eyes of wonder.[12] Painting, sculpture, poetry, music,

---

11. John of Damascus, "Apologia against Those Who Decry Holy Images," 16.

12. For J. R. R. Tolkien, fantasy literature creates a fantastic world that effects a kind of recovery when crossing back over into reality. Tolkien writes: "Recovery (which includes return and renewal of health) is a re-gaining—regaining of a clear view. I do not say 'seeing things as they are' and involve myself with the philosophers, though I might venture to say 'seeing things as we are (or were) meant to see them'—as things apart from ourselves. We need, in any case, to clean our windows; so that the things seen clearly may be freed from the drab blur of triteness of familiarity—from possessiveness." According

architecture, or story can be seen as a recognition that all matter is hallowed by the incarnation, that material can be a charmed portal to the immaterial. An encounter with matter can activate the soul. As James K. A. Smith puts it, "What is mesmerizing and haunting about a Bach cantata is the miraculous way that these indentations of airwaves on membranes inside our heads can nonetheless transport us onto a plane of contemplation that feels just barely tethered to the earth, our souls walking a tightrope of elation and longing that feels infinite."[13] In this brief phenomenology of poiesis, we can see what is at stake for Smith and Milbank. Still, his conclusions do not only rely on a phenomenology, but also depend on its fundamental theological importance.

Verbum as Transcendental

John Milbank elevates poiesis to the status of a transcendental—an aspect of all being, convertible with truth, goodness, and beauty, and perfected in God. Milbank considers poiesis to be important not only as a calculated response to modernity but as theologically inescapable, especially since "creative making" is an attribute of God and a requisite of all being. Patristic theologian Nicholas of Cusa first spoke of the Second Person of the Trinity as the "Art" of God and declared eternal "making" an aspect of the Father's "begetting of the Son," which renders "God's inner creativity definatory of the divine essence."[14] Milbank agrees with philosopher Giambattista Vico, who employs the Latin term *Verbum* for the second person of the Trinity. While the Greek term *Logos* has been commonly used for the second person of the Trinity, he feels this has been stripped of its significance by the modern connotation of "Word" as static and stable, as a noun. In Milbank's view, God is divine creative utterance and so in a sense is already "the world," since the Second Person of the Trinity, as *Verbum*, freely extends God's speaking/making power from inside God to outside God.

---

to Tolkien, the fairy tale's chief aim is desire, for example, for the ability to speak to animals and "surveying the depths of space and time." These desires point the reader back to an Edenic relationship with the world, one of intimate connection, of difference but not division. If a fairy tale has awakened desire, according to Tolkien, it has succeeded. Tolkien, *Tales from the Perilous Realm*, 373.

13. Smith, "Resurrecting the Imagination."

14. Milbank, *Theology and Social Theory*, 27–30, 82–84, 126–32.

For Nicholas of Cusa, *creation* rather than *being is* the principal philosophical category.[15] Milbank affirms a theory of making in which the truth is precisely what is made. While, as we have seen, Descartes's *cogito* or "thinking self" is a subject problematically suspended in a timeless, suprahistorical realm of essences, Milbank agrees with Vico that we are caught in "the unfolding and carnality of time," being shaped by and shaping culture.[16] For Milbank, the human participates with the divine not simply by passive contemplation (against Plato and Descartes), but also by means of poiesis or "making."[17]

Poiesis as Gift

Milbank's favorite theological topics, including poiesis, rely in part on his conception of gift.[18] The notion of gift has a long philosophical heritage. French philosopher Jacques Derrida, in his philosophy of gift, controversially insists that it is contradictory to imagine a gift as a free unconditional donation, since it holds an implicit expectation of reciprocity. Milbank rejects Derrida's understanding of gift, since it involves a Kantian sense of persons as abstractions with discrete and separable interests,[19] which Milbank sees rooted in a transactional instead of a theological economy. For Milbank, persons and their gifts must be defined by interrelationality and cannot be thought of apart, except as an act of violence. Milbank envisions an original gift as inspiring and energizing a further "return" gift such that it becomes impossible to distinguish the end of giving from the beginning of receiving. Milbank sees that it is the nature of gifts to be given as "nonidentical repetition."[20] To give a return gift is, in a sense, a repetition of the original gift, but it must not be identical, since giving the identical gift as

15. Milbank, *Theology and Social Theory*, 22.

16. Mazzotta, *The New Map of the World*, 27.

17. Already programmatically as a conclusion to the first volume of his Vico study: "An alternative version of modernity" (Milbank, *The Religious Dimension*, 327–35).

18. Milbank, *Being Reconciled*, 201.

19. See Milbank, "Can a Gift Be Given?," 119–61. In this article, Milbank discusses Jean-Luc Marion's and Jacques Derrida's notions of the gift. For Milbank, the divine gift does not precede being (Marion). And it is not an impossible possibility (Derrida). Milbank's trinitarian metaphysics is characterized by the participation between persons (perichoresis) and the participation of creation in the trinitarian life.

20. Milbank observes that for Augustine, in *De Trinitate*, "Gift" is a name for the Holy Spirit. Milbank, *The Word Made Strange*, 55–83, esp. 60–61, 70–71.

quid pro quo effectively removes the person from the giving.[21] But when a gift is unexpected or nonidentical, it can represent a personal giver seeking communion. For Milbank, communion is a more fundamental human category. Gifting must be seen as relative to communion and not abstracted as a transaction.

Identity is not a static category but resides in the flow and communion of gift-giving and receiving, which points to the plenitude of God and the communion of the Trinity. According to Milbank, from creation through redemption, God gives gifts through the Spirit and brings humanity into a Trinitarian gift exchange.[22] In receiving divine gifts, the human is involved in "active reception" in which one gives the love one receives from God to one's neighbor in return.[23] The gift "is not prior to but coincident with relation" such that they are inseparable.[24] It is impossible to receive God's gift while refusing to give to one's neighbor.[25]

For Milbank doxological glory must not be seen as a static event but is manifest in flow of giving and receiving of gifts. This description characterizes the entire cosmos as properly liturgical and doxological in its mutual receiving and giving. In this metaphysical understanding of gifting, Milbank understands poiesis as a means of participating in God by extending beauty in a way that constitutes a liturgical response filled with eros and glory, but which can never be final.

Anthropology of Poiesis

Milbank reclaims an ancient Greek and early Christian anthropology which sees that the human soul is, as Aristotle said, "in a manner all things."[26] The soul is not some ghostly aspect of our interiority but rather the orientation of the body in its linguistic, sacramental, relational, and cultural aspects,

21. Even when repeating the exact stanzas, the poet adds a different emphasis, pairs a phrase with a novel facial expression, or stresses different syllables. In this way, *mutatis mutandis,* the poem contains the potential for an infinite variety of performances.

22. Milbank, *The Word Made Strange,* 124, 143–47.

23. Milbank coins the term "active reception" in an essay on Gregory of Nyssa and the Gift. The phrase is helpful in expressing Milbank's constructive alternative to theologies of "passive" reception, a theme dominating his essays on the Gift. See Milbank, "Gregory of Nyssa," 95.

24. Milbank, "Can a Gift Be Given?," 137.

25. Milbank, "Can a Gift Be Given?," 136.

26. Aristotle, *De Anima,* iii.

which give it form and make it to live. Rather than standing above time in Cartesian bodiless contemplation, the soul is within time, subject to change and mutation, capable of discerning. Spiritual progress is not just temporally inward and upward but spatially outwards into the ecclesia and society, in a sense of shared embodiment in social and liturgical symbolic interaction and ritualized practice. Even the categories of objective and subjective are thoroughly entangled in this ancient understanding of the soul.

As a capacity of soul, poiesis is not reserved only for the extraordinarily gifted but is the ordinary mode of human knowing. Milbank observes that we normally have an intuitive sense of the depth of things: "We take the surface of things as disclosing or promising such a depth . . . There is a necessary 'taking together' or reading of the conjunction, over and above what merely appears . . . To know is basically to select, to desire and to construct 'aesthetically preferred patterns' which we should not mistake, as did Kant, for necessary logic."[27] Poiesis is key to our perception of the world. As I confessed earlier, my creative reception of Lulu—rendering her as an interplanetary emissary, a spiritual guide—is not merely a flight of whimsy but is key to rightly perceiving her. My language for her is at once invention and discovery. In giving poetic expression to my relationship with her, I can see her more truly.

Hence the human self's relationship to truth is principally active and generative; the true is coterminous with the "made." While, for Descartes, the *cogito* (the thinking self) is an abstracted homunculus, for Milbank, the self is a work of art constituted by its imagination, storytelling, and making in relation to the world—a work of soul. Milbank imagines truth as remaining close to the ground of desire, mystery, and beauty in the world, which awakens our senses and bears witness to God. If, as Timothy Brennan puts it, Descartes fails "to capture human action in its transformative encounter with materialities,"[28] Milbank produces a theory of "making as participation" in which, following Vico, "the true is precisely what is made"[29] and, therefore, "the first truth is in God, because God is the first Maker."[30]

Viewing the human's relationship to truth as active and generative suggests a dynamic view of humanity and culture and a stronger role for

27. Milbank, *Philosophy*, 24–31.
28. Brennan, *Borrowed Light*, 38.
29. Milbank, *The Religious Dimension*, 1, 108.
30. Quoted in Bull, *Inventing Falsehood, Making Truth*, 30.

mediation of God.[31] Made in God's image, humanity is *homo faber*. Just as the Father is never without his eternal "Art/Son," so human artifacts are not a secondary reality grafted onto a more basic "natural" existence but "fully equiprimordial" with humanity itself.[32] The boundaries between nature and culture are thus blurred or evacuated. A theological vision must not see creation as pure nature, but includes a role for human creativity, and any vision for human selfhood must involve our creative making in the world.[33] Furthermore, since human making reflects the eternal Trinity and the continually creative work of God, it is also a reaching for transcendence, an imitation of and participation in the ongoing creative action of God.

Milbank shows that there is no knowledge that is separate from the made product. The real knowledge of the artistic product, for example, is the finished product itself. Milbank says, "We do not really know what we are going to do until we have decided what to do and therefore have already done the thing. To decide is but to mime the action in advance."[34] This means that we don't make things merely to bring preexisting ideas to public expression; the idea is formed and conveyed in making the thing.

The analogy of the artist can help us understand Milbank's poietic epistemology. While an artist may be moved by the sense of a landscape, this knowledge is not complete until it is rendered in artistic making. Only when the product is rendered as form do the originating intuitions of beauty and depth become concrete knowledge. So it is not possible to posit a thinking subject that "uses" language, since this understates the role of language. Since we think in language, the "thinking I" is not extricable from its having thoughts using words, its continual self-expressing with language and culture. For human beings, making and knowing have an important element of uncertainty. If we complete or make a product, it means that we finally have knowledge of it. Thus, we know nothing finally or definitively but are constantly striving toward the completion of our knowledge, which lies in God.[35]

31. Milbank, *Theology and Social Theory*, 150–53.

32. Milbank, *Theology and Social Theory*, 31, 88, 101.

33. Here, Christian educators may recall Maria Harris's refrain, "We create the forms, and the forms create us," Harris, *Fashion Me a People*, 171–73, 177–81.

34. Milbank, *Theology and Social Theory*, 177.

35. See, e.g., Milbank, *The Religious Dimension*, 130, where Milbank paraphrases Vico: "Whereas God is *infinitum*, humanity is *quod tendit ad infinitum*. *Explicatio* certainly implies a constant uncertainty as to our proper substance, but in escaping from our incompletion towards the divine *comprehensio*, we travel towards an unreachable point

The Poiesis of the Church: Making Strange

In a chapter from *The Word Made Strange,* titled "A Christological Poetics,"[36] Milbank speaks of Christ not only as the sum total of the signifying chain of Hebrew theology poetically imagined in the Old Testament but also as occupying a certain "originating place" in the chain, as Logos.[37] So "on the night before he was betrayed," Jesus Christ performs and repeats the story of the passing over in Egypt but in a radically new way that includes the command to love one another, with the example of washing his disciples' feet, an act that the church has been performing and remembering for two millennia. As we said earlier, when Pope Francis in 2016 washed the feet of Muslim prisoners in the context of the Maundy Thursday rites, he performed Christ in a radically new way. And who knows what potential meanings are yet still to come as signs are made newly strange? Milbank argues that Christian faith is not merely reclaiming or repeating a pristine original Word since it is the nature of the Word or *Verbum* that it demands to be "made strange" if truth is to be heard. Contemporary meaning should feature texts that linger and words that explode, disrupting and reconfiguring contemporary constructions of the self and the social order.

Christ's creativity or "making strange" includes his ministry to proclaim good news to the poor, to proclaim freedom for the prisoners and recovery of sight for the blind, and to set the oppressed free and proclaim the year of the Lord's favor (Luke 4:18–19). The church's Christological creativity is expressed when we create, discover, and thus partake in the church's ministries as creative acts. Milbank asserts that the power of creativity is "restored to us in the Incarnation and even newly augmented by it."[38] He writes:

> Because the creative human being is "inspired," and because she does not fully grasp or command the new thing which she has brought about, there is no absolute creation here; the new thing invented is also "discovered," given to the creator herself as a mysterious new potency." Human creativity is understood as a

where our exact substance is known and realised . . . Createdness properly belongs to us as becoming, as *facere,* but our full particularity is sustained by the completion of this createdness, within the godhead itself."

36. Milbank, *The Word Made Strange,* 123–44.

37. This term comes from Certeau, "How Is Christianity Thinkable Today?," 143.

38. John Milbank, *Beyond Secular Order,* 198.

"participation in the transmission of this power to humanity in the person of Jesus Christ."[39]

Perhaps the most radical aspect of Milbank's thought is his suggestion that the final shape of the church's narrative is not yet written but emerges in an imaginative transformation. Milbank's vision is not undisciplined; it lives under the sign of the cross, within a society of unlimited reciprocity among friends. Christ remains homeless, an exile wandering the world, finally pushed out on to the cross where the church is to follow him as a new community without familiar barriers. The church can only proclaim peace when it is most ready to be uneasy and constructively suspicious, when it too is in exile and homeless. The church is to be "like a trained revolutionary cell," tearing up false treaties of peace and breaking up deceptive harmonies.[40] Jesus' homelessness creates our home, a place for us to live.[41] And it is here that the church finds its mission. Milbank evokes the image of a gothic cathedral, a living ruin steeped in history and particularity but always growing, through new additions, styles, and extensions.[42] This is a construction that speaks of transcendence in its archways, vaultings, ceilings, and colored windows but also of the limits and failures of human imagination in its breakages and architectural anomalies.

The church involves an ongoing experimental embrace of difference, constantly making harmonies out of emerging identities. In this creative harmonizing we out-narrate the secular stories of conflict and competition. The church does not constitute a seamless or unassailable system of thought or a utopian vision; it stands ever as an interruption of history, a critique of human sociality that tells an alternative story that exposes history to judgment. The church appears as a community of peace but also as a radically antagonistic community that explodes into the middle of history. The church embraces difference, trusting that peace rather than chaos lies at the heart of reality.

Christian formation of modernity assumes a stable, preexisting self, unilaterally receiving the truth of texts, practices, and doctrines as stable (typically, rational) substances. As we have seen, John Milbank rejects these

---

39. Milbank is quoting Ambrose, who draws a connection between the word of Christ creating the world ex nihilo and the word of Christ changing the nature of the eucharistic elements. Milbank, *Beyond Secular Order*, 196.

40. Williams, *The Truce of God*, 75.

41. Williams, *The Truce of God*, 81.

42. Milbank, *Theology and Social Theory*, 276.

modern assumptions and affirms the priority of the imaginative, the poetic, and the mythic capacities of soul as strategies that resist the modern impulse to objectify and freeze thought and retain a stronger role for God's mediation in the making of culture.

If Charles Taylor decries a secular disenchantment or flattening, Milbank sees poiesis as restoring the world's enchantment by continually "making strange"—by poietically renewing and refreshing our encounter with beauty and the depths of being. Because the world is brimming with beauty that opens to God's depths and because we are ensouled beings with imagination and desire that intend toward God, human poiesis can illumine God in our midst and animate our spiritual senses. As Milbank makes clear, if Christian formation is to take beauty seriously, then neither our faith nor our formation can be divorced from creativity, continual poiesis, "making strange." Milbank's focus on poiesis suggests a significant revision of our modern approaches to Christian formation that emphasize frozen ideas and practices.

EDUCATIONAL AIMS

Given that truth of the world, self, or God is infinitely beautiful, deep, relational, and fluid, we cannot transmit frozen ideas to be passively received. Instead our creative making becomes the crucial way of knowing. Therefore, pedagogies for Christian formation that recognize the significance of poiesis seek to do three things:

1. *They seek to receive the sources of the Christian tradition as gifts of unique beauty.* The foundational texts, doctrines, liturgies, practices of the Christian tradition—indeed Christ himself—are too often conveyed as frozen concepts to be mastered, which, as such, cannot evoke delight, gratitude, joy, or transformation. Pedagogies for poiesis seek to illumine these sources as poietic responses in a historical economy of joyful gifting and invite learners to participate in this economy.

2. *They invite responses that return the tradition's gifts in new creative forms with fresh accent or inflection for others to receive as truth.* Just as a story may be improved in its retelling and a liturgy of foot washing given new significance when performed in a prison or refugee camp, so do the ideas and practices of Christian faith attain new significance as they are reworked in our hands and with our tongues. In

such telling and retelling, making and remaking, the church makes the gospel ever strange as it expands its field of metaphors, images, meanings, and responsive acts, in which we glimpse God's glory in the exchange of our creative gifts. As old stories are told and performed with new inflection, new meanings are opened and old meanings are given new significance.

3. *In all things, they seek to respond to the surpassing beauty of Christ's incarnation and offer gifts fitting to its original donation.* In this field of unfolding meanings, we are formed as Christians, as creative beings under the sign of the cross. Christian formation is above all a creative response to the gift of Christ encountered as poiesis prompting our poiesis. As such, our ongoing poiesis bears witness to the original gift of Christ.

Christian educators have long recognized the power of such poiesis. Maria Harris saw that the church's ministries are akin to artistic forms. She declared, "we create the forms and they create us."[43] As we have seen, some Christian educators have embraced Jewish educator Peter Pitzele's bibliodramatic approach to engaging Scripture creatively, dramatizing it in order to see new meanings. Others, like Fred Edie, engage adolescents in the gestures of liturgy and adapt them creatively for life beyond the chapel. Still others, like Craig Dykstra and Dorothy Bass, see that Christian practices are creative adaptations and must be adapted in each new historical context.[44] Frank Rogers observes that creating stories involves a kind of vital flourishing or spiritual healing.[45]

We will survey them and others as we consider the practices of poiesis as an approach to Christian formation.

FOUR EDUCATIONAL PRACTICES OF A PEDAGOGY FOR POIESIS

How do we teach and form Christians in a pedagogy for poiesis? As we saw in Balthasar's thought, when beauty is perceived we are ecstatically caught up in creative response. The initiative lies in the object of beauty. Yet, the work of teachers is to explore ways to make space in which beautiful

43. Harris, *Fashion Me a People*, 171–73, 177–81.
44. Bass, *Practicing Our Faith*; Dykstra, *Growing in the Life of Faith*.
45. Rogers, *Finding God in the Graffiti*, ch. 5.

objects—or the "great things," as Parker Palmer names them—can have their formative effects. The following represents practices that teachers employ in fostering formation that features creative responses to beauty.

The first practice involves creating, performing, getting our hands dirty amidst the materiality. Christian formation does not primarily involve transmission of frozen ideas but must also include creative engagement with the materials of the tradition—its texts, narratives, liturgies, and practices. Before artists give shape to their art, they linger with a material object, intuit the mysterious depths of its form, and engage experientially and experimentally with it. Engagement with the material forms from the Christian tradition sparks creativity and freshness of heart but also intellectual curiosity and thought. We do not extract the wisdom of a tradition from a distance as autonomous beings deducing its rationality but by entering into the field of its "game" to try and test its limits and potentials. Just as a painter must explore different angles, lighting options, and a variety of color pallets and modes of composition in order to express the truth of an object, so do Christians know the truth of created being and of Christ by imaginatively handling its materials.

Pedagogies that feature poiesis engage two materials—forms of revelation and our lived experience. As we saw above, for Courtney Goto, poiesis involves play with Christian materials—nuns playing with Christ dolls, holy fools playing with Christ's subversions, playing with visions of a redeemed cosmos amidst our lived experience.[46] Dori Baker's LIVE practice, elaborated in *Doing Girlfriend Theology* and *The Barefoot Way*, focuses on stories—handling lived experience, theological reflection, and new meanings and ethical responses as materials that prompt reflection on hidden meanings. Anne Wimberly's story-linking approach invites participants to engage and handle a variety of materials—personal stories, Scripture stories, and African American heritage stories—as wisdom is discerned amidst the imaginative interplay of these stories.[47] Augusto Boal's theater games prompt participants to explore and experiment with bodily sensations, memory, guided imagery, and creative performance, to create new narratives from the oppression and hope of ordinary life. For Walter Wink and Peter Pitzele, the bodily performance or handling of Scripture sheds new light on more creative and faithful possibilities for living and

46. Goto, *The Grace of Playing.*
47. Wimberly, *Soul Stories.*

acting.[48] Spiritual directors know that asking directees to create a painting or drawing of their relationship to their "true self" yields insight that cannot be gained simply by reflecting. Spiritual insight cannot be marshalled by thought, but when our bodies and souls encounter the materials of our lives and Christian revelation.

Mihaly Csikszentmihalyi sees that creative people are absolutely fascinated by their subject; then, they take their intuition seriously, looking for patterns where others see confusion and making connections between discrete areas of knowledge.[49] It is difficult to generalize about how people engage in creative process across all media. Some writers will brainstorm to see what connections can be made; others use timed writing or journaling to make space, as Parker Palmer says, for the "shy soul to speak."[50] But finally, artists know that there is no substitute for "getting our hands dirty," diving into the materiality of our work, the images, ideas, grammar, and patterns in their particularity. Christian educators have long intuited that a creative process in which we get our hands dirty in the messiness of the materials not only produces great art but reveals hidden meanings.

In classes conducted by Professor Frank Rogers, he directs students working in small groups to engage the biblical story of Ishmael to rework it as a press release in the newspaper, a popular song, a poem, or a television show. This assignment requires students to engage the biblical story, discern its features and subtle depths, comprehend the requirements of the particular genre, and give shape to new constructions to express the biblical text.

At Marymount School in Manhattan, Sister Clevie Youngblood asks eleventh-grade students to write a creative account of the faith journey of Abraham, Sarah, Hagar, Isaac, Rebekah, Esau, or Jacob. Using the biblical account as a framework, they creatively fill in the details, telling a story of the character's faith and imagine how it changes over the course of his or her life. Students' stories, she advises, may take whatever form they choose—for example, dialogue with another character, diary entries, an appearance on a talk show. Their stories must include at least two lessons from the character's story: one lesson about the faith journey and one lesson about God. Kim Boykin, from the same school, invites religion students to create short videos in which their pets are characters in one of Jesus' parables. These assignments yield new insights into biblical texts that are now forever

48. Wink, *Transforming Bible Study*; Pitzele, *Scripture Windows*.

49. Csikszentmihalyi, *Creativity*.

50. Palmer, *A Hidden Wholeness*, 59, 60.

etched into the imaginations of learners. In order to perceive its "strangeness," learners must "get their hands dirty" in the materiality of the text and the forms.

The second practice involves imaginative free play, creating and engaging imaginative worlds that express the depths and ends toward which our souls reach. Artists play by creating new worlds in order to reveal truths that cannot be rendered any other way. As we saw previously, J. R. R. Tolkien created Middle Earth; C. S. Lewis created Narnia; Flannery O'Connor fashioned a Southern gothic world. Poets play with images or metaphors that create worlds that guide the poem in its unfolding. In the Christian tradition, worship liturgies play with the world by crafting stories, songs, prayers, feasts, words, and architectural forms that constitute a new and subversive habitus.

Walter Wink's *Transforming Bible Study* approach invites participants to playfully dramatize a biblical scene as they imagine it. These performed scenes provided an imagined "world" that prompts further reflection about texts. In Peter Pitzele's *Bibliodrama* Bible study approach, participants perform biblical narratives imagining and improvising roles suggested by the texts.[51] As participants move in this biblical world and play with its characters, new meanings are created and old meanings given new texture.

One of Augusto Boal's foundational games is one in which participants together build a "machine" of images with moving parts representing dynamics of a particular context.[52] This game creatively renders the relationships and dynamics of a community as an image. In this game the community "workshops" these characters, dynamics, and their motivations. In creating a machine of images that represent its distortions and oppression, the community permits itself to play with their lives amidst systems and structures; they begin to envision the machine as it might ideally look as redeemed.

The third practice involves accessing our hidden desires and their appropriate ends. Axiomatic to poiesis is that it seeks to express those undercurrents of desire that seek or inhibit our search for the good. As desiring and imagining creatures, our "making" reflects our intention toward the world in the gravitational pull of God's eros "under the sign of the cross." The creative work we do participates in God's own endless creating, guided by our restless desire for Beauty. For example, J. R. R. Tolkien, in creating Middle Earth, is making manifest a hidden desire to commune with

51. Pitzele, *Scripture Windows.*

52. Boal, *Games for Actors and Non-Actors,* 94.

animals and trees, to fight darkness, to honor small acts of goodness, as in the habits of hobbits. Flannery O'Connor's fiction makes manifest a desire for the redemption of entrenched Southern racism and poverty. When Christians narrate their testimony, they are not simply providing a factual account; they are expressing something of their yearnings or hopes which Christian faith addresses. Especially in a culture that assigns us to gross political, ethnic, racial, gendered, and sexual categories, poiesis can reveal the deeper mysteries of our goodness and of the world around us.

At its best, Christian formation helps us to resist our distorted desires and deepen our love for God and neighbor. Christians have utilized various techniques to make concrete in order to clarify their desires. As mentioned earlier, Ignatius's practice of Examen prompts participants to consider each morning or night their desires—their consolations and desolations—that make them most alive and those that drain life. In Augusto Boal's theater games, as participants construct a scene that demonstrates a situation of their oppression, they are prompted to "freeze" the action to reflect on the desires of each character, especially the antagonist and protagonist. Only when the desires of the characters are made concrete by dramatization can there be reconciliation. Only in playing with the materiality of the world and Christian revelation can we access our hidden desires.

The fourth practice involves inviting return gifts of non-identical repetition. We are formed as Christians in an economy of receiving the gifts of the past of other communions and giving our gifts in response. In Milbank's view, God's glory is not found in stable substances but in the back and forth of gift-giving and -receiving.

We see such reciprocal gift-giving in the work of many educators. In Augusto Boal's theater games, the community identifies a limit situation and enacts a variety of resolutions to the situation. Participants take turns observing their fellow "spect-actors"—receiving their gifts—but at crucial points individuals may shout, "Freeze!" and step into the scene to offer a different ending—thus offering their gifts.[53] Dori Baker's LIVE practice does not seek a settled conclusion regarding a story's significance but is designed to honor the multiplicity of connections as participants playfully offer their insights without critique or comment.[54] Instead of clinging to a single settled theological or practical conclusion, participants sit amidst the shared images, lingering in their wisdom and beauty. Jack Zipes invites participants to

53. Boal, *Theatre of the Oppressed*, 95–113.
54. Baker, *The Barefoot Way*.

workshop the damaging gender stereotypes found in traditional fairy tales. Students offer their updated interpretations as gifts.[55] Each week in Christian worship, preachers engage Scriptures, liturgies, and stories as fragments as they weave their sermons. These sermons do not add up to a monolithic orthodoxy but a field of tensive and paradoxical images, metaphors, and meanings—ever receiving old and returning new gifts. As Milbank observes, the power of such formation is in its charged and reciprocal gratuity. While there is certainly a place for dogma, Christian formation finds its power in the ecstatic flux of poietic gift-giving and -receiving.

* * *

This chapter has probed the question of how the poietic nature of God, the world, and Christian tradition points to different pedagogical priorities and practices for Christian formation. I have wagered that the truth of the world, God, and us can best be seen not by forcing a confession, as Billy Collins fears, but by entering a room, turning on a light, running its maze, putting an ear to its hive. In this view Christian formation is a bit like how I imagine my relationship with my dog, Lulu, not best comprehended in terms that are merely factual that can be instructed. Christian formation must include a perpetual array of texts that linger and words that explode, disrupting and reconfiguring contemporary constructions of the self and the social order.

---

55. Zipes, *Creative Storytelling.*

PART III

Liturgy as Art, and Art as Liturgy

NOT ONLY ARE BEAUTY and poiesis aspects of a forgotten social imaginary that might be reclaimed for a postmodern world; they are essential dynamics of the church's worship, qualities of the "other world" it establishes. They are also key for understanding the church's art, which expresses its Referent, manifests its laments, and keeps alive its hope for a world redeemed. As we have seen, creative poiesis is not only a response to created beauty; it is part of the ordinary life of the church—its texts, liturgies, visions of redemption, ordinary practices, its testimonies and stories. In a sense, this book stands on the shoulders of Alexander Schmemann, who sees human vocation as receiving God's good gifts and returning our gifts in naming them. In this view, we are formed not in the mere reclaiming of a pristine past, but in the flow of perpetual naming—in worship and art that is forever trying to say God's name more adequately, expressing the Referent that eternally outstrips its efforts. The following chapter elaborates and responds to recent writings of James K. A. Smith, who prioritizes aesthetics, especially the role it plays in Christian formation. As we noted at the outset, art and music seem to constitute something of a refuge for those who reject organized religion. With Smith, we must wonder if this moment presents us with the possibility of reaching these refugees by emphasizing the overlap between art and Christian truth, especially the truth of the incarnation. The final chapter reveals how prophetic art in particular finds common cause with the Christian incarnation, which joins the material with the spiritual hope with lament. These final chapters blur any hard distinction between worship and art.

5

Another World in Liturgy

A group of children who were sheltered in Le Chambon-sur-Lignon, a town
in southern France. Le Chambon-sur-Lignon, France, August 1942.

We do not want merely to see beauty, though, God knows, even that is bounty
enough. We want something else which can hardly be put into words—to be
united with the beauty we see, to pass into it, to receive it into ourselves, to bathe
in it, to become part of it.

—C. S. LEWIS, *THE WEIGHT OF GLORY*[1]

1. First preached by Lewis as a sermon in the Church of St. Mary the Virgin, Oxford,

"ONE DAY IN 1942, two khaki-colored buses pulled into Le Chambon, a little Huguenot village in the mountains of southern France. They were the buses of the Vichy French police, and they had come to round up the Jews who were hiding there. The police knew that Le Chambon had become a refuge for them, so they rousted everyone into the village square. The police captain stared straight into the face of the pastor of the Protestant church, Andre Trocme, 'warning him that if he did not give up the names of the Jews they had been sheltering in the village he and his fellow pastor, as well as the families who had been caring for the Jews, would be arrested.' The pastor refused, and the police, after a thorough and frightening search, could find only one Jew. They loaded him into an otherwise empty bus. Before they drove off, 'a thirteen-year-old boy, the son of the pastor, passed a piece of his precious chocolate through the window to the prisoner, while twenty gendarmes who were guarding the lone prisoner watched. Then the rest of the villagers began passing their little gifts through the window until there were gifts all around him—most of them food in those hungry days of the German occupation of France.'"[2]

Craig Dykstra regards this true story from *Lest Innocent Blood Be Shed* by Philip Haillie as singularly important for Christian educators. Haillie's book is subtitled *The Story of the Village of Le Chambon and How Goodness Happened There*, although he never seems to quite explain these people and their goodness. During World War II, five thousand Chambonais gave protection, shelter, and food to approximately five thousand Jews fleeing the Nazis. This community's acts of kindness, done at great risk and considerable cost, were remarkable. But random they were not. Nor were they utilitarian calculations, since the simple act of shoving their gifts to the young prisoner endangered the entire community. Dykstra asserts that years of engaging Christian practices had prepared them to give such hospitality.

The worship and tactile practices of the people of Le Chambon created a certain open space in their hearts for hospitable acts, for God's redeeming work. The Scriptures, testimonies, songs, proclamations, gestures of peace, prayers, Eucharist, and baptismal rites all bear witness to a God who created a hospitable world for creatures, called a people to be a blessing for the nations, and inaugurated a new reign of welcome for the poor, sick, oppressed, and marginalized. According to Dykstra, the gestures of

---

UK, on June 8, 1942.

2. Haillie, *Lest Innocent Blood Be Shed*, 3. As told by Craig Dykstra in *Growing in the Life of Faith*, 56.

worship infused the ordinary lives of the Chambonais and prepared them to answer a knock at their door, to reach out their hands, and to offer their gifts. As Dykstra explains, "In the midst of their practice, the people of Le Chambon found that it was not really their practice. It was the practice of Another."[3] Their hospitality bore witness to this Other.

Sadly, in some quarters of the church, it is common to set in binary opposition supposed "empty rituals" over against the "vibrant spontaneity of the Spirit," as if these were intrinsically opposed. In truth, worship and the tactile Christian practices that unfold from it are places in our lives for habitations of the Spirit. Christians have long affirmed that worship is not merely a field from which to distill rational concepts that can only then be applied to life. As Debra Dean Murphy says, "the breaking of the bread together in the Eucharist does not *mean* that Christians are called to be in solidarity with the poor; the act itself constitutes a people so defined."[4] Liturgist and theologian Don Saliers says that worship is an activity "where people are characterized, given their life and their fundamental location in the world."[5] Worship is the site at which we are trained in physical, linguistic, and affective skills, where our bodies are produced as worshipping bodies, our hearts as worshipping hearts. Worship constitutes the church, bestows to us our life and community, and participates in God's universal redemption.

In a story that has by now the status of legend, Flannery O'Connor was in New York, visiting with friends and a couple of what she called "Big Intellectuals." She reports:

> Well, toward morning the conversation turned on the Eucharist, which I, being the Catholic, was obviously supposed to defend. Mrs. Broadwater said when she was a child and received the Host, she thought of it as the Holy Ghost, He being the "most portable" person of the Trinity; now she thought of it as a symbol and implied that it was a pretty good one. I then said, in a very shaky voice, "Well, if it's a symbol, to hell with it." That was all the defense I was capable of but I realize now that this is all I will ever be able to say about it, outside of a story, except that it is the center of existence for me; all the rest of life is expendable.[6]

3. Dykstra, *Growing in the Life of Faith*, 64.

4. Murphy, *Teaching that Transforms*, 15. Emphasis mine.

5. Saliers, "Liturgy and Ethics," 17.

6. O'Connor, *Habit of Being*, 124–25.

Liturgy is not a material ladder to be kicked away once we have ascended the heights of abstracted ideas. We are changed by worship's materiality that is immediate, bodily, social, and continuous with life beyond the sanctuary. For O'Connor, the Eucharist was not a mere sign of some distant truth but a material reality with the power to transform our lives.

According to Duke practical theologian Fred Edie, the church once understood that

> the ordo constitutes a living communal ecology: one that included initiating persons into Christian faith through baptism (bath), then continued to nurture them in faithfulness to their baptismal callings through sustained participating in the Bible (book), Eucharist (table), and Christian seasons and sabbath keeping (time). Thus, the ordo "'ordered'" not only worship life on Sundays but the entirety of the church's life before God.[7]

For the early centuries of the church's life, "evangelism was organic to the practice of baptism. Hospitality took its cue from Eucharist. Justice was practiced because of and by way of a common bath, shared cup, and a preference for Sabbath rest over pursuit of personal empire."[8]

Patterns for worship were also the patterns for belief and communal living (*Lex orandi, lex credendi, lex vivendi*) that bear witness to God's kingdom. For centuries Christians have ordered their lives according to the Rule of St. Benedict, a sixth-century primer for monastic living, in which doxology is recognized as a mode of existence; liturgy and life, worship and ethics, are of a piece.

Christians have long affirmed the necessary relationship between who we are and what we love and deem worthy of our praise. For Augustine, even our very personhood, our self, is disclosed in and through the doxological and intimately bound up with knowledge of God. In the "Soliloquies" he prays, "Oh God, who art ever the same, let me know myself and Thee."[9] As Balthasar observes, biblical witnesses of glory fall to the earth, their faces downcast or shielded or, in Paul's case, blinded, giving way to worship. Such encounters are perceived as a grace the Spirit of God brings to people as a kind of death and new life. Balthasar suggests that this is what happens to every hearer of God's word; he or she "perceives God by being transported outside of himself or herself . . . They are no longer their own

---

7. Edie, *Book, Bath, Table, Time*, 7.

8. Edie, *Book, Bath, Table, Time*, 8.

9. "*Deus semper idem, noverim me, noverim te*." Augustine, "The Soliloquies," 41.

but are conscripted for obedience in mission, thus revealing God's holiness to the world."[10]

Today, a growing chorus of Christian educators seeks to reclaim worship as key for Christian formation.[11] Some consider the aesthetic, narrative, and kinesthetic material of worship to be bound up with the surpassing beauty of Christ, God's Art, and in ongoing acts of poiesis. The heroic Chambonais were not simply conforming to ideas or compelled by the weight of tradition but were responding to the beauty of Christ's own hospitality made manifest in their worship. As Dionysius the Areopagite saw, God's beauty is truly surpassing so we come back each day in liturgy to express more adequately (but always through a glass darkly) God's beauty. While only partial and fragmentary such beauty continues to life our gaze to the Infinite. In this chapter, we will consider worship's analogy to art, including its significance for Christian formation.

WORSHIP AND THE FORMATION OF DISPOSITION

How does worship educate and form us as Christians?

Many accounts of liturgy rely on Aristotle's understanding of habits as internal dispositions intending toward appropriate ends.[12] When habits are aimed at the good, we call them virtues; when they are not, we call them vices. Human virtue does not simply appear but is habituated by repeated practice. As we saw in Le Chambon, liturgical and tactile Christian practices helped to create a space in the hearts of the Chambonais in which the

10. Balthasar, *Engagement with God,* 13.

11. Among Christian educators there has been a growing chorus of voices who have given attention to worship, including John Westerhoff, Suzanne Johnson, Debra Dean Murphy, Mary Elizabeth Moore, Michael Warren, Craig Dykstra, Jerome Berryman, and Fred Edie, among others. Smith's work on liturgies, as he acknowledges, stands in continuity with the work of Craig Dykstra and Dorothy Bass in the 1990s (and C. Ellis Nelson and Maria Harris some decades earlier), who expanded our vision of Christian education by introducing practices as liturgically significant and characterizing for the church. Smith employs the tools of a philosophical theologian and improves upon the theory of previous work of Dykstra and Bass by providing theological nuance and insight about cultural relevance. A recent interpreter of liturgy and formation is James K. A. Smith, whose books, especially *Desiring the Kingdom* and *Imagining the Kingdom,* have helped to clarify the significance of liturgy for the church's ministry of formation.

12. Aristotle's conception of moral dispositions or "habits" is presented within a systematic ethical framework. The substance of his discussion of habit is found in Book II of the *Nicomachean Ethics.*

virtue of hospitality could flourish. Over time, habits work in preconscious ways to condition our bodies and souls. We have many terms for this kind of preconscious knowing—feel, touch, zone, flow, form, proprioception, kinesthesia, control, reflex, soul. Our preconscious habits and dispositions orient and express our desire for the good; they make us who we are. These dispositions are not biologically hardwired as first nature but are woven by habit into virtuous character as second nature. Such habits and dispositions usually function below the level of conscious intent and do not simply yield to intellectual control. Athletes and musicians, for example, work tirelessly to refine their responses, to make them automatic, functioning beneath their consciousness.[13] In fact, attempting to think one's way through an athletic or musical performance tends to inhibit our fluidity.

James K. A. Smith is a recent scholar who appeals to a neo-Aristotelian view of tradition, narrative, practices, and virtues to elucidate the formative significance of worship. Smith observes:

> Being a disciple of Jesus is not primarily a matter of getting the right ideas and doctrines and beliefs into your head in order to guarantee proper behavior; rather, it's a matter of being the kind of person who loves rightly—who loves God and neighbor and is oriented to the world by the primacy of that love . . . We are made to be such people by our immersion in the material practices of Christian worship.[14]

Smith concludes that Christian formation involves the kinesthetic and aesthetic senses inscribed by worship's gestures, images, and narratives, a kind of know-how by feel for what faith demands. The gestures of Christian worship, he notes, are akin to children bicycling in their neighborhoods, absorbing its geography into their bones with each turn of the pedal. Years later, with their embodied sense of the place, they could lead you anywhere, even when not able to recall street names. Instead of erecting an edifice of Christian ideas, liturgy cultivates "know-how"—a tacit sense by which we navigate the world. This points to the irreducible genius of Christian liturgy as a "hearts and minds" strategy that "trains us as disciples precisely by putting our bodies through a regimen of repeated practices that get hold of our hearts and 'aim' our love toward the kingdom of God."[15]

---

13. Hint: If you want to defeat your brother-in-law at golf, give him a book to read that forces him to "think" about his stroke.

14. Smith, *Desiring the Kingdom*, 32.

15. Smith, *Desiring the Kingdom*, 33.

Smith is not suggesting that liturgy functions merely as a kind of oper-ant conditioning. Smith states, "Because our hearts are oriented primarily by desire, by what we love, and because those desires are shaped and molded by the habit-forming practices in which we participate, it is the rituals and practices . . . that shape our imaginations and how we orient ourselves to the world."[16] Liturgy helps to create a social and personal imaginary; its bodily gestures embed us within a certain narrative (and embed a certain narrative in us) account of the world. Contained in the fact that we are liturgical crea-tures is that we are narrative creatures. Smith says, "The heart has reasons of which reason knows nothing—which is just to say that the heart has a story to tell and loves to hear one told. The heart drinks up narrative like it's mother's milk."[17] The gestures of worship combine with the narratives they embody to train our affective and emotional core. Smith says:

> Liturgy is the shorthand term for those rituals that are loaded with a story about who and whose we are, inscribing in us a habitus by marshaling our aesthetic nature. Liturgies are "cunning" peda-gogies that extort what is essential while seeming to demand the insignificant, precisely because they are stories that are told by— and told upon—our bodies, thereby embedding themselves in our imagination, becoming part of the background that determines how we perceive the world. Liturgies are those social practices that capture our imaginations by becoming the stories we tell ourselves in order to live.[18]

The shaping of our character is accomplished by stories embedded in liturgical gestures that captivate us by narrating a "good life," complete with values, behaviors, and versions of personhood they authorize. We act in re-sponse to liturgy's narratives that have consciously or unconsciously captured our imaginations, trained our emotions, and conditioned our perceptions.

The bodily gestures and language of worship constitute a thick mate-riality akin to the materiality of art. According to Smith:

> In the same way that the "understanding" embedded in the paint-ings in the Sistine Chapel is not just a substitute for a treatise on Pauline theology, or vice versa . . . the distillation of the Christian worldview in terms of creation-fall-redemption-and-consum-mation can never adequately grasp what is understood when we

16. Smith, *Desiring the Kingdom*, 25.
17. Smith, *Imagining the Kingdom*, 38.
18. Smith, *Imagining the Kingdom*, 138, 139.

participate in communion and eat the body of Christ, broken for the renewal of a broken world . . . The rhythms and rituals of Christian worship are not the "expression of" a Christian worldview, but are themselves an "understanding" implicit in practice—an understanding that cannot be had apart from the practices. It's not that we start with beliefs and doctrine and then come up with worship practices that properly "express" these (cognitive) beliefs; rather, we begin with worship, and articulated beliefs bubble up from there.[19]

The meaning of a worship, like a work of art, is bound up with its irreducibly material form in a way resonant with our own material bodies. According to phenomenologist Maurice Merleau-Ponty, "our body is comparable to a work of art. It is a nexus of living meanings."[20] The truth of a story is understood with what Merleau-Ponty calls "motor intentionality,"[21] on the register of *praktognosia*—a kind of practical wisdom we absorb in the betweenness of our incarnate existence. For Merleau-Ponty and Smith, the nexus of living meanings created in liturgy's narrative is not limited to its sign function but is inextricably bound to a material habitus that resonates in our bodies.

Smith states, "A liturgical anthropology is rooted in both a kinaesthetics and a poetics—an appreciation for the 'bodily basis of meaning' (kinaesthetics) and a recognition that it is precisely this bodily comportment that primes us to be oriented by story, by the imagination (poetics)."[22] If we are innately liturgical and doxological beings, *homo liturgicus*, so is culture inescapably liturgical, replete with its own ubiquitous liturgies—in shopping malls, football stadiums, college campuses, and beer commercials—which involve patterned activities that exert their own formation by recruiting our desires and habits through their gestures and narratives.

In *Imagining the Kingdom*, Smith refers to the work of sociologist and philosopher Pierre Bourdieu, who describes "pedagogies of insignificance" as occasions in which micro-practices contain entire cosmologies.[23]

19. Smith, *Desiring the Kingdom*, 69–70.

20. Merleau-Ponty, *Phenomenology of Perception*, 175.

21. "Motor intentionality" is a concept used by Merleau-Ponty to indicate that we are not mere passive recipients of knowledge; there is a kind of aesthetic construction we do at the level of our bodies within environments to find meaning. This idea is also explored by Lakoff and Johnson in their view of body schemas in which the positionality of the body conditions our metaphors. See Lakoff and Johnson, *Metaphors We Live By*.

22. Smith, *Imagining the Kingdom*, 29.

23. Smith, *Imagining the Kingdom*, 138.

Bourdieu was studying non-Western cultures when he discovered that he couldn't rely on the accuracy of self-reporting, not because subjects were dishonest but because they were formed by influences below the level of their consciousness. He realized that within cultures are micro-practices— for example, when a child is taught to "sit up straight" or to "hold your knife in your right hand"—that instill a whole cosmology.[24] These seemingly insignificant things constitute a covert pedagogy. In posture and cutlery, a whole way of life is taught.

To illustrate, Smith recounts a beer commercial depicting a group of young men leaving work bedraggled, preparing to climb together into a junky car, when one of them (inexplicably) pops open a can of beer and suddenly a new sports car appears where the old car once stood. One of the young men swipes his hand from left to right, as if swiping a computer screen to change pages, and when he does (and since this is a beer commercial), they are suddenly transported to a beach. Off in the distance (and since this is a sexist beer commercial), they spot attractive young women. One of the young men gestures with his fingers, a reverse pinch, as if enlarging a photo on an iPhone. Suddenly the young women are no longer distant; they are now immediately present, and (again, since this is a beer commercial) they seem attracted to the young men, apparently because they are drinking a certain kind of beer. Together they go to a night club where they find a DJ playing "lame" music. As the men and women look at each other knowingly, one of them again swipes the scene from left to right with his hand, which makes appear a really "cool" DJ playing music they prefer.[25]

Cultural liturgies contain embedded visions of the good that become inscribed upon our bodies and in our imaginations, conditioning what we love and what we imagine as normative behavior. According to Smith, this beer commercial demonstrates Bourdieu's "pedagogies of insignificance." Seemingly innocent commercials, with their stories and gestures, can smuggle an entire cosmology. When a beer commercial features "swiping" and "enlarging" iPhone gestures, it inscribes what we might otherwise call an egoistic or objectifying narrative as a vision of the good. Since there is no neutral site that does not exert its own liturgical influence, formation is happening constantly, often beneath the level of our awareness.

In Christian worship, by engaging in song, prayer, passing the peace, joining at table, we are internalizing a Christian story in our core. We are

24. Smith, *Imagining the Kingdom*, 98.
25. Story paraphrased from Smith, *Imagining the Kingdom*, 143.

training our hearts and bodies to perceive and respond to world Christianly. Worship should be seen as the site of a formation that can confirm or disaffirm the formation of cultural liturgies of the mall, university, social media, or beer commercials. Worship must not be seen simply as an arena for our expression but also for the sanctification of our perception.

According to the modern intellectualist account, we first see a situation and assess the options available to us—including risks, rewards, and consequences—and only then make a conscious choice. What the intellectualist model misses is the fact that we never simply perceive the so-called facts of the matter. As soon as the situation is perceived, an evaluation has already occurred. As soon as I confront a situation, I "take in" the situation, influenced by affective dispositions I bring to the encounter. Psychiatrist and writer Iain McGilchrist notes, "One's feelings are not a reaction to, or a superposition on, one's cognitive assessment . . . the affect comes first, the thinking later. Some fascinating research confirms that our affective judgment is not dependent on the outcome of a cognitive process."[26] According to McGilchrist, "Emotion and the body are at the irreducible core of experience: they are not there merely to help out with cognition. Feeling is not just an add-on, a flavoured coating for thought: it is at the heart of our being, and reason emanates from that central core of the emotions, in an attempt to limit and direct them, rather than the other way about."[27] To take in a situation is already to be recruited by obligations embedded within the situation that functions beneath our consciousness. For this reason, generating virtuous action is dependent upon training our emotions to take in and evaluate situations well. As David Brooks says in his book *The Social Animal:*

> Seeing and evaluating are not two separate processes, they are linked and basically simultaneous. The research of the past thirty years suggests that some people have taught themselves to perceive more skillfully than others. The person with good character has taught herself, or been taught by those around her, to see situations in the right way. When she sees something in the right way, she's rigged the game. She's triggered a whole network of unconscious judgments and responses in her mind, biasing her to act in a certain manner.[28]

26. McGilchrist, *The Master and His Emissary,* 184.
27. McGilchrist, *The Master and His Emissary,* 185.
28. Brooks, *The Social Animal,* 127.

The kinesthetic link between story, body, and imagination is implicit in Christian wisdom as it links spiritual formation and liturgical practice. In Christian worship, the narrative of the life, death, and resurrection of Jesus Christ infuses each physical gesture in their liturgical enactment. Worship not only tells a story but illumines a tradition, a living communal habitus into which we are absorbed. The acquisition of a habitus is described by Pierre Bourdieu as a slow process of co-option, initiation, and incorporation.[29] The social body of the church recruits my body through the most mundane means: through bodily postures, repeated words, ritualized cadences that effectively "deposit" an affective orientation within. There is an irreducibility to stories that can only be grasped by the imagination. The meaning of a story cannot be abstracted from its material form nor indiscriminately transposed from one form to another.

Smith's embrace of Merleau-Ponty's notion of resonance between the materiality of art and the materiality of the human body suggests a consideration of worship as an object of art. While Smith's appropriation of Merleau-Ponty is extremely helpful, there is perhaps more to say about the analogy of art and worship. In the following section, I consider liturgy's role as an object of art, specifically as an opening to "another world." Further, as I will argue, viewing liturgy as an art can be further clarified by considering a more determinative role for beauty.

WORSHIP AS ART: OPENING ANOTHER WORLD

Merleau-Ponty's notion of the interrelationship between the materiality of art and the materiality of bodily knowing combines kinesthetics with poietics. Smith appropriates this idea and conceives worship an art form which resonates in our bodies. However, he is not alone in perceiving liturgy as art. Evelyn Underhill once wrote, "Liturgical worship shares with all ritual action the character of a work of art. Entering upon it, we leave the lower realism of daily life for the higher realism of a successive action which expresses and interprets eternal truth by the deliberate use of poietic and symbolic material."[30] Liturgical worship, like art, transports participants into a different world through the use of its rich materiality, its gestures, and the story they embody.[31] Liturgy, like the expressed world of art, creates

29. Bourdieau, *Logic of Practice*, 68.
30. Underhill, *Worship*, 111.
31. Underhill, *Worship*, 111.

a finite totality through which the "world" of the work shows both its form and content and solicits feeling and reflection. Just as art creates an expressive world for participants to enter, in worship the church offers "another place" that is felt, sensed, and inhabited.

Alexander Schmemann also insists that worship inhabits another world and sees that world as determinative for our life and mission.[32] He says, "There is no point in converting people to Christ if they do not convert their vision of the world and of life, since Christ then becomes merely a symbol for all that we love and want already—without Him. This kind of Christianity is more terrifying than agnosticism or hedonism."[33] For Schmemann, the conversion of the world relies on transforming people's palpable sense of the world as an eschatological reality. The Christian account tells us of a world transfigured into a new heaven and a new earth, an eschatological reality that has come in Jesus and culminates in an eschatological banquet begun in the eucharistic meal. The bread and wine of the Eucharist are not only the foretaste of our eschatological destiny; they create the world anew in time and space.

The world of worship like that rendered by art is concrete and totalizing, difficult to control. According to philosopher Mikel Dufrenne, the art object has initiative; it compels me to submit to its requests. The aesthetic world summons us to participate in its alterity, moving us out of our comfortable world.[34] Worship, like art, constitutes a form of "alienation," since "I must surrender to the enchantment, deny my tendency to seek mastery of the object, and conjure up the sensuous so as to lose myself in it."[35] To be successful we must partake in its exploration, become party to its movements. Philosopher Hans-Georg Gadamer, in *The Relevance of the Beautiful*, explains that art involves submitting to the norms and requirements of the work of art, much as we might enter into a game.[36] Much like a game, art and worship exert a normative authority over recipients which, through their aesthetic address, challenges the participant to rethink their existence. Gadamer states:

32. Schmemann, *For the Life of the World*, 26–28.

33. Excerpted from his entry of Friday, October 12, 1973. Schmemann, *The Journals*, 16.

34. Dufrenne, *The Phenomenology of Aesthetic Experience*, 513.

35. Dufrenne, *The Phenomenology of Aesthetic Experience*, 231.

36. Gadamer, *The Relevance of the Beautiful*, 23.

The attraction of the game, the fascination it exerts, consists precisely in the fact that the game tends to master the players . . . The real subject of the game (this is shown in precisely those experiences in which there is only a single player) is not the player, but instead the game itself. The game is what holds the player in its spell, draws him into play, and keeps him there.[37]

This is not to say that liturgies, like games or artistic renderings, are stable or unchangeable. Every fiction writer knows what it is like to alter a plot to better fit one of the developing characters or vice versa, in which case the story is not subject to the writer but to the demands or internal logic of the story itself. Likewise, liturgy takes on a concrete existence but is capable of being changed as participants seek to be more internally consistent with the truth it glimpses, the world it manifests.[38] But any change must come from inside the experience, under the condition of its materiality, and not from a distance as an abstract reflection.

Gadamer suggests that the expressed world of art is like the "soul of the world," which surpasses itself toward its meaning. A work of art focuses our attention; it condenses and intensifies our sense of the world or some aspect of it. Artistic truth drags from the contingency of the world the fullness of its being and represents it creatively.[39] Dufrenne says that a work of art is like "a faint light in which the thing is revealed and in which everything that is perceptible in this light is disclosed."[40] In the world created by art, a spotlight has been shone on a particular facet, allowing it to become universal. A catharsis results when we are able to accept that its reality is a reality for us and a vehicle towards our own self-knowledge. To artfully express the idea of a thing is to further its transcendence toward the luminescence of its meaning. The joy of recognition for Gadamer is in knowing that more is known than just the thing known; there is a sense of excess—a form of recognition, a new remembering and seeing what is true in relation to one's own life. Liturgy, like art, has the capacity to "show" the hidden depths of human existence by employing the material means available to it. Liturgy makes present a referent that can be encountered concretely, but which also points beyond itself. So, in liturgy, we come back

---

37. Gadamer, *Truth and Method*, 95–96.

38. This idea harkens to Milbank's notion of poiesis.

39. Heidegger's notion of *alethia* is similar to Gadamer's notion of the manifestation of truth. Balthasar might refer to this as the depths or lumen.

40. Dufrenne, *The Phenomenology of Aesthetic Experience*, 182.

each day to name and respond to what we have glimpsed of God, knowing that God is always more.

Worship does not simply articulate the doctrinal structure of Christian existence, but, like art, it must be materially dense enough to convey its feel. According to Dufrenne, the artist's task is not to represent the physical object in a figurative manner but to convey an emotional "essence" or significance. The art object manifests a certain quality which words cannot fully express which communicates itself in arousing a feeling.[41] According to Dufrenne, "Feeling is that in me which relates to a certain quality of the object through which it manifests its intimacy as depth."[42] He states, "Van Gogh's bedroom is not merely a room where someone lives. It is a room which is haunted by Van Gogh's spirit and which . . . urges us to sense the mystery of the night which the painter could not enter without being overwhelmed. The aesthetic object carries the world which reveals itself."[43] To see Van Gogh's bedroom as art does not involve simply making out the figures of his bed, chair, and window, or the story they tell, but feeling the world it discloses. Like works of art, liturgy provides aestheticized gestures, images, and stories that participate in the inbreaking kingdom of God; its gestures provide a feel of grace, forgiveness, celebration, peace, and reconciliation. Like art, worship expresses the hidden depths of the world it manifests, while paradoxically frustrating any attempt to reveal fully what it seeks.

The expressed world of liturgy, like art, has the power to transform the world beyond the aesthetic object. Dufrenne states, "The function of representation is . . . not to imitate the real as to serve the expression which allows the real to be grasped."[44] He adds that "we need to allow the feeling that the aesthetic object awakens to be deposited in us—a feeling which in turn illumines the world where such an object can appear."[45] For instance, an affectively toned recognition of the "soft delicate tranquility" of a Vermeer interior might lead us to experience an indeterminate range of other objects in terms of "tranquility."[46] Art provides a means of relating to the world differently, with changed affect and behavior. The work of art may lead us to a sense of revelation through the affective. Dufrenne confesses:

41. Wynn, *Emotional Experience and Religious Understanding*, 153.

42. Dufrenne, *The Phenomenology of Aesthetic Experience*, 276.

43. Dufrenne, *The Phenomenology of Aesthetic Experience*, 227.

44. Dufrenne, *The Phenomenology of Aesthetic Experience*, 526.

45. Dufrenne, *The Phenomenology of Aesthetic Experience*, 527.

46. Wynn, *Emotional Experience and Religious Understanding*, 153.

It matters little that one does not understand Latin when one listens to a *Missa Solemnis*. When I listen to the affective quality expressed, I feel something in-depth, not a sentiment; "What is expressed is something more profound and more necessary—a revelation" . . . And, although nothing is revealed to me except a light, I know that the real can appear through it. Nothing is given to me except a key but I know it can open doors. I know that the real can be seen in this way and even that it calls for such seeing.[47]

Theologian Karl Barth is said to have listened for one hour each day to recordings of Mozart's music. In a speech made at a Mozart festival in Basel, he said: "Whenever I listen to your [Mozart's] music I feel led to the threshold of a world which is good and well-ordered in sunshine and thunderstorm, by day and by night. If a man really digests your musical dialectics he can be young and become old, he can work and relax, he can be gay and depressed, in short he can love."[48] Barth was moved by Mozart's music to feel the world that it served, conveying an emotional essence that moved Barth toward the music's object, a feeling that prompted him to seek God's kingdom in this world.

Like art, liturgy beckons worshippers to feel the world it expresses.[49] Worship engenders a mode of feeling that makes possible a different quality of engagement in the world beyond the sanctuary. The performance of what is significant spills over into an affective and perceptual reworking of the external world. Liturgical materiality, like art, becomes the means for feeling reality differently.[50] The church's worship becomes a place for feeling "another country" that bursts forth in ritual space, prompting a desire for the life made present in sacred performance. As Underhill writes, "Christian worship is . . . a response in which man moves out towards Reality, sheds self-occupation, and finds the true basis of his life."[51]

By no means do these points of comparison constitute an exhaustive phenomenology of art or worship, but they demonstrate how the analogy of art enhances our understanding of worship and its formation. Worship is best understood as another world to whose enchantments we surrender, in which we perceive hidden depths that are always outstripping the truth

47. Dufrenne, *The Phenomenology of Aesthetic Experience*, 518–19.

48. Barth, *Wolfgang Amadeus Mozart*, 22.

49. García-Rivera, *A Wounded Innocence*.

50. Loughlin, *Alien Sex*, 54.

51. Underhill, *Worship*, 339.

we glimpse, but in which we discover a characterizing feeling, a sense of the real that decenters and recenters our lived worlds.

BEAUTY, WORSHIP'S TELOS

As we have seen, liturgy's power to form us lies in its habituating gestures and stories that shape our imaginations, but also in the world it creates. Yet, with these insights in view, we must ask, why these gestures? Why this imaginary? Why this world? Why should we trust the Christian liturgy and what it embodies over, say, the liturgy of the mall, stadium, or social media?

As we have seen in previous chapters, Christian truth relies not on a superior argument waged dispassionately, but on its surpassing rhetoric, its incarnate beauty. God chose to articulate God's Word as an aesthetic form—a word (*Verbum*) that makes its appeal by persuasion. Beauty is the telos of Christian worship and life. The gifts of God's beautiful creation and the beauty of Christ's self-giving love motive us to worship, compelling us to offer our gifts of gesture, song, word, prayer, and practices in return. As we have seen, in the ancient tradition, beauty was the self-validating source and telos, erotically drawing all things to itself.[52] Alexander Schmemann articulates the church's ancient rationale for liturgy as beauty:

> Beauty is never "necessary," "functional" or "useful." And when, expecting someone whom we love, we put a beautiful tablecloth

52. Smith frequently uses terms such as "erotic comprehension," "comprehension of desire," or understanding that "reverberates with our bodies" to describe the resonance of our bodies to liturgical forms, yet without acknowledging a source or final telos of erotic appeal. Smith states explicitly his discomfort with a strong role for beauty. He says, "Christian formation, in worship or education, must be characterized by a fundamentally aesthetic aspect—not merely in the sense that such formative practices should be 'beautiful' or attractive or 'pleasing,' but in the sense that such practices should tap into our incarnate significance, should pluck the strings of our embodied attunement to the world. If the practices of Christian formation are truly going to reform our manners and deflect our dispositions to be aimed at the kingdom of God, then such practices need to engender rightly ordered erotic comprehension by renewing and reorienting our imaginations. Sanctifying perception requires restor(y)ing the imagination. Note two aspects of this: first, this transformation of the imagination is a re-story-ing of our understanding. Sanctifying perception requires aesthetic measures that resonate with the imagination and affect us on an affective level, in the 'between' of our incarnate significance . . . So sanctifying perception involves re-story-ing our being-in-the-world. But second, the sanctification of perception for Christian action requires restoring rightly ordered perception—training us to take the right things for granted" (Smith, *Imagining the Kingdom*, 3).

on the table and decorate it with candles and flowers, we do all this not out of necessity, but out of love. And the Church is love, expectation and joy. It is heaven on earth, according to our Orthodox tradition; it is the joy of recovered childhood, that free, unconditioned and disinterested joy which alone is capable of transforming the world. In our adult, serious piety we ask for definitions and justifications, and they are rooted in fear—fear of corruption, deviation, "pagan influences," whatnot. But "he that feareth is not made perfect in love" (1 Jn. 4: 18). As long as Christians will love the Kingdom of God, and not only discuss it, they will "represent" it and signify it, in art and beauty. And the celebrant of the sacrament of joy will appear in a beautiful chasuble, because he is vested in the glory of the Kingdom, because even in the form of man God appears in glory. In the Eucharist we are standing in the presence of Christ, and like Moses before God, we are to be covered with his glory. Christ himself wore an unsewn garment which the soldiers at the cross did not divide: it had not been bought in the market, but in all likelihood it had been fashioned by someone's loving hands. Yes, the beauty of our preparation for the Eucharist has no practical use.[53]

As Schmemann insists, to see the church's ministries, including its liturgical celebrations, as other than a witness to God's beauty risks reducing them as instrumental goods. The church's ministries in the world may do much good, but as theologian William Cavanaugh has stated, our job is not to fix the world but to bear witness to how God is redeeming the world.[54] It is the wager of this book that God's way of redemption, revealed in Christ's incarnation, is beauty in the style of love. Unless the church's ministries bear witness to God's beauty "in the style of love" they also cannot form in us joy.

What does the notion of beauty add to our conversation about Christian formation? The telos of beauty adds to Smith's understandings of kinesthetics and poiesis by reminding us of ecstasy. As Balthasar said, in Scripture, "every hearer of God's word . . . perceives God by being transported outside of himself or herself . . . They are no longer their own but are conscripted for obedience in mission, thus revealing God's holiness to the world."[55] In beauty we are decentered in a kind of death experienced as gift and joy.

53. Schmemann, *For the Life of the World*, 30.
54. Cavanaugh, "Don't Change the World."
55. Balthasar, *Engagement with God*, 13.

Worship's habits, gestures, narratives, imaginaries, its art, powerfully form us, especially when they serve the ends of beauty. Clearly the gestures and narratives of worship are powerful shapers of human disposition, but the beauty of Christ remains a powerful driver of Christian formation. Apart from the surpassing beauty of the incarnation, our preference for Christian liturgy is arbitrary. In Christian worship, beauty is encountered in our poietic songs, testimonies, gestures, poems, architecture, and practices that bear witness to Beauty Incarnate. According to Milbank, "our 'total hermeneutic situation' regards Christ aesthetically as he is given (Balthasar) and poetically as he is still being given, re-born, through our spirit-inspired constructions."[56] Here, Jesus is beauty incarnate who is constantly being re-narrated by the church. Christ cannot be made static as frozen meanings but is known in the ongoing poiesis of the church, including the poiesis of liturgy. For Milbank, the beauty of Christ is made visible in the beauty of the church, its communal life and liturgy, and its love extended to the world in practices that mirror Christ's own love. Milbank writes: "Poesis is an integral aspect of Christian practice. Its work is the ceaseless re-narrating and 'explaining' of human history under the sign of the cross."[57] In and through the church's poiesis the cosmos is harmonized, redeemed form and spirit, in beauty.

ENHANCING THE FORMATIVE POWER OF LITURGY

Attending to beauty as a context for Christian formation brings into greater focus the following intentional liturgical activities. Since liturgy in its thick materiality, constituted of stories, songs, words, gestures, art, and architecture, form Christians in conscious and preconscious ways, the following are possible ways to enhance the formative efficacy of liturgy:

1. *Church leaders might attend closely to the historic rhythms of its worship, the ordo,* including invocation, confession, and pardon, passing the peace, songs, prayers, proclamation, reading Scripture, testimony, baptism, Eucharist, and benediction. These forms should be continual sources of contemplation, reflection, and ongoing poiesis, creating and recreating these forms ever more beautifully.

---

56. Milbank, *The Word Made Strange,* 142.
57. Milbank, *The Word Made Strange,* 32.

2. *Church leaders might take care to artfully craft the worship encounter using beautiful forms of music, poetry, flowers, images, and gestures of welcome, care, and forgiveness and reconciliation that bear witness to Christ's own beauty in the style of love.*

3. *Church leaders might teach young and old how to participate in worship*—its gestures, words, testimonies, songs, and prayers. Catechesis should include more than an introduction to history and doctrine; it must also teach members to engage its embodied practical rhythms with excellence, to joyfully attend to its beauty with openness to the demands made by its material artistry, to respond appropriately in praise and ecstasy.

4. *Church leaders might cultivate seasonal and episodic liturgies that extend worship,* such as the feasts, fasts, baptisms, vigils, healings, exorcisms, clearness and discernment practices, service to the poor, hospitality to strangers, public witnesses of justice, and end-of-life rites. These liturgies punctuate our lives with stories, habits, and artistry, and witness to the beauty of Christ and the poiesis of the church.

5. *Church leaders might make spaces to teach practices of appropriate contemplation of the beauty of the Christ form as manifested in its eucharistic meal and all its gestures*—in its words, songs, art and architecture, and its ordinary practices to discern the depths disclosed by these forms.

6. *Church leaders might recognize that liturgy's beauty involves a natural impulse to respond creatively, artistically, and actively.* Liturgy is a font of the church's visible holiness. Leaders must create space for members to respond to liturgy's beauty, in art, prayer, discussion, and action.

7. *Church members might make audits of the cultural liturgies that shape our imaginations and habits* through their stories and activities and their potential to distort or enhance our love of God and neighbor, noting especially any tensions with the normative Christian ordo.

8. *All of the church's gatherings might be punctuated by liturgy and prayer.* As these liturgical and poetic forms invite participants into "another world," the affect discovered there will affect the work to be done in these spaces.

6

Lament and Hope

The Christian should see two realities at once, one world (as it were) within another: one the world as we all know, in all its beauty and terror, grandeur and dreariness, delight and anguish; and the other the world in its first and ultimate truth, not simply "nature" but "creation," an endless sea of glory, radiant with the beauty of God in every part, innocent of all violence. To see in this way is to rejoice and mourn at once, to regard the world as a mirror of infinite beauty, but as glimpsed through the veil of death; it is to see creation in chains, but beautiful as in the beginning of days.

—DAVID BENTLEY HART, *THE DOORS OF THE SEA*

THEOLOGIAN WILLIAM CAVANAUGH TELLS of a community of people in the Philippines, on the fringes of Manila, who live beside a garbage dump and scavenge whatever can be sold from what others have discarded. According to Cavanaugh, "When Father Danny Pilario says Mass for people in this community, he says that the sign of the cross he makes over the eucharistic elements serves a dual purpose: to consecrate the elements, and to brush away the flies from the chalice."[1] In the midst of the cosmic mystery of the Eucharist, the same gesture blesses the blood of Christ and defends against the insects that infest the rotting dump. For Fr. Pilario, there is a close association between the sacred and the profane, between the Eucharist he celebrates with the community and the political work they do together to improve the lives of the people there.

A factor inhibiting wider engagement with theological aesthetics is the unavoidable question of evil and suffering in the world. Given the tragic reality of suffering, one might be forgiven for wondering whether a focus on beauty, art, and liturgy can contribute much good in the world. Would not our time be better spent directly addressing suffering with whatever resources we have at hand, fighting at the barricade or ballot box? How can Fr. Pilario invest such confidence in liturgy as anything more than other-worldly spirituality as a suitable response to injustice and suffering? How do Christianity's beauty and poiesis constitute a response to suffering in the world? How are aesthetic and liturgical approaches to Christian formation appropriately attentive to suffering and evil?

Before any proper response to these questions can be considered, it is important to understand this historical moment and its fundamental disenchantment. As James K. A. Smith explains, the naturalism of our age struggles to find the intellectual or imaginative resources to either decry evil or engender hope.[2] Under its own terms, naturalism can only refer to the pseudo-sovereignty of chance and genetic destiny which prohibit the possibility of lament or hope. Having formally rejected religion, late-modern thought has lost important resources for speaking of values that undergird all of life and its purpose. Our persistent cultural inclination to name evil relies to some degree on the borrowed capital of religious faith, or at least its vague memory. Late-modern thought has imagined itself into an untenable impasse, and the only way beyond it must begin by enlarging its imaginative resources. While we must remain open and hopeful about

1. Cavanaugh, "The Eucharist as Politics."
2. Smith, "Resurrecting the Imagination."

resources from any number of sources, we should at least recognize that the Christian liturgical and aesthetic tradition provides unique resources for navigating evil and suffering.

This chapter elaborates theoretical and pedagogical resources for training a Christian imagination for resisting evil and embracing good in the world.

THEORETICAL UNDERPINNINGS

Detoxifying and Reforming the Imagination

As we saw in the first chapter, according to Charles Taylor, our social imaginary is "not expressed in theoretical terms,[3] but carried in images, stories, and legends," shaped by those who weave a myth about the nature of the world and our place in it.[4] As stated above, the modern social imaginary has collapsed all meaning into the immanent sphere, excluding anything more than provisional and utilitarian value. So white supremacy, militarism, greed, gender violence, nationalism, exploitive forms of capitalism, or state-sponsored totalitarianism, for example, are not simply failures of reason; they are more essentially failures of imagination, the failure to see beauty where it exists, and the mistrust of accounts of human ends that point to beauty.

Christians do well to remember that Jesus' parables involved correcting and enlarging our imagination. When faced with a lawyer's question, "Who is my neighbor?" Jesus told a parable about imagination and its miscarriages. "Who is my neighbor?" is not a question of geography or jurisdiction; it's a question of imagination. To see the person before me as a foe or alien is a failure of imagination; to perceive a neighbor is an achievement of the imagination. If the church is to be a school of beauty "in the style of love," then, following Jesus, we must train our imaginations. As Fr. Pilario knew, the Eucharist is an imaginative act, an enacted narrative in which we

---

3. As we have seen, modernity has created a Manichean world, which distinguishes, on the one hand, the center of (economic, scientific, political) life necessitating the use of power, and on the other, the marginal space allowed for religious cultic life and devotion. One sphere is deemed real, rational, empirical; the other is the realm of the imaginary, irrational, and speculative. Yet here at the far end of modernity, we can affirm that there is no purely non-imaginary sphere. The term "imaginary" wrongly assumes or designates a sphere that is not imaginary, not subject to such things as intuition or speculation.

4. Taylor, *Modern Social Imaginaries*, 23.

do not simply break and consume elements but in which we are mysteriously broken and consumed on behalf of the world.

Our imagination is not just the capacity for invention or innovation but, as we saw previously, it involves our *feel for the world* by a faculty lodged somewhere between intellect and instinct. Imagination is our default mode of navigating the world—a perception that is pretheoretical and largely unarticulated, but which is inextricably intertwined with our acting. According to James K. A. Smith, philosophers Martin Heidegger and Maurice Merleau-Ponty describe our imaginary as constituting a kind of "attunement." As Smith puts it, "My feel for the world is like a song my body knows how to sing, or a story of the world I carry in my bones."[5] As we saw earlier, embodiment is fundamental to imagination; attunement is absorbed on a bodily register. It is not hardwired like instinct, but it can become second nature through habits of perception, through the learned bodily disposition to the world.

At the root of many of our social ills today is not just what people believe, profess, or enact, but our habits of perception, our feel for the world. How we unthinkingly imagine others determines our action in the world. At this moment, in the early 2020s, many have been twisted by stories that imagine others as threats or otherwise dehumanize them. Our habits of perception have been skillfully "attuned" by social media, cable and internet news, political rhetoric, and other sources, to imagine others as invaders, competitors, and adversaries, and so we default to individualism and self-preservation.

As Smith notes, perceptual distortion is not new; it is a staple, for example, of American racism. Smith sees in James Baldwin's writings an insightful analysis of how our perceptions are distorted. Smith says:

> One of the distinguishing features of Baldwin's searing prose is his remarkably generous—and what I can only call *spiritual*—insight into the ways white racism devours the soul of the racist. "In evading my humanity," Baldwin says, "you have done something to your own humanity." My imagination needs to undergo detoxification, not just for the sake of the other but because it corrodes my own soul.
>
> Baldwin argues that the United States—"this peculiar purgatory which we call America"—is a distinct case, not because racism doesn't exist elsewhere, but because the history of America is a history of dehumanizing fellow image-bearers in such close proximity. Unlike the British or French colonialists for whom exploitation was an abstraction on a distant shore, "the American found himself

5. Smith, "Healing the Imagination."

in a very peculiar position because he knew that black people were people." This proximity of the enslaved demanded imaginative acrobatics that became habits of perception for centuries. In Baldwin's estimation, "the attempt to avoid this"—the proximate fact of Black humanity—is "one of the keys to what we can call loosely the American psychology" that "created in Americans a kind of perpetual, hidden, festering, and entirely unadmitted guilt." How to suppress that guilt? Tell yourself a story that denies what you see. To filter Didion through Baldwin: white people tell ourselves a story (about Black people) in order to live (with their reduction to chattel and ongoing repression).

Guilt is like a film projector that casts a story onto others as if this could somehow expel it from our own souls. Baldwin notes "the ways in which we manage to project onto the Negro face, because it is so visible, all of our guilts and aggressions and desires. And if you doubt this, think of the legends that surround the Negro to this day. Think, when you think of these legends, that they were not invented by Negroes, but they were invented by the white Republic. Ask yourself if Aunt Jemima or Uncle Tom ever existed anywhere and why it was necessary to invent them." These are *images*, each one invoking and confirming a story that rattles around in a collective imagination, thereby shaping what many see before we look.[6]

Baldwin argues that white American soul-sickness is rooted in the relationship between our historic racial violence, our guilt, and the stories we tell in order to live. Smith sees in Baldwin's analysis of race a paradigmatic example of how imagination and narrative function in relation to suffering and injustice.

With Baldwin, Smith thinks we are only healed of our racist imagination by means of detoxification, a reshaping of our social imaginary, the myths and stories that have created and that supported our racist perception. This much seems obvious in this historical moment. Smith wagers that Christian liturgy is a key locus for detoxifying our imagination, shattering our racism, and fostering a true imagination in which we perceive and lament suffering in the world and hope for the world's complete healing. While the example of James Baldwin focuses on racism, there are, after all, many spells that normalize evil and suffering and need to be broken. We must not be content to fight against sin and suffering only at the barricades or ballot box but also at worship, in prayer, armed with ancient stories, visions, and sacraments, as creative souls before empty canvases or blank pages.

6. Smith, "Healing the Imagination."

Breaking the spell of imaginaries that validate evil and suffering requires that Christians attend to lament and hope as key aspects of the Christian imagination. The Christian imaginary abides in the tension between lament and hope, portrayed by Christ in his interval between the cross and the resurrection. The theologians of the church, from Athanasius to Anselm, agree that Christ had to take on the full weight of humanity with all its sin and guilt and wretchedness in order to heal it. The cross becomes the place where that sin and wretchedness are most acutely visible, as the ugliness without which the cross could never be beautiful. According to the church fathers, what is to be redeemed must be assumed—and in the process it becomes visible to us as ugliness in which the full beauty of God's love is most profoundly revealed in sin's defeat. Christ reveals the form of God in a new way, as self-emptying love. In this sense, the cross clarifies Christ's life as the action of God in history and as an extension of the kenotic life of the Trinity. For this reason, the Christian imagination grounded in Christ's beauty "in the style of love" lives in the tension between lament and hope.

Both Christian liturgy and art constitute a counter-formation to late modernity that struggles to name evil and project hope and without which the world does not change. If, as Augustine saw, Christian liturgy generates our selfhood precisely as it performs the ugly-beauty of the cross, so perhaps we may consider art a form of liturgy at least in the sense that it shares with Christian liturgy the project of counter-formation, of detoxifying our imagination.

Below we will consider how lament and hope are fostered in liturgy and in art and certain devotional practices, as formative contexts that point to other pedagogies.

Liturgy: Remembering the World

Despite modernity's tendency to divide the sacred from the mundane, the scandal of Christian truth is that it holds together the spiritual with the material, faith with public life, the individual with corporate life, the aesthetic with the practical, lament with hope. We see this unity enacted in the eucharistic liturgy, the memorial of Christ, the mystery of cosmic remembrance. As Alexander Schmemann states, "God remembers us. Remembrance is an act of love, a restoration of love as the very life of the world."[7] In Christ, the church remembers the world and all creatures, and offers it in love as gift to

7. Schmemann, *For the Life of the World*, 8.

the Father. According to Schmemann, liturgy includes two aspects, remembering the kingdom in its beauty and remembering the world—analogues of hope and lament.[8] The liturgy manifests God's harmonious reign and reveals the hopeful destiny of all human and created suffering. The liturgy of the church, which participates in Christ's eucharistic gift to the Father, provides an experience of the kingdom: "The very goal of this [liturgical] movement of ascension is to take us out of 'this world' and to make us partakers of the world to come . . . But this is not an 'other' world, different from the one God has created and given to us. It is our same world, already perfected in Christ, but not yet in us."[9]

This understanding of liturgy, far from being an escape from the world, propels us, as Fr. Pilario knew, back into the world with new vision guided by the beauty of the kingdom. The eucharistic gestures, narratives, and images are not reducible to abstracted ideas, commodities to be consumed, or mere private spiritual enrichment. In performing the eucharistic words and gestures, God generates the church and characterizes us as selves bearing witness to God's beauty in the midst of an ugly and suffering world.[10] As William Cavanaugh concludes, "The Eucharist is a way of constructing a different kind of world, a world redeemed."[11] Thus, it constitutes us by performing a body politic with its own ethos, as Paul saw, bearing witness against the Roman Empire.

In the ancient Greek and Roman world, where citizenship was limited to property-owning men, Paul sees a new type of body in which participation is offered to all: "There is no longer Jew or Greek, there is no longer slave or free, there is no longer male and female; for all of you are one in Christ Jesus" (Gal 3:28). Not only are the weakest members not excluded, but there is a preferential option for the weakest in the body: "The members of the body that seem to be weaker are indispensable, and those members of the body that we think less honorable we clothe with greater honor" (1

8. This is a summary of Schmemann's eucharistic theology, elaborated in Schmemann, *For the Life of the World*, 8.

9. Schmemann, *For the Life of the World*, 42.

10. In the *Soliloquiorum*, Augustine states he wants to know the soul and God, but only pages later he prays, "Oh God, who art ever the same, let me know myself and Thee." Augustine says, *"Deus semper idem, noverim me, noverim te"* (Augustine, "The Soliloquies," 41). Also, he says, "As often as we eat this bread and drink this cup we receive the mystery of ourselves: our identity as the body of Christ—taken, blessed, broken, and shared with a suffering world" (Sheerin, *The Eucharist*, 94).

11. Cavanaugh, "The Eucharist as Politics."

Cor 12:22–23). This new politics demands a different nervous system in which "if one member suffers, all suffer together with it; if one member is honored, all rejoice together with it" (1 Cor 12:26). The common end that holds the body together is the love of God.

According to biblical scholar N. T. Wright, Paul's missionary work implies a high and strong ecclesiology in which the scattered and muddled cells of people loyal to Jesus as Lord form subversive little groups when seen from Caesar's point of view, but which, when seen Jewishly, are a foretaste of the time when the earth shall be filled with the glory of the God of Abraham and the nations will join Israel in singing God's praises (cf. Rom 15:7–13).[12] Cavanaugh suggests that this counter-empire claims to be the true reality of which Caesar's empire is only a parody.[13] The church models genuine humanness, the justice, peace, and unity across traditional racial and cultural barriers of which Caesar's empire wrongly boasted. Early Christians thought of the church as a kind of political body, as an anticipation of a different kind of city, the city of God, as St. Augustine would write. The church anticipates the heavenly city that descends to earth in the last chapter of the book of Revelation. So the church is not simply concerned with another world but with the transformation of this cosmos, a new heaven *and* a new earth anticipated in a body of people who order material life in a new way.[14] The Eucharist is a kind of politics, a way of ordering the world that draws the world into the very life of the Trinity through the body of Christ.

Just as Fr. Pilario brushes away the flies and consecrates the bread and wine in one spiritual and practical gesture, in the Eucharist, we are spiritually awakened by Christ's beauty as we join in the church's politics, its beautiful practices of love, including lamenting and hoping. Christian liturgy

---

12. Wright, "Paul's Gospel and Caesar's Empire," 182–83.

13. Cavanaugh, "The Eucharist as Politics."

14. According to Schmemann, the meaning of the world is not found in itself; God has given the physical world to be "transparent to God," and "the world is meaningful only when it is the 'sacrament' of God's presence" (Schmemann, *For the Life of the World*, 16). Readers will recall that this is similar to Balthasar's view that the beauty of all beings involves a "splendor" that draws our gaze beyond it to God, perfect beauty, perfect light. All things, in their beauty, are an analogy to Perfect Beauty. In Balthasar's reading of *Divine Comedy*, Dante is led by Beatrice's beauty in a journey to union with God, fulfilled in the beatific vision (Balthasar, *The Glory of the Lord: 3*, 34–53). As we saw, the Greeks and many Patristic writers, including Dionysius, Gregory Nyssa, and Augustine, understood the created world as containing a gravity pulling all creatures to their Source and Perfection, in which all things find their meaning. Christ has surely come "for the life of the world," restoring nature as sacrificial gift, as a blessing to the Father.

reveals a Christ who is practical because he is first beautiful;[15] he is beautiful because of the life he lived in love, as God's expression of lament and hope. Liturgy defines the church's response to suffering as remembering the world in lament and the beauty of God's reign of love in hope. It establishes an imaginary in which evil and suffering can be named and lamented, with the expectant hope of the redemption of all things.

Art and Our Imaginative Capacity for Lament and Hope

Today, as we are caught between secularism's rejection of religion and a felt need for fullness and transcendence, many find refuge in the arts. Some gravitate to art precisely for its rare capacity to express the human hunger for restoration while honoring the sorrow of our present pilgrimage, a capacity it shares with Christian faith. Smith is again worth quoting at length:

> Christian eschatology nourishes a distinct imagination that refuses to be constrained by the catalogue of economic, political, or scientific alternatives currently available; it instead imagines a new world breaking into the present. Christian faith has the intellectual and imaginative resources to name evil as an immanent eruption in the cosmos, one that God himself overcomes. Christian hope can imagine a world without evil, not by denying its existence but based on the first fruits of the resurrection of Christ, a sign that death and all death-dealing will die. It is hard to imagine a gracious God speaking to a more humane desire than the assurance at the end of the book of Revelation, where God promises to "wipe away every tear from their eyes." "There will be no more death or mourning or crying or pain, for the old order of things has passed away." The king who sits on the throne in this kingdom still bears scars on his hands and yet announces, "Behold, I make all things new." There is nothing more scandalous in Christian eschatology, and yet nothing speaks more directly to a hurting fearful world.[16]

---

15. Schmemann maintains that faith (as beauty) must not be instrumentalized. He opposes a Christianity that seeks to "help" rather than to manifest Christ's trinitarian beauty. He sees an instrumental desire to "help" as part of a capitulation to secularism stemming from a duality between spirituality and materiality. If the church is a sacrament, it must be experienced on its own terms. If church becomes merely relevant or utilitarian, it risks losing its sense of the wholeness of creation and is seeking to simply meet material (or spiritual) needs, assuming a division between the two. Schmemann, *For the Life of the World,* 17.

16. Smith, "Resurrecting the Imagination."

Letitia Huckaby. "Suffrage
Project: Sugar and Spice", 2018.
Pigment on vintage cotton-
picking sack. 72 x 24 inches.

It is precisely this eschatological orientation, suspended between an intuition of the "already and not yet," that art expresses. Smith tells of a recent print entitled "Sugar and Spice,"[17] which depicts a young African American girl who looks despondent; her protest sign simply says "Enough" as it rests on her shoulder—her own version of "How long, O Lord?"[18] The print appears on a vintage cotton-picking sack, conjuring the long history of oppression and marginalization, while contradictorily the girl wears a pink skirt that evokes a ballerina's tutu. This image, Smith says, "births in us a longing to see this young girl dance, to see her despondency turned to joy, to trade the now necessary sign of protest for a banner of praise."[19]

Like liturgy, art can play a prophetic role by inhabiting the tension between lament and hope. Yet it does not merely transmit a message. Like liturgy, it enacts what it embodies; it performs in our imagination this transformation of mourning into dancing. There is a long history of prophetic art which honors our experience of the heartbreak of the now and gives voice

17. Huckaby, "Suffrage Project: Sugar and Spice." This print features an image of Huckaby's ten-year-old daughter holding a sign that says "Enough." Her pose evokes Norman Rockwell's *The Problem We All Live With,* an iconic image of the civil rights movement. The image is printed onto a six-foot vintage cotton-picking sack. The word "Enough" was taken from a recent speech by Martin Luther King's nine-year-old granddaughter, Yolanda King, at the March for Our Lives rally in Washington: "I have a dream that enough is enough, and that this should be a gun-free world. Period" (Kalfas, "I Have a Dream").

18. Huckaby, "Suffrage Project: Sugar and Spice."

19. Smith, "Resurrecting the Imagination."

to our longings for fullness. It neither glamorizes tragedy nor escapes in sentimental naivete; it embodies the tension between lament and hope.

According to Smith, "Lament without hope is just anger; hope without lament is a lie about the present. Lament is one of those practices that the church's hymn book, the Psalms, teaches us. Lament is this paradoxical blend of naming what's not supposed to be to God, as if God is accountable for that."[20] Lament, for Christians, isn't just unbridled anger. It is anger that always has a lilt of hope echoing in it, out of which we respond in action. So, we lament and we protest, and we work against the way it's not supposed to be; we act, construct policy, destroy and build institutions, with the hope or foretaste of shalom. Anger and protest characterize lament; as such, the public lamentation of the church can be a gift to the wider society.

As we have seen in the poetry of James Baldwin and in Letitia Huckaby's "Sugar and Spice," the arts are a particularly powerful force that can embody something akin to an eschatological imagination that laments and hopes. This capacity of art to hold together lament and hope may be why it has become a safe harbor for many who are influenced by the cultural shift away from religion but also by their unyielding hunger for transcendence and hope. Art can be a liberation from the claustrophobia of our unimaginative materialism in late modernity; it can be a window to God and the soul. If this happens paradigmatically in eucharistic liturgy, it is mirrored in artistic expressions that "detoxify" our imaginations by focusing our attention upon lament and hope.

Complete story cloth embroidered by Wendy, asylum-seeker from El Salvador, 2020

20. Smith, "Resurrecting the Imagination."

Ex-Votos

Between the sites of liturgy and art there exists a form of spiritual practice that blurs the distinction between art and liturgy, or better, makes art an extension of liturgy. In the example of "Sugar and Spice," we saw lament and hope performed, spanning the gap between injustice and the joyful dance of a little girl.

My colleague and Bible scholar Dr. Gregory Cuellar and his students at Austin Presbyterian Theological Seminary, as part of a comprehensive response to the humanitarian crisis on the southern border, travel there for the purpose of collecting the artwork created by children and families from Central and South America upon crossing the border. Dr. Cuellar and his students distribute art materials to children and invite them to draw, sketch, or paint their perilous journey. Some children depict parents and siblings in the desert weighted down by belongings, physical exhaustion, unbearable heat, thirst, and hunger, the sadness of loss, and the uncertainty of what will greet them on the other side. Others draw pictures of being unexpectedly detained on the US side. In their depictions of struggle and suffering, many also include the surprising image of a theophany—an angel, Our Lady of Guadalupe, Christ on a cross, a saint, the Spirit, the Trinity, an guardian ancestor, or a shining visage—overseeing their journey, protecting them from harm, and guiding their safe passage to a new home.

The practice of artistically representing their travail in migration stands in continuity with an older Mexican tradition of *retablo* or *ex-voto*,[21] which is a small devotional painting commonly placed in church foyers or home shrines. *Ex-votos* are typically composed of three elements: a scene depicting a tragedy or someone with a grave illness or injury, a depiction of the intervention of a saint or theophany on behalf of the afflicted, and an inscription describing the tragic event and giving thanks for the divine intervention.

---

21. Votive paintings in Mexico go by several names, such as *ex voto, retablo,* or *lámina,* which refer, respectively, to their purpose, place often found, or material from which they are traditionally made. The painting of religious images gives thanks for a miracle or favor received. The form that most votive paintings take, from the colonial period to the present, was brought to Mexico by the Spanish. As in Europe, votive paintings began as static images of saints or other religious figures, which were then donated to a church. Later, narrative images, telling the personal story of a miracle or favor received appeared. These paintings were first produced by the wealthy and often on canvas; however, as sheets of tin became affordable, lower classes began to have these painted on this medium. The history of this form of devotion can be found in Durand and Massey, *Miracles on the Border.*

Ex-votos are used as icons transparent to God's loving providence, used in prayer for naming and lamenting evil and hoping for God's redemption.

In *ex-votos* and the similar images drawn by children, the borderlands are not a neutral space; they are charged with a memory of the long history of imperial colonization and exploitation in which the border was forced southward by means of military domination and political treachery, coopting approximately half of Mexico's land, people, and resources. In seeing the images, an entire history of oppression and suffering travels from our gut to our spine to our heart, finally stopping in the lump in our throat.[22] We do not need our brains to gather data to be cognized as thought. Such art may not access our rational mind, yet we now know something we didn't before. Just as landscape painters create visual paths to guide our eyes to points of interest, *ex-votos* guide our hearts and birth in us a longing to see these travelers find rest, food, shelter, and welcome, to see their misery turned to joy. As such, the *ex-votos* are consistent with Christian liturgy and practices in which suffering is not ignored or normalized but lamented in light of God's promises of redemption.

It would be a grave mistake to think that *ex-votos* or the collected art of migrant children are merely decorative or in service of wish fulfillment or an otherworldly spirituality. The functions they perform are at once spiritual and embodied, metaphysical and existential, political and personal, and formative for imagining the world and our place in it. While art and liturgy can lift our gaze to God, their spiritual effects cannot be divorced from political work that proceeds from lament and hope.

As Fr. Pilario knew, liturgy is not a spiritual addition; it forms us as political bodies of remembrance and hope that spill into our streets and homes. As James K. A. Smith observes, all of our cultural practices—in the mall, the stadium, social media, the university—are liturgical in the sense that they form us as they recruit our bodies and enact stories with certain ends. Therefore, it is not too much to claim that art, like other cultural liturgies, can play a role in Christian formation. When immigrants paint pictures and icons of their journey and God's providence, they are not engaging in mere wish fulfillment or whimsy. They are rehearsing a sustaining vision of God's provision as a prayer of gratitude, reinforcing their commitment to God's ongoing work of redemption. They are remembering the concrete ways in which they experience suffering and God in their particular journeys. Not only do these images help to name God and establish

22. This approximates an image used in Smith, "Resurrecting the Imagination."

our personhood; they also become acts of worship, receiving God's gifts, naming them, and offering them back as return gift.

As we turn our attention from theological clues and the formative significance of liturgy and art, we can ask what other intentional pedagogies can detoxify and renew our imaginations in lament and hope intrinsic to Christ's form.

EDUCATIONAL AIMS

Pedagogies that foster Christian imagination teach us to remember the world, to lament its brokenness, and to perceive the world as created, loved, and redeemed by God, as the condition for lamenting. Perceiving and lamenting the world's brokenness and hoping for its healing begins with an intuition of its goodness and its promised redemption. If the world is not felt as fundamentally beautiful or good, if we do not expect it to be set right, then we would not be able to lament. Brokenness and suffering would simply be what we expect as normal. For this reason, hope and lament are bound together in the Christian imagination.

Pedagogies that foster lament and hope seek to do three things:

1. *They seek to attend closely to the concrete particularity of people and situations, to glimpse their real and potential beauty as a backdrop against which their brokenness and suffering can be seen and lamented.* Such pedagogies seek to discover human and created depths and hold them respectfully, and sometimes paradoxically, alongside other discoveries. These pedagogies hold interpretations loosely in humility and openness, in respect for the surpassing complexity and depth of human personhood. These pedagogies seek to resist reductionistic descriptors. Ideological, political, racial, gender, theological categories can say something about a person but can never fully capture the mystery, depth, and beauty of being human. Because pedagogies of lament resist reductive flattening, conclusions often cannot be articulated by simple propositions but instead require poetry, narrative, and art that allow for paradox and mystery.

2. *They seek to concretely represent particular experiences of human suffering in order to elicit compassion, solidarity, healing, and reconciliation.* To lament is to give empathic expression to the suffering we have experienced or witnessed, even as we cry for wholeness. It seeks a

solidarity that can be redemptive; it mirrors Christ's own solidarity with God's creatures. In the Christian imaginary, reconciliation is most possible when sin is named and lamented. If remembrance attends to the beauty of people and creatures as they are created and made whole, we do not truly remember them if we do not also lament their suffering and brokenness.

3. *They seek glimpses of hope in hidden wholeness, foretastes of how life would be and will be when their suffering is healed.* If lament is not to descend into bitterness and hatred on the one hand or naivete on the other, it must inhabit the tension between suffering and hope. Pedagogies of Christian formation appropriately engage lament by expressing the hoped-for joy that lies on the far side of suffering, by imagining life redeemed in the fullness of shalom—as dancing, welcome, freedom, justice, peace, and harmony.

THREE EDUCATIONAL PRACTICES OF PEDAGOGIES OF LAMENT AND HOPE

Pedagogies that foster lament and hope involve three essential practices.

The first practice is to perceive our own or another's life in concrete particularity as remembrance. In recent decades, Christian educators have developed pedagogies of remembrance, especially in forms of practical theology that begin with close readings of contexts, persons, social structures, powers, and principalities. For example, Richard Osmer's approach involves four moments: descriptive-empirical (What is going on?), interpretive (Why is this going on?), normative (What ought to be going on?), and pragmatic (How might we respond?).[23]

Approaches to practical theology, especially in the descriptive moment, often employ qualitative research methods which seek to provide a thick description of human contexts and phenomena.[24] Common types of qualitative research—including phenomenological, ethnographic, grounded theory, historical, case study, and action research—involve techniques such as observation, focus groups, interviews, and narratives. But from the beginning, qualitative researchers acknowledged the limits and risks of their approaches, including the impossibility of data unsullied by prior

23. Osmer, *Practical Theology,* 4.
24. See for example, Moschella, *Ethnography as a Pastoral Practice.*

expectations or hidden commitments. At their best, qualitative methods provide much needed texture and depth over quantitative approaches that presume clinical neutrality. Yet, unfortunately, at times qualitative research methods collect observable facts and force them into a coherent rational explanation. In a rush to systematize or rationalize our conclusions we risk smuggling ready-to-hand, fully formed interpretations and strategies that can exclude intuitions of mystery, beauty, depth, and poiesis. Some are constrained in their interpretive moment by an overreliance upon social science, which leaves little room for discerning aesthetic depth or imaginative poiesis (as such, tragically, could never discern the regal air or spiritual mission of my Golden Retriever). At other times, such approaches seem to force their strategic moment into a pragmatic straitjacket, pressing them into immediate relevance to address limit situations.

Unless we discern carefully a situation's hidden beauty and alterity, and the radical beauty of Christ's form, we risk only replicating what is culturally familiar and reducing the gospel to instrumental utility. As stated earlier, Christian formation is not merely about solving problems but also bearing witness to the beauty of God's creation and redemption, resisting all that distorts this beauty, and participating in how God is saving the world. To truly remember the world, we must remember its mystery and the Mystery whose image we bear and resist all forms of reductionism.

Some religious educators gravitate to aesthetic approaches that do not simply conform to systematic interpretations or reductionistic strategies but instead seek to describe the depths of persons and situations. For example, as Frank Rogers illumines in his brilliant book *Finding God in the Graffiti*, our lives are narratively constructed, calling for greater attention to story as foundational for religious formation, personhood, creative vitality, and the common good. Rogers's narrative approaches do not rush to explain the lives of young people in existing social science terms, but they seem to mine the hidden true self—the surprising, subversive, vital and spiritual—in order to foster its agency. Further, Rogers sees that such true selfhood and agency cannot be attained as an abstraction or from a distance, but only from within the materiality of story.

In one of his frequent invitations to give leadership to narrative projects in local schools, Rogers met an African American boy named Spencer who felt isolated in his mostly white school by his differences of color, weight, interest, and ability.[25] Over time, as Rogers introduced a variety of

---

25. Rogers, *Finding God in the Graffiti*, ch. 2, "Narrative Pedagogy and Personal Identity."

folk tales, Spencer gravitated to the Danish folktale of the ugly duckling and chose to write himself into the story of a baby eagle who was lost and raised by barnyard chickens. In Spencer's story, the young eagle discovered by accident that he was not an earthbound chicken but was born to fly, to soar, that despite the mocking taunts of the chickens, he was a noble creature. The true self that Spencer discovered through identification with the eagle could only have been discovered in practices of reading and writing which unearthed his hidden lament and practices of retelling of his story that surfaced his hope. In the story of the ugly duckling, Spencer was able to glimpse his own truth as an act of remembrance.

Rogers highlights the importance of mobilizing the hidden or true self in examining the hidden cultural narratives in folk tales, commercials, bourgeois gender roles, and so forth, to criticize them, resist them, and recreate new and more life-giving stories. Rogers's work reveals the aesthetic and narrative nature of identity, life, faith, and flourishing. Stories provide a way to lament suffering and to imagine hope. Spencer struggled to name his suffering and to perceive his higher possibilities until he was inspired to seize the analogy of an eagle relegated to being a barnyard animal.

Dori Baker's LIVE approach begins with a slice-of-life story, an account of a moment without obvious religious significance.[26] But when the story is told, the gathered community makes connections to their own lives and reflects on how they were moved by the story, where God may exist, and how God may be calling them. This approach, like Rogers's narrative approaches, provides a true glimpse into a person's experience, including their suffering and hope, and invites the community to join in lamenting and hoping in light of how God is at work.

Similarly, Anne Wimberly's story-linking approach begins with a story of a limit situation, of suffering and lament.[27] But unlike many qualitative research approaches, the story is not interpreted by a scientific coding of statements and interpreting them systematically. Like Baker's, Wimberly's approach does not provide a solitary interpretation but juxtaposes an original story with diverse other stories, images, impressions, memories, and songs. For example, Wimberly's approach juxtaposes original stories to Bible stories and to African American heritage stories in which figures navigate similar situations and faithfully and wisely resolve them.

26. Baker, *The Barefoot Way*; Baker, *Doing Girlfriend Theology*.
27. Wimberly, *Soul Stories*.

These approaches allow for contemplative and aesthetic reflection on the depths and mysteries of a person's life and context. In them we attend to a person's story as the community helps identify how God may be speaking without forcing interpretations or solutions. Even as liturgy juxtaposes gestures, texts, images, narratives, architecture, and songs, so do these pedagogies juxtapose stories with other stories and images.[28] The approaches of Rogers, Baker, and Wimberly all weave in and out of story, experience, analogy, and imagery, as participants engage the depths of each other's lives without reduction, in wonder.

The second practice is to express particular experiences of human suffering in order to elicit compassion, solidarity, healing, and reconciliation. As we have seen, each of the approaches above, from Rogers, Baker, and Wimberly, create space in which stories highlight suffering and invite the gathered community to lament and hope. Augusto Boal's "theatre of the oppressed" approach is designed explicitly for participants to identify occasions of oppression and suffering, especially as they relate to social institutions and structures.

Initially, Boal worked among rural communities in South America who understood their lives to be fated to be poor and oppressed; they had no hope or expectation of resolution or wholeness. In *Theatre of the Oppressed*, Boal argues that theater is inherently political and that Aristotelian tragedy is a coercive system to enforce lawful behavior in the viewer, suppressing any desire for rebellion. According to Boal, Aristotle's tragic hero has one flaw, a characteristic that is antisocial or rebellious. The audience empathizes with this flaw and with the virtuous character. When the flaw leads the character to tragedy, the audience pities the character and fears for themselves. Through the character's downfall, whatever empathy has been fostered for the character is released in a catharsis and the trait is suppressed in the audience. Boal, following Brecht, calls this "bourgeois theater" because it reproduces elite visions of the world and pacifies spectators. Bourgeois theater is "finished" theater; the bourgeoisie already know what the world is like and so simply present it onstage.

In contrast to bourgeois theater, in Boal's approach "the people" are empowered with agency and do not yet know what their world will be like. Boal's theater is therefore unfinished and can provide space to rehearse different possible outcomes. As Boal says, "One knows how these experiments will begin but not how they will end, because the spectator is freed

28. See Lathrop, *Holy Things*, 10,11, 54, 58, 68–69, 163–64, 206, 219.

from his chains, finally acts, and becomes a protagonist."[29] Boal explored ways in which the people can become participants in the theater instead of passive spectators. People use theater exercises as a means to discuss their lives and the oppressive situations that they confront. Instead of the Aristotelian play that includes a static event which the audience watches and absorbs, in Boal's approach the audience determines the outcome of the action. Instead of passively observing, empathizing, and purging, the audience is not released from their conflictual feelings but uses them in becoming participant-creators, entering the play, feeling the complexity of the characters and their social contexts, and rehearsing alternate responses and resolutions to the conflict.

The most widely recognized form of theatre of the oppressed is *forum theatre*, which presents a scene that is first run from beginning to end. Then, it is rerun, but this time, spectators can interrupt the action (by shouting, "Stop!") and take the place of an actor. Usually, the scene depicts a type of oppression—workers on strike confronting a manager, a racist swimming pool attendant demanding papers from a Black family, an authoritarian father throwing his daughter out for getting pregnant, and so on. "Spect-actors," who become actors, take on the role of the oppressed person and try out alternative responses. The facilitator or "joker" invites alternate "spect-actors" to contribute a solution to the dramatized problem. Boal's approach allows for a wide range of perspectives and interpretations. Often, in preparation for forum theatre, the joker invites participants to workshop the characters in order to clarify what they want and fear.

The aim of theatre of the oppressed is not to identify a single solution to the situation of oppression but to consider and rehearse a range of possibilities. The range and number of interpretations of these situations is often stunning. It is possible to linger with characters and to perceive their beauty and depth and to imagine solutions that are creative and redemptive.[30] Boal's theatre is shared with the larger community so that they might

---

29. Boal, *Theatre of the Oppressed*, 142.

30. Too often, Boal's method focuses so entirely on structural problems of oppression that it can foster an adversarial perspective and foster reductionistic binaries—such as oppressed-oppressor. Maintaining a nuanced and generous perspective can be challenging, especially when the antagonist is not present. Again, it is possible for the joker to introduce complexity if he or she is willing to speak generously of the antagonist. Theatre of the oppressed was initiated by Boal in response to extreme economic and structural disparities that in reality did pit those with power against those without power. Often, as Freire discovered (*Pedagogy of the Oppressed*), people in impoverished communities were so subdued by those in power that they lacked a sense of agency, oblivious to how

share its lament and hope. Boal's approach might be seen as an extension of the eucharistic liturgy of remembrance.

The third practice is to seek glimpses of hope in hidden wholeness, fore-tastes of how life would be and will be without suffering. In the Christian imagination, to lament is to hope for some higher and more beautiful existence, free from the limits of suffering and evil. Most of us are fortunate enough to have lives filled with beauty and goodness. We have parents who love us, sun that warms us, food that fills us, friends that delight us, gifts in which we lose ourselves. Erik Erikson speaks of a "basic sense of trust" in the experience of a world good enough to encourage children to explore the world and find a place in it.[31] For those fortunate enough to know this basic trust in the world's goodness, complete flourishing in seamless goodness and beauty seems always just ahead, around the corner. But for others, flourishing is only ever a distant dream amidst what seems like a life of seamless suffering.

As Christians, we look forward to the waking dream of God's reign of perfect shalom, life, love, communion, and joy. According to Jurgen Moltmann, Christ's resurrection inaugurated a hope that animated Christian life and practice. Only in light of this hope and expectation can suffering seem anomalous. Letitia Huckaby's "Sugar and Spice" would not be nearly as compelling without the hint of a tutu foreshadowing the hope of the young girl's dancing. Mexican *ex-votos* would not be as compelling without the guiding images of a providential theophany and the promise of being welcomed home.

Boal's theatre of the oppressed is also an example of an approach that explicitly includes an imaginary of hope. As noted earlier, Boal's approach culminates in a forum theatre event. However, in order to achieve the clarity and capacity for expression needed in forum theatre, Boal's process includes a series of image theater games, in which participants take turns sculpting images and tableaus with their bodies to express their experiences, which

their fates were subject to their own intelligence, power, and will. In these cases, especially lines between adversaries were starkly drawn, and it was crucial to draw attention to such binaries. While understanding and resisting unequal and oppressive forms of power must still be a project of the church, not every tensive relationship should be seen in binary terms. Further, sometimes even situations of unequal power and dominance can be addressed by means that not only pit people as adversaries but cast them as brothers and sisters of a single human family or part of Christ's body. If the work of the liturgy is to "remember" the world, then remembrance would seem to involve truly seeing and being seen by others and not being reduced as categories in a binary.

31. Erikson, *Childhood and Society.*

will later become material for the forum theatre skits. Boal also instructs participants to construct an "ideal image"—an image of the ideal situation, the way they wished the situation existed. The sculptor sculpts the actors into her ideal image. This is the most important image, the bridge between the two worlds. Boal calls this scene "the change, the transformation, or the revolution."[32]

Boal recalled his experience with image theater in a small village in Peru where a young woman sculpted the participants into a recent event. The leader of the peasant rebellion had been captured by government landlords and publicly castrated. The woman's actual image showed a man pushed down on the ground with his hands tied behind his back. Around him stood the faces of dominance and oppression. Men stood in aggressive positions with "air" guns. Sculpted female figures in the scene were kneeling in prayer; others were held in restraining positions by government landlords and military police. Boal remembers: This was the image that person had of her village, a true reflection of something that had actually taken place.[33] When the woman was asked to show her ideal image, she altered the "statues" and reorganized them as people working in peace and loving each other. Participants will use such ideal images as background for considering ways to mobilize for transition to the ideal.

Anne Wimberly's story-linking approach also employs ideal images from across the range of personal, biblical, and African American heritage stories. Wimberly relates a story of one of Harriet Tubman's harrowing trips on the way from slavery to freedom through the Underground Railroad. During the trip, the freedom-seekers encountered rain, sleet, hail, wind, and cold. Their clothes were tattered and soaked. Wimberly recounts:

> The soles of their feet gradually took the place of the disappearing soles of their shoes. They ran out of rations. Hunger overtook them. Several in the party sat down on the ground and said to Harriet that they simply could not go on through the storm. Harriet, who became known as the Moses of our people, looked down at them and said quietly but firmly, "Get up and move," knowing that if they did not do so, they would be found and likely beaten or killed, and the way ahead would be discovered. When they remained seated and cried out their inability to go on, Harriet replied with a bit firmer tone, "Get up and move." Following the continued protestations of those seated on the ground, Harriet reached into

32. Boal, *Theatre of the Oppressed,* 135.
33. Boal, *Theatre of the Oppressed,* 131.

her cloak, pulled out a gun, pointed it at the protesters, and said resolutely, "Move or die!" They moved![34]

Wimberly asks the group: "What do these stories say to us in our stories of moving from one point to another in our lives in the midst of the storms of adversity?" One of the most powerful statements given by a group member was this:

> To give up on ourselves and on life is tantamount to pronouncing our own death. We don't see a way out. So, our boat sinks and we drown. Sometimes that happens. Another way to put it is that we don't need Harriet's gun pointed at us. In essence, we point it at ourselves and sometimes "shoot ourselves in the foot," meaning we stop ourselves in our tracks and don't get anywhere. But, we must not allow ourselves to do this. We must and we can get up and move! I do it by calling on the name of the Lord daily, knowing that I'm going to get an answer and strength to help others to move.[35]

Anne Wimberly and Sarah Farmer recently coauthored a book titled *Raising Hope: 4 Paths to Courageous Living for Black Youth* in which they review four pedagogical pathways that are directed towards forming a courageous hope in youth. These pathways are the narrative pathway, a creative pathway, a peacemaking pathway, and a pathway of exposure. The chapters describe a variety of ways that black youth can be empowered and equipped with a courageous hope by using storytelling and creative arts and teaching communication and relational skills to offset the violence in their culture and by engaging them in multidimensional experiences that foster positivity and purpose in their lives.

While the pedagogies employed in this chapter are meant to illustrate their key dynamics, by no means do they exhaust the possibilities for pedagogies that remember and lament. Mark Yaconelli's storytelling practice invites participants to identify lament and hope in their stories.[36] Some

---

34. Wimberly, *Soul Stories*, 23.

35. Wimberly, *Soul Stories*, 23.

36. Mark Yaconelli is the founder of a program in southern Oregon known as the Hearth in which stories are told in community that confront a social problem, bridge divisions, and embody a new awareness or understanding. His work of storytelling assists communities in discerning the actions their stories invite. Often this means creating safe and transformative settings where marginalized and suffering people feel empowered to share their experiences. In Yaconelli's philosophy, honest storytelling can be playful, evoking humorous self-recognition, delight, and gratitude for the pleasures of life. The Hearth is committed to transforming residents into neighbors, enemies into friends,

spiritual direction approaches invite spiritual directees to draw or create in clay an image of their true self (an image of hope) and what inhibits them (sometimes in suffering but surely to be lamented) from living truthfully.[37]

In this chapter, I have tried to suggest how aesthetic pedagogies address serious evil and suffering in the world. I have highlighted the importance of cultivating a Christian imaginary that includes lament and hope. If our pedagogical practices do not make space for lament and hope, we risk normalizing suffering and evil. Without hope, lamenting can devolve into the prison of anger and bitterness. Without lament, hope can take flight into naive fantasy. Lament and hope must be held together in our experience of faith and in our pedagogies. The internal goods of lament and hope are many. When we lament, we cry to God for help, but we also invite the community to join us in our lonely suffering. When we remember our hope that God promises to redeem our suffering, our imaginations are enriched with the possibility of healing and reconciliation. In hope, we find courage to act against status quo structures at whose hands we suffer. In lament and hope, we awaken from our late-modern slumber that struggles to find a reason for hope and, thus, struggles to lament, given the dearth of resources for imagining what should be or bemoaning what is.

---

and towns into communities. Ultimately, gathering to share stories is one of the deepest, most transformative, and most pleasurable activities we do as human beings. In 2010, Yaconelli joined with Austin Seminary in hosting an event titled Breaking Down Walls, a powerful, much needed night of stories from people who have suffered under US immigration policies. Mark is the author of *The Gift of Hard Things; Wonder, Fear, and Longing; Downtime; Growing Souls;* and *Contemplative Youth Ministry.*

37. See, for example, Paintner, *Awakening the Creative Spirit.*

Conclusion

I Will Open My Mouth in Parables

Jesus spoke to the multitudes in parables, and he was not speaking to them without a parable, so that what was spoken by through the prophet might be fulfilled, saying, "I will open my mouth in parables, I will utter things hidden since the foundation of the world."

—MATTHEW 13:34–35

IN THE GOSPELS, JESUS is seen speaking constantly in parables in which he drew outrageous comparisons about an even more far-fetched realm. The kingdom of heaven is like—a mustard seed, yeast that a woman mixed into flour, a merchant looking for fine pearls, a net let down into the lake, a landowner who went out in the morning to hire workers, a king who prepared a wedding banquet for his son, ten virgins who took their lamps and went out to meet the bridegroom, or a man going on a journey who called his servants and entrusted his wealth to them.

Despite using ready-to-hand images and experiences, parables do not yield their meanings in straightforward lessons, nor do they illustrate more basic ideas or theological meanings. Bishop William Willimon quips,

> In my Christian experience, the funny, shocking, surprising, subversive teaching of Jesus has often been quenched by analysis and exposition. We're not good listeners. It's hard for us to stay in the moment with Jesus the Storyteller. We want the explanation, the moral, the lesson. We want the punchline to be clear, the message to be practical and edifying. We resist being left hanging. We don't want Jesus to respond to our questions with even harder questions. We're impatient. We want the answers so that we can pass the test. Now.[1]

Parables are not so much communiques as lumps of coal compressed into diamonds, condensed metaphors that catch the flicker of something infinite, bejeweled thresholds of another world. They are not transparent like windows, but through their surfaces they refract light that might otherwise blind us or else pass unseen. Parables participate in the reality they express; thus, they always contain an excess beyond what can be conveyed. They are the residue of something ineffable filtering from the depths where the kingdom accomplishes its work of germinating mustard seeds, blooming yeasts, preparing banquets, finding pearls, or setting on a journey. We do not so much think as feel our way into parables. In experiencing their mystery, we sense that we do not understand them after all, but they understand us.

This book has sought to illumine forgotten strands of the Christian tradition in which all created things speak as parables. Not only do mustard seeds, pearls, yeasts, and wedding feasts mediate God's kingdom; so does each dust mote, each child's chubby grin, and each chirping cricket. All created things, like parables, contain hidden depths that bear witness to mysteries obscured by a necrophilic modernity that reduces things as dead quantities for our calculation and mastery. The beauty of the cosmos does

1. Willimon, *Why Jesus?*, 26.

not submit to being consumed, mastered, or exhaustively comprehended. As we have seen, the beautiful forms of the cosmos announce themselves, gaze upon us, and invite our love, knowledge, and mutual becoming in relation. Christianity's aesthetic tradition sees all creatures dripping with glory; they do not reduce to mere efficient causality or economic determinism. This is paradigmatically true with Christ's beauty in the style of love, which can be expressed but not exhausted by doctrine. In this tradition, we do not so much "understand" the gospel as submit to being understood by it. It can be critically engaged, but only as we submit to its immediacy in response to the divine light that shines from beyond it. In the moment we are captured by beauty we are compelled to respond in grateful worship by returning our gifts of prayer, art, and action that bear witness to their original donation. We are hence called by the beauty of Christ into personhood and mission.

If such ecstatic knowing, loving, and making seems like a dream, it is because we remain under the spell of a modern social imaginary which is reinforced daily and hourly by our materialistic economic system, flattened political rhetoric, and mechanistic scientism. Perceiving beauty—in the cosmos, others, God, and ourselves—is inhibited by the sheer ubiquity of modernity's objectifying trance and the interlocking web of institutions that rely on its spell. In a sense, this has always been the location of the church. Even Jesus' disciples seemed annoyed by his reluctance to narrate the kingdom in familiar and straightforward terms. Like Jesus' disciples, we stand today as spellbound and reluctant followers desiring that the word be made "familiar"—spoken in the idiom of our tribe, consistent with our politics or doctrinal formulations. We fear losing ourselves in the unfamiliar detail of each other's stories and in the depths of the world's alterity, in God's perichoretic infinity. We prefer a world we can master over one filled with strange surprises and risks, even if such represents the possibility of our healing.

Today, in some quarters, the beauty and depth of the gospel is obscured by teaching rigid doctrinal formulations, while in others it is obscured by teaching rigid moralism. We wrongly assume that the value of our pedagogical approaches is found only in mastery of concepts or of ethical action. We imagine that Christian faith ascends the ladder of aesthetic materiality—the narratives, forms, parables, liturgies, and practices—that can then be kicked away as we achieve the abstractions of doctrine, ideology, or moralism. It bears repeating that although this book reclaims and highlights our aesthetic formation, it does not negate the significance of systematic thought and reflection. While neither concepts nor acts should be seen in themselves as negative, their highest value is found when they are humbled relative to beauty and its mysteries. The rush to know or act can obscure other virtues, such as love, generosity, and compassion, which beauty can awaken.

Glossing over beauty can render the Christ form an instrumental afterthought in the service of predetermined actions. Such an instrumental use functions rather like Pierre Bourdieau's notion of "pedagogies of insignificance" that carry in themselves a microcosm of the culture's tacit curriculum. Just as instructions in etiquette instill a whole cosmology, a way of life, so does a hasty rush to ideological or practical conclusions. Unfortunately, knowledge and action without a sense of the world's depth and mystery can lead to a purely utilitarian vision of the world, to anger, violence, and ineffectiveness. Approaches to Christian formation that over-emphasize its active aspect can narrate a world in which mystery, beauty, and God is evacuated. This book locates our practices, including social activism, theological reflection, and Christian formation, as a creative liturgical response to beauty's depths.

This book can be seen as a rejection of modern rational reductionism, and a partial response to Charles Taylor's lament that we live in a world disenchanted, as something of a loss. More specifically, I am reclaiming a tradition that sees re-enchantment as fundamental to Christian faith, a tradition that conditions the aims and techniques for Christian formation.

Yet, learning to see with new eyes and hear with new ears does not involve a single choice but an ongoing formation. Jesus daily invited his disciples into this new world where sheep, seeds, lamps, bridegrooms, and servants hold deep meaning. He walked beside them and invited them to see beauty in children, Samaritans, women, tax collectors, those sick and imprisoned. Jesus persuaded his followers to ponder and pivot by means of the rich detail in narratives, images, metaphors, parables, and the artistic life he manifested in their midst. In this way did the world open to them in love, joy, and communion. Today, we need practices that can teach us to attend to beauty and its depths, subvert the tyranny of our egos, and respond creatively in worship—offering our return gifts of art, music, language, practices, and acts of charity and justice that bear witness to God's own beauty and creativity. Like the disciples, we need those who walk alongside us as Jesus did, awakening our spiritual senses.

By no means have I said all that can be said about the possibilities for Christian formation enlightened by beauty and poiesis; I have only made a start, offering but a glimmer of its luminous facets. I have acknowledged, however inadequately, that existing approaches—such as those that feature narrative, contemplation, and play—can enlarge our spiritual senses by the quality of attention they demand. If the church is to awaken our spiritual senses in order that we feel our way into the parables of creation and kingdom, we must boldly explore practices that deepen our encounter with beauty's depths—practices, for example, such as those familiar to artists and contemplatives. Church teachers must learn and teach the habits of artists who linger before their objects to perceive their hidden truths. We must learn and teach habits of contemplatives who hear God speaking in silence, texts, bodies, in consolations and desolations. We must notice and develop the aesthetic dimensions of existing pedagogical approaches. We need better language for discussing how beauty is a dimension of truth and goodness, ideas and activism. Our pedagogies need to clarify how the broken world is changed by our response to beauty's call.

The thought of Balthasar and Milbank and the traditions they retrieve point to a reconsideration of the church's ministry of formation, including active involvement in creating and appreciating music and art. Not only liturgists but artists and musicians engage in a vocation of remembering and "naming" God's creatures. In fact, art itself, even apart from formal pedagogical approaches, can be powerfully formative, enlarging our spiritual senses of wonder, joy, and gratitude. Not a few medieval musicians, artists, and architects bear witness to a lovely Referent. Today, Christian music must not simply derive its forms from contemporary popular music but must seek to express the deep beauty and mystery of our encounter with the holy. It is worth noting that even some atheists who reject the apologetics of the church are caught up in wonder before the liturgical masterpieces of, for example, Mozart or Bach or Beethoven.

While this book attempts far too much, it admittedly does not achieve enough. This book ambitiously explores theological questions about the true nature of knowledge and formation yet has only nodded to the vast bodies of research, for example, in psychology, human development, multiple intelligence, narrative studies, contemplative practices, brain research, and continental philosophy that may perhaps confirm the theological assertions of this book. My hope is that Christians who care about education and formation will continue to explore the ground tilled by educators like

Harris, Smith, Edie, Rogers, Moore, Baker, Wimberly, Goto, and others who see pedagogical value in story, drama, play, liturgy, and contemplation.

We must imagine beauty beyond its use as a technique. Beauty and creativity are not additives to spice up a doctrinal or moral lesson. Beauty and creativity are key to the nature of all things, perfected in God, a key aspect of our redemption. As Jurgen Moltmann once suggested "man's free self-representation has to be the human echo to the pleasure of god in his creation. The glorification of God lies in the demonstrative joy of existence. Then man in his uninhibited fondness for this finite life and by his affirmation of mortal beauty shares the infinite pleasure of the creator."[2] In Christ, God opens humanity and all creation to "a noble game" of doxological freedom, abundant rejoicing in God, and free play with the grace of God. Play begun in God's act of creation is continued in eternity. Moltmann elaborates:

> Christian eschatology has never thought of the end of history as a kind of retirement or payday or accomplished purpose but has regarded it totally without purpose as a hymn of praise for unending joy, as an ever-varying round dance of the redeemed in the Trinitarian fullness of God, and as the complete harmony of soul and body . . . Christian eschatology has never painted the joy of existing in the new, redeemed, and liberated creation in colors of this life damaged by trouble, labor, and guilt, but it has painted it in colors which for all of us—in Ernst Bloch's beautiful phrase— shine back into our childhood, namely the colors of unhindered laughter, devoted vision of the marvelous riches and goodness of God and of new innocence. Christian eschatology has painted the end of history in the colors of aesthetic categories.[3]

So, at the end of history all creatures shall "play with heaven and earth, the sun and all the creatures," says Luther. "All creatures shall have their fun, love and joy, and shall laugh with thee and thou with them, even according to the body."[4]

In the midst of my recent isolation due to the global COVID pandemic, I found great delight in YouTube videos of flash mobs, where the ordinary lives—of shoppers, strollers, mothers scolding their children, messengers making deliveries on bikes, businessmen taking a break from whatever urgent matters occupy them—are interrupted by the entirely

2. Moltmann, *A Theology of Play*, 21.
3. Moltmann, *A Theology of Play*, 34.
4. Moltmann, *A Theology of Play*, 37.

extraordinary surprise of choraliers or dancers who offer their gifts, the inbreaking of another world, a fleeting glimpse of the world's soul. With the revelation of these gifts, mothers, children, delivery persons, businessmen, and shoppers are immediately stopped in their tracks as smiles erupt from their previously unaffected or morose faces. Some bystanders cannot resist the impulse to sing along or dance alongside. Many stand frozen after the music has stopped, as if hoping for more. It is not hard to imagine that in the aftermath of such experiences, days become brighter, moods softened, relationships momentarily strengthened, and commitments reconsidered. At a fundamental level, the possibility of giving gifts is kindled in our imaginations again.

Much like Jesus' outlandish comparisons in his parables, this book suggests that the church is like a flash mob interrupting the stale treaties of work, consumption, and governance to say a new word in a strange way that takes our breath and compels us to join in its joy. A vision of Christian formation adequate for this historical moment recognizes that beauty, creativity, poiesis, is a means by which we participate in God who is eternally at play, generating, creating, intoning, painting, composing, sculpting. The church bears witness to God's inbreaking beauty, forever erupting into new song. This is a formation that is most truly Christian.

Let it be so.

Bibliography

Aersten, Jan A. *Medieval Philosophy and the Transcendental: The Case of Thomas Aquinas.* Leiden: Brill, 1996.

Anderson, Ray S. *The Shape of Practical Theology: Empowering Ministry with Theological Praxis.* Downers Grove, IL: InterVarsity, 2001.

Aristotle. *Aristotle De Anima.* Translated and edited by R. D. Hicks. Cambridge, UK: Cambridge University Press, 1907.

———. *Nicomachean Ethics.* Translated by H. Rackham. Cambridge, MA: Harvard University Press, 1968.

Aquinas, Thomas. *The Pocket Aquinas.* Translated by Vernon J. Bourke. New York: Washington Square, 1965.

———. "De Principiis Naturae" ("On the Principles of Nature"). In *Aquinas on Matter and Form and the Elements: A Translation and Interpretation of the De Principiis Naturae and the De Mixtione Elementorum of St. Thomas Aquinas,* translated by Joseph Bobick, 1–102. Notre Dame, IN: University of Notre Dame Press, 1998.

———. *Summa Theologica.* Translated by Fathers of the English Dominican Province. Westminster, MD: Christian Classics, 1981.

Arcand, Denys, dir. *Jesus of Montreal.* Toronto: Cineplex Odeon Films, 1989.

Arieti, James A. *Springs of Western Civilization: A Comparative Study of Hebrew and Classical Cultures.* Lanham, MD: Lexington, 2017.

Augustine. "The Soliloquies (*Soliloquia*)." In *Augustine: Earlier Writings,* edited and translated by John H. S. Burleigh, 23–63. Philadelphia: Westminster, 1953.

Augustine. *The Confessions of St. Augustine.* Translated by Rex Warner. New York: Penguin Group, 1981.

Baker, Dori Grinenko. *The Barefoot Way: A Faith Guide for Youth, Young Adults, and the People Who Walk with Them.* Louisville: Westminster John Knox, 2012.

———. *Doing Girlfriend Theology: God-Talk with Young Women.* Cleveland: Pilgrim, 2005.

Balthasar, Hans Urs von. *Apokalypse der deutschen Seele: Studien zu einer Lehre von letzen Haltunger.* 3 vols. 3rd ed. Einsiedel, Germany: Johannes Verlag, 1998.

———. *Engagement with God: The Drama of Christian Discipleship.* San Francisco: Ignatius, 2008.

———. *The Glory of the Lord: A Theological Aesthetics.* Vol. 1, *Seeing the Form.* 2nd ed. Edited by John Riches. Translated by Erasmo Levia-Merikakis. San Francisco: Ignatius, 2009.

————. *The Glory of the Lord: A Theological Aesthetics. Vol. 2, Studies in Theological Styles: Clerical Styles.* Edited by Brian McNeil and John Riches. Translated by Andrew Louth, Francis McDonagh, and Brian McNeil. San Francisco: Ignatius, 1984.

————. *The Glory of the Lord: A Theological Aesthetics. Vol. 5, The Realm of Metaphysics in the Modern Age.* Edited by Brian McNeil and John Riches. Translated by Oliver Davies et al. Edinburgh: T. & T. Clark International, 1981.

————. *The Glory of the Lord: A Theological Aesthetics. Vol. 6, Theology: The Old Covenant.* Edited by John Riches. Translated by Levia-Merikakis and Brian McNeil. Edinburgh: T. & T. Clark International, 1991.

————. *Love Alone Is Credible.* San Francisco: Ignatius, 2004.

————. *Maximus the Confessor: Cosmic Liturgy: The Universe According to Maximus Confessor.* Translated by Brian E. Daley. San Francisco: Ignatius, 2003.

————. "Movement toward God." In *Explorations in Theology*, translated by Brian McNeil, 3.15–55. San Francisco: Ignatius, 1993.

————. *My Work in Retrospect.* San Francisco: Ignatius, 1993.

————. *Mysterium Paschale.* Translated by Aidan Nichols. San Francisco: Ignatius, 1990.

————. *Origines Geist und Feuer: Ein Aufbau aus Seinen Schriften.* Salzburg: Otto Müller, 1938.

————. "Personlichkeit und Form." *Gloria Dei* 7 (1952) 1–15.

————. *Theo-Drama: Theological Dramatic Theory. Vol. 1, Prolegomena.* Translated by Graham Harrison. San Francisco: Ignatius, 1988.

————. *Theo-Drama: Theological Dramatic Theory. Vol. 2, The Dramatis Personae: Man in God.* Translated by Graham Harrison. San Francisco: Ignatius, 1993.

————. *Theo-Drama: Theological Dramatic Theory. Vol. 5, The Last Act.* Translated by Graham Harrison. San Francisco: Ignatius, 1998.

————. *Theo-Logic: Theological Logical Theory.* 3 vols. Translated by Adrian J. Walker. San Francisco: Ignatius, 2000.

————. *A Theology of History.* San Francisco: Ignatius, 1994.

————. *Word and Revelation.* New York: Herder and Herder, 1954.

Barnes, Julian. "Nothing to Be Frightened Of." *New York Times*, October 3, 2008.

Barth, Karl. *Wolfgang Amadeus Mozart.* Eugene, OR: Wipf and Stock, 1986.

Bass, Dorothy. *Practicing Our Faith: A Way of Life for a Searching People.* San Francisco: Jossey-Bass, 1997.

Benedict XVI, Pope. "Meeting with Artists." November 22, 2009. https://www.vatican.va/content/benedict-xvi/en/speeches/2009/november/documents/hf_ben-xvi_spe_20091121_artisti.html.

Berryman, Jerome W. *How to Lead Godly Play Lessons.* New York: Church, 2002.

————. *Teaching Godly Play.* Nashville: Abingdon, 1995.

Boal, Augusto. *Games for Actors and Non-Actors.* New York: Routledge, 1992.

————. *The Rainbow of Desire: The Boal Method of Theatre and Therapy.* Translated by Adrian Jackson. New York: Routledge, 1995.

————. *Theatre of the Oppressed.* Translated by Charles A. McBride. New York: Theatre Communications Group, 1979.

Boersma, Hans. *Heavenly Participation: Weaving a Sacramental Tapestry.* Grand Rapids: Eerdmans, 2011.

Bourdieau, Pierre. *The Logic of Practice.* Stanford, CA: Stanford University Press, 1990.

Brennan, Timothy. *Borrowed Light: Vico, Hegel and the Colonies.* Stanford, CA: Stanford University Press, 2014.

Bibliography

Brooks, David. *The Social Animal: The Hidden Sources of Love, Character, and Achievement.* New York: Random House, 2011.

Browning, Don S. *A Fundamental Practical Theology: Descriptive and Strategic Proposals.* Minneapolis: Fortress Press, 1991.

Buber, Martin. *I and Thou.* Translated by Walter Kaufman. New York: Charles Scribner's Sons, 1970.

Bull, Malcolm. *Inventing Falsehood, Making Truth: Vico and Neapolitan Painting.* Princeton, NJ: Princeton University Press, 2013.

Burghardt, Walter J. "Contemplation: A Long Loving Look at the Real." In *An Ignatian Spirituality Reader,* edited by George W. Traub, 89–98. Chicago: Loyola, 2008.

Buytendijk, Frederik Jacobus Johannes. *Het Spel van Mensch en Diet als Openbaring van Levensdriften.* Amsterdam: Herder, 1932.

Bywater, I. "Aristotle's DIalogue on Philosophy." *Journal of Philology* 7.13 (1876).

Caldecott, Stratford. "An Introduction to Hans Urs von Balthasar." *Catholic Education Resource Center,* 2001. https://www.catholiceducation.org/en/culture/catholic-contributions/an-introduction-to-hans-urs-von-balthasar.html.

Caldwell, Elizabeth F. *I Wonder: Engaging a Child's Curiosity about the Bible.* Nashville: Abingdon, 2016.

Cameron, Julia. *The Artist's Way.* 25th anniversary edition. New York: TarcherPerigee, 2016.

Cavanaugh, William T. "Don't Change the World." Lecture, Biola University Center for Christian Thought, La Mirada, CA, July 13, 2017. https://cct.biola.edu/dont-change-world/.

———. "The Eucharist as Politics." Lecture, Basilica of Notre-Dame de Fourvière, Lyon, France, November 9, 2016. https://www.youtube.com/watch?v=XXDMJ4X-IfI.

———. "'A Fire Strong Enough to Consumer the House': The Wars of Religion and the Rise of the State." *Modern Theology* 11 (1995) 397–420.

———. *Migrations of the Holy: God, State, and the Political Meaning of the Church.* Grand Rapids: Eerdmans, 2011.

Certeau, Michel de. "How Is Christianity Thinkable Today?" Translated by Frederick Christian Bauerschmidt. In *The Postmodern God: A Theological Reader,* edited by Graham Ward, 142–55. Malden, MA: Blackwell, 1997.

Chesterton, G. K. *Orthodoxy.* 1908. Reprint, Grand Rapids: Regent College Publishing, 2004.

Collins, Billy. *The Apple that Astonished Paris.* Fayetteville, AR: University of Arkansas Press, 1996.

Csikszentmihalyi, Mihaly. *Creativity: Flow and the Psychology of Discovery and Invention.* New York: Harper Perennial, 1996.

———. *Flow: The Psychology of Optimal Experience.* New York: Harper and Row, 1990.

De Mello, Anthony. "The Finest Act of Love." *DeMello Spirituality Center,* January 1, 2021. https://www.demellospirituality.com/the-finest-act-of-love/.

———. *The Way to Love: The Last Meditations of Anthony de Mello.* New York: Doubleday, 1991.

Dickinson, Emily. "'Hope' Is the Thing with Feathers." In *The Complete Poems of Emily Dickinson,* edited by Thomas H. Johnson, 116. Cambridge, MA: The Belknap Press of Harvard University Press, 1951.

Dostoevsky, Fyodor. *The Brothers Karamazov.* Translated by Larissa Volokhonsky. New York: Farrar, Straus and Giroux, 2002.

————. *The Idiot.* Translated by Constance Garnett. New York: Bantam, 1981.

Dionysius the Areopagite. *The Collected Works of Dionysius the Areopagite.* Translated by John Parker. Morrisville, NC: Solace, 2015.

Dufrenne, Mikel. *The Phenomenology of Aesthetic Experience.* Evanston, IL: Northwestern University Press, 1973.

Durand, Jorge, and Douglas S. Massey. *Miracles on the Border: Retablos of Mexican Migrants to the United States.* Tucson, AZ: University of Arizona Press, 1995.

Dykstra, Craig. *Growing in the Life of Faith, Second Edition: Education and Christian Practices.* 2nd ed. Louisville: Westminster John Knox, 2005.

Edie, Fred. *Book, Bath, Table, Time: Christian Worship as Source and Resource for Youth Ministry.* Cleveland: Pilgrim, 2007.

Eichrodt, Walter. *Theology of the Old Testament.* 2 vols. Translated by J. A. Baker. Philadelphia: Westminster, 1965.

Einstein, Albert. "Religion and Science." *New York Times Magazine,* November 9, 1930.

Erikson, Erik. *Childhood and Society.* New York: W. W. Norton & Company, 1963.

Francis, Pope. *Encyclical Letter, Laudato Si' of the Holy Father Francis on Care for our Common Home.* Rome: Vatican, 2015.

Freire, Paulo. *Pedagogy of the Oppressed.* New York: Continuum, 2007.

Gadamer, Hans-Georg. *The Relevance of the Beautiful.* London: Cambridge University Press, 1986.

————. *Truth and Method.* London: Continuum, 1975.

Ganss, George. *The Spiritual Exercises of St. Ignatius.* Chicago: Loyola, 1992.

García-Rivera, Alejandro R. *A Wounded Innocence: Sketches for a Theology of Art.* Collegeville, MN: Liturgical, 2003.

Gilson, Etienne. *The Arts of the Beautiful.* London: Dalkey Archive, 2000.

Gopnik, Alison, Andrew N. Meltzoff, and Patricia K. Kuhl. *The Scientist in the Crib: Minds, Brains, and How Children Learn.* New York: William Morrow, 1999.

Goto, Courtney. *The Grace of Playing: Pedagogies for Leaning into God's New Creation.* Eugene, OR: Pickwick, 2016.

Greenblatt, Stephen, et al, eds. "Gerard Manley Hopkins." In *The Norton Anthology of English Literature,* 2.1513–26. 8th ed. New York: W. W. Norton & Company, 2006.

Greene, David, dir. *Godspell.* Culver City, CA: Columbia Pictures, 1973.

Groome, Thomas. *Sharing Faith: The Way of Shared Praxis.* San Francisco: HarperCollins, 1991.

Haillie, Philip. *Lest Innocent Blood Be Shed: The Story of the Village of Le Chambon and How Goodness Happened There.* New York: Harper and Row, 1979.

Harris, Maria. *Fashion Me a People: Curriculum in the Church.* Louisville: Westminster John Knox, 1989.

Hart, David Bentley. *The Beauty of the Infinite.* Grand Rapids: Eerdmans, 2003.

————. *The Doors of the Sea: Where Was God in the Tsunami?* Grand Rapids: Eerdmans, 2005.

————. *The Experience of God: Being, Consciousness, Bliss.* New Haven, CT: Yale University Press, 2014.

————. *The Offering of Names.* London: T. & T. Clark, 2005.

Henrici, Peter. "Hans Urs von Balthasar: His Cultural and Theological Education." In *The Beauty of Christ,* edited by Bede McGregor and Thomas J. Norris, 49–63. Edinburgh: T. & T. Clark, 1994.

———. "Hans Urs von Balthasar: A Sketch of His Life." In *Hans Urs von Balthasar: His Life and Work*, edited by David L. Schindler, 7–43. San Francisco: Ignatius, 1991.

Hopkins, Gerard Manley. "God's Grandeur." In *Gerard Manley Hopkins: Poems and Prose*, edited by W. H. Gardner, 27. London: Penguin Classics, 1985.

———. *The Poetical Works of Gerard Manley Hopkins*. Edited by Norman H. MacKenzie. Oxford: Oxford University Press, 1990.

Huckaby, Letitia. "Suffrage Project: Sugar and Spice." https://huckabystudios.com/body/suffer-rage/.

Hugo, Victor. *Les Miserables*. Savoie, Belgium: A. Lacroix, Verboeckhoven & Cie, 1862.

James, Bill. *The New Bill James Historical Baseball Abstract*. New York: Free Press, 2001.

James, William. *The Principles of Psychology*. Vol I. New York: Dover, 1950.

Jewison, Norman, dir. *Jesus Christ Superstar*. Universal City, CA: Universal, 1973.

John of Damascus. "Apologia against Those Who Decry Holy Images." In *On Holy Images*, translated by Mary H. Allie, 1–54. London: Thomas Baker, 1898.

John Paul II, Pope. "The Trinity: Fountain of Love and Light." *L'Osservatore Romano*, January 26, 2000.

Johnson, Junius C. "Christ and Analogy: The Metaphysics of Hans Urs von Balthasar." PhD diss., Yale University, 2010.

Kalfas, Jennifer. "'I Have a Dream That Enough is Enough.' Martin Luther King Jr.'s Granddaughter, 9, Gives Powerful Speech at March For Our Lives." *Time*, March 24, 2018.

Keats, John. *The Poems of John Keats*. Edited by E. de Selincourt. New York: Dodd, Mead and Co., 1905.

Kierkegaard, Søren. *Either/Or*. 2 vols. Edited and translated by Howard V. Hong and Edna H. Hong. Princeton, NJ: Princeton University Press, 1987.

———. *Kierkegaard's Writings, II, Volume 2: The Concept of Irony, with Continual Reference to Socrates/Notes of Schelling's Berlin Lectures*. Edited by Howard V. Hong and Edna H. Hong. Princeton, NJ: Princeton University Press, 1989.

———. *Practice in Christianity*. Edited and translated by Howard V. Hong and Edna H. Hong. Princeton, NJ: Princeton University Press, 1991.

Koontz, Dean. *The Darkest Evening of the Year: A Novel*. New York: Random House, 2007.

Kosloski, Philip. "How to Pray with Icons." *Aleteia*, September 12, 2018. https://aleteia.org/2018/09/12/how-to-pray-with-icons-a-brief-guide/.

Lakoff, George, and Mark Johnson. *Metaphors We Live By*. Chicago: University of Chicago Press, 1980.

Lathrop, Gordon. *Holy Things: A Liturgical Theology*. Minneapolis: Fortress, 1998.

Lewis, C. S. *The Chronicles of Narnia*. New York: HarperCollins, 1994.

———. *The Weight of Glory*. San Francisco: Harper San Francisco, 2001.

Liebert, Elizabeth. *The Way of Discernment: Spiritual Practices for Decision Making*. Louisville: Westminster John Knox, 2008.

Locke, John. *The Works of John Locke, Esq: In Three Volumes, Fifth Edition*. London: Birt, Browne, Longman, Shuckburgh, Hitch, Hawes, Hodges, Oswald, Millar, Beecroft, Rivington, Ward, and Cooper, 1751.

Loughlin, Gerard. *Alien Sex: The Body and Desire in Cinema and Theology*. Oxford: Blackwell, 2004.

Mahan, Brian J. *Forgetting Ourselves on Purpose: Vocation and the Ethics of Ambition*. San Francisco: Jossey-Bass, 2002.

Maximus the Confessor. "Ambigua 41." In *On Difficulties in the Church Fathers,* edited and translated by Nicholas Constas, 2.103. Cambridge, MA: Harvard University Press, 2014.

Mazzotta, Giuseppe. *The New Map of the World: The Poetic Philosophy of Giambattista Vico.* Princeton, NJ: Princeton University Press, 1999.

Maurer, Armand. *About Beauty: A Thomistic Interpretation.* Houston, TX: Center for Thomistic Studies, 1983.

McCarraher, Eugene. *The Enchantments of Mammon: How Capitalism Became the Religion of Modernity.* Cambridge, MA: Belknap, 2019.

McGilchrist, Iain. *The Master and His Emissary.* New Haven, CT: Yale University Press, 2009.

McInroy, Mark. *Balthasar on the Spiritual Senses.* Oxford: Oxford University Press, 2014.

———. "Origen of Alexandria." In *The Spiritual Senses: Perceiving God in Western Christianity,* edited by Paul L. Gavrilyuk and Sarah Coakley. Cambridge, UK: Cambridge University Press, 2012.

Merleau-Ponty, Maurice. *Phenomenology of Perception.* Translated by Colin Smith. New York: Routledge, 2007.

Milbank, John. *Being Reconciled: Ontology and Pardon.* New York: Routledge, 2003.

———. *Beyond Secular Order.* Malden, MA: Wiley Blackwell, 2013.

———. "Can a Gift Be Given? Prolegomena to a Future Trinitarian Metaphysics." *Modern Theology* 11 (1995) 119–61.

———. "Gregory of Nyssa: The Force of Identity." In *Christian Origins: Theology, Rhetoric, Community,* edited by Lewis Ayres and Gareth Jones, 94–116. London: Routledge, 1998.

———. *Philosophy: A Theological Critique.* Hoboken, NJ: Wiley, 2014.

———. "Reality is a poem." Twitter, February 12, 2020. twitter.com/johnmilbank3/status/1227658861416460289.

———. *The Religious Dimension in the Thought of Giambattista Vico (1668–1744).* Lewiston, NY: Edwin Mellen Press, 1992.

———. "The Soul of Reciprocity Part One: Reciprocity Refused." *Modern Theology* 17 (2001).

———. *Theology and Social Theory: Beyond Secular.* Malden, MA: Blackwell, 2006.

———. *The Word Made Strange: Theology, Language, Culture.* Cambridge, MA: Blackwell, 1997.

Milbank, John, Catherine Pickstock, and Graham Ward. *Radical Orthodoxy: A New Theology.* London, Routledge, 1998.

Moltmann, Jürgen. *A Theology of Play.* New York: Harper and Row, 1972.

Mongrain, Kevin. "Balthasar's Way from Doxology to Theology." *Theology Today* 64 (2007) 58–70.

Moore, Mary Elizabeth Mullino. *Teaching as a Sacramental Act.* Cleveland: Pilgrim, 2004.

Moschella, Mary. *Ethnography as a Pastoral Practice: An Introduction.* Cleveland: Pilgrim, 2008.

Murphy, Debra Dean. *Teaching that Transforms: Worship as the Heart of Christian Education.* Grand Rapids: Brazos, 2004.

Nehemas, Alexander. *Only a Promise of Happiness: The Place of Beauty in a World of Art.* Princeton, NJ: Princeton University Press, 2007.

Nelson, C. Ellis. *Where Faith Begins.* Louisville: John Knox, 1967.

Neville, Gwen Kennedy, and John H. Westerhoff. *Learning through Liturgy*. New York: Seabury Press, 1978.

Nichols, Aidan. *A Key to Balthasar: Hans Urs von Balthasar on Beauty, Goodness, and Truth*. Grand Rapids: Baker Academic, 2011.

———. *Say It Is Pentecost: A Guide through Balthasar's Logic*. Washington, DC: The Catholic University of America Press, 2001.

———. "The Theo-logic." In *The Cambridge Companion to Hans Urs von Balthasar*, edited by Edward T. Oakes and David Moss, 158. New York: Cambridge University Press, 2004.

———. *The Word Has Been Abroad: A Guide through Balthasar's Aesthetics*. Edinburgh: T. & T. Clark, 1998.

O'Connor, Flannery. *Habit of Being: Letters of Flannery O'Connor*. New York: Farrar, Straus and Giroux, 1988.

O'Donnel, John. "Hans Urs von Balthasar: The Form of His Theology." In *Hans Urs von Balthasar: His Life and Work,* edited by David L. Schindler, 213–14. San Francisco: Ignatius, 2011.

Osmer, Richard Robert. *Practical Theology: An Introduction*. Grand Rapids: Eerdmans, 2008.

Paintner, Valters. *Awakening the Creative Spirit: Bringing the Arts to Spiritual Direction*. Harrisburg, PA: Morehouse, 2010.

Palmer, Parker. *The Active Life: A Spirituality of Work, Creativity, and Caring*. San Francisco: Jossey-Bass, 1999.

———. *The Courage to Teach: Exploring the Inner Landscape of a Teacher's Life*. San Francisco: Jossey-Bass, 1997.

———. *A Hidden Wholeness: The Journey Toward an Undivided Life*. San Francisco: Jossey-Bass, 2004.

———. *To Know as We Are Known: Education as Spiritual Journey*. San Francisco: HarperSanFrancisco, 1983.

Pickstock, Catherine. *After Writing: On the Liturgical Consummation of Philosophy*. Oxford: Blackwell, 1998.

Pieper, Joseph. *"Divine Madness": Plato's Case against Secular Humanism*. Translated by Lothar Krauth. San Francisco: Ignatius, 1995.

Pitzele, Peter. *Scripture Windows*. Los Angeles: Alef Design Group, 1998.

Plato. *The Republic*. Translated by W. H. D. Rouse. New York: Penguin, 1955.

Portmann, Adolf. *Biologie und Geist*. Freiburg: Herder, 1963.

Potter, R. "St. Irenaeus and Recapitulation." *Dominical Studies* 4 (November 1951) 192–200.

Progoff, Ira. *At a Journal Workshop: Writing to Access the Power of the Unconscious and Evoke Creative Ability*. New York: Penguin, 1975.

Rohr, Richard. *A Spring within Us: Daily Meditations*. Albuquerque: Center for Action and Contemplation, 2016.

Rogers, Frank, Jr. *Finding God in the Graffiti*. Cleveland: Pilgrim Press, 2011.

Saliers, Don E. "Liturgy and Ethics: Some New Beginnings." In *Liturgy and the Moral Self: Humanity at Full Stretch before God*, edited by E. Byron Anderson and Bruce T. Morrill, 16. Collegeville, MN: Liturgical, 1998.

Sammon, Brendan Thomas. "The Beauty of God: Beauty as a Divine Name in Thomas Aquinas and Pseudo-Dionysius the Areopagite." PhD diss., The Catholic University of America, 2012.

Scarry, Elaine. *On Beauty and Being Just*. New Haven, NJ: Princeton, 1999.

Schindler, David L. *Hans Urs von Balthasar: His Life and Work*. San Francisco: Ignatius, 1991.

———. "Sanctity and the Intellectual Life." *Communio* 20.4 (1993) 652–72.

Schindler, D. C. *Hans Urs von Balthasar and the Dramatic Structure of Truth: A Philosophical Investigation*. New York: Fordham University, 2004.

———. "Surprised by Truth: The Drama of Reason in Fundamental Theology." *Communio* 31 (Winter 2004) 587–611.

Schmemann, Alexander. *For the Life of the World: Sacraments and Orthodoxy*. New York: St. Vladimir's, 1998.

———. *The Journals of Fr. Alexander Schmemann, 1973–1983*. New York: St. Vladimir's, 2000.

Schwarz, Alan. *The Numbers Game: Baseball's Lifelong Fascination with Statistics*. New York: St. Martin's, 2005.

Sheerin, Daniel. *The Eucharist: Message of the Fathers of the Church*. Wilmington: Michael Grazier, 1986.

Sheffield, Frisbee. *Plato's Symposium*. Oxford: Oxford University Press, 2009.

Smith, James K. A. *Desiring the Kingdom: Worship, Worldview, and Cultural Formation*. Grand Rapids: Baker Academic, 2009.

———. "Healing the Imagination: Art Lessons from James Baldwin." *Image: Art, Faith, Mystery* 107 (2020) 3–6. https://imagejournal.org/article/healing-the-imagination-art-lessons-from-james-baldwin/

———. *How (Not) to Be Secular: Reading Charles Taylor*. Grand Rapids: Eerdmans, 2014.

———. *Imagining the Kingdom: How Worship Works*. Grand Rapids: Baker, 2013.

———. "Resurrecting the Imagination." June 11, 2020. https://www.youtube.com/watch?v=ik6CZS6jN4w.

———. *A Secular Age*. Cambridge, MA: Harvard University Press, 2007.

Stern, Daniel. *The Interpersonal World of the Infant: A View from Psychoanalysis and Developmental Psychology*. New York: Basic, 1985.

Stenberg-Lee, Kaisa. "Encountering God with Children & Three Playful Nature Prayer Practices for Adults and Children." September 6, 2021. https://www.kutsucompanions.com/post/encountering-god-with-children-three-playful-nature-prayer-practices-for-adults-and-children.

———. "Wonder Walks and Listening to God with Children." December 27, 2020. https://babydevotions.com/2020/12/27/wonder-walks-and-listening-to-god-with-children/.

Taylor, Charles. *Modern Social Imaginaries*. London: Duke University Press, 2007.

———. *A Secular Age*. London: Belknap, 2018.

Tolkien, J. R. R. "On Fairy-Stories." In *The Monsters and the Critics*, edited by Christopher Tolkien, 109–61. London: George Allen and Unwin, 1983.

———. *Tales from the Perilous Realm*. Boston: Meriner, 2021.

———. *The Return of the King*. New York: Ballantine, 1965.

Tracy, David. *The Analogical Imagination: Christian Theology and the Culture of Pluralism*. New York: Crossroad, 1981.

Underhill, Evelyn. *Worship*. Eugene, OR: Wipf and Stock, 1989.

Von Rad, Gerhard. *Old Testament Theology*. Vol. 1. Translated by D. M. G. Stalker. New York: Harper and Row, 1962.

Weber, Max. *The Sociology of Religion*. London: Methuen, 1971.

Weil, Simone. *Waiting for God*. London: Routledge, 2010.

Bibliography

White, David F., and Sarah Farmer, eds. *Joy: A Guide for Youth Ministry.* Nashville: Higher Education and Ministry, 2020.

Wilder, Thornton. *Our Town: A Play in Three Acts.* New York: Coward-McCann, 1938.

Will, George F. *Men at Work: The Craft of Baseball.* New York: Macmillan, 1990.

Williams, Rowan. *The Truce of God.* Grand Rapids: Eerdmans, 2005.

Willimon, William H. *Why Jesus?* Nashville: Abingdon, 2010.

Wimberly, Anne. *Soul Stories: African American Christian Education.* Nashville: Abingdon, 2005.

Wimberly, Anne, and Sarah Farmer. *Raising Hope: 4 Paths to Courageous Living for Black Youth.* Nashville: Wesley's Foundery, 2017.

Wink, Walter. *The Bible in Human Transformation: Towards a New Paradigm for Biblical Study.* Philadelphia: Fortress Press, 1973.

———. *Transforming Bible Study: A Leader's Guide.* Eugene, OR: Wipf and Stock, 2009.

Wise, Jean. "How Does Art Enhance Prayer?" *Healthy Spirituality,* December 18, 2018. https://healthyspirituality.org/how-does-art-enhance-prayer/.

Wright, N. T. "Paul's Gospel and Caesar's Empire." In *Paul and Politics: Ekklesia, Israel, Imperium, Interpretation,* edited by Richard A. Horsley, 160. Harrisburg, PA: Trinity Press International, 2000.

Wynn, Mark. *Emotional Experience and Religious Understanding: Integrating Perception, Conception, and Feeling.* Cambridge, UK: Cambridge University Press, 2005.

Yoder, Timothy J. "Hans Urs von Balthasar and Kenosis: The Pathway to Human Agency." PhD diss., Loyola University Chicago, 2013.

Yaconelli, Mark. *Contemplative Youth Ministry: Practicing the Presence of Jesus.* Grand Rapids: Zondervan, 2006.

———. *Downtime: Helping Teenagers Pray.* Grand Rapids: Zondervan, 2008.

———. *The Gift of Hard Things: Finding Grace in Unexpected Places.* Westmont, IL: InterVarsity, 2016.

———. *Growing Souls: Experiments in Contemplative Youth Ministry.* Grand Rapids: Zondervan, 2007.

———. *Wonder, Fear, and Longing: A Book of Prayers.* Grand Rapids: Zondervan, 2009.

Zipes, Jack. *Creative Storytelling: Building Community/Changing Lives.* New York: Routledge, 1995.

Index

Index

radiance, 37, 39

reason, 4–6, 11, 22, 25, 36, 44, 45, 49, 74, 91, 125, 128, 140, 176

Rogers, Frank, vii, 22, 67, 86, 110, 112, 153–55, 166, 175

Rohr, Richard, 60, 61, 175

Roman Catholic, 6, 11

Saliers, Don E., 121, 175

Sammon, Brendan Thomas, 31, 32, 35, 36, 175

Scarry, Elaine, 26, 28, 29, 175

Schindler, D.C., 51, 53–55, 74, 82, 173, 175, 176

Schmemann, Alexander, 46, 47, 98, 117, 130, 134, 135, 143–46, 176

Schwarz, Alan, 21

Smith, James K.A., 7, 9, 10, 15, 22, 23, 102, 117, 123, 124, 125- 127, 129, 134, 135, 139, 141, 142, 146–48, 150, 166, 174, 176

social imaginary, v, 4, 7, 12, 13, 17, 24, 31, 117, 140, 142, 163

Socrates, 19, 27, 36, 173

soul, 3, 5, 6, 8, 10, 11, 25, 32, 33, 49, 51, 52, 53, 64, 71, 96, 97, 102, 104, 105, 109, 111, 112, 113, 124, 131, 141, 142, 144, 148, 154, 159, 160, 166, 167, 174, 177

spiritual senses, 9, 23, 48–50, 59, 71, 109, 164, 165, 174

Streaty-Wimberly, Anne, 71, 111, 154, 155, 158, 159, 166, 177

Sugar and Spice, 147–49, 157, 173

Summa Theologica, 34, 37, 169

Stern, Daniel 29, 176

Taylor, Charles, 4–7, 38, 99, 109, 140, 176

The Artist's Way, 60, 171

The Divine Names, 32, 35

The Song of Songs, 39

Theo-Drama (Theo-Dramatics), v, 72, 75, 78, 79, 80, 82, 83, 170

Wilder, Thornton, 46, 177

Tolkien, J.R.R., 30, 47, 48, 66, 101, 102, 113, 176

totus Christus, 77, 83, 86

transcendentals, vi, 33, 34, 102, 169

Tracy, David 84, 176

Trinity, 35, 58, 75, 86, 102, 104, 106, 121, 143, 145, 149, 173

Trocme, Andre, 120

Tubman, Harriet, 86, 158

Underhill, Evelyn 129, 133, 176

United Methodist, 11

Van Gogh, Vincent, 132

Verbum, vi, 102, 107, 134

Vermeer, 10, 132,

Vico, Giambattista, 102, 103, 105, 106, 170, 171, 174

virtues, 21, 33, 86, 123, 124, 164

von Balthasar, Hans Urs, 6, 15, 40, 41, 48–60, 63, 64, 69, 70–81, 83–89, 91, 93, 98, 99, 110, 122, 123, 131, 135, 136, 145, 165, 169, 171–77

von Rad, Gerhard, 39, 176

Weil, Simone, 28, 176

White, David F., 89, 177

Will, George F., 21

Williams, Rowan, 98, 177

Willimon, William, 162, 177

Wink, Walter, 92, 95, 111–13, 177

Wind in the Willows, 97

Wittgenstein, 29

wonder, v, 2, 13–15, 24, 27, 35, 42, 46, 48, 53–55, 57, 58–60, 64–67, 71, 83, 87, 88, 91, 92, 101, 155, 160, 165, 171, 176, 177

Word, 3, 23, 41, 55, 74, 75, 76, 77, 79, 80, 82, 99, 102–4, 107, 108, 134, 135, 170, 174, 175

worship, vi, 3, 25, 36, 38, 42, 49, 87, 101, 113, 115, 117, 120–130, 132–34, 136, 137, 142, 151, 163, 164, 172, 174, 176

Wright, N. T., 145, 177

Yaconelli, Mark 159, 160, 177

Made in the USA
Middletown, DE
18 August 2022

71548589R00109